THE LAST ONE OUT OF TOWN
TURN OUT THE LIGHTS

The Epic 1975 Foxcroft Academy Basketball Season

DAVE ALBEE

T0349394

Down East Books

Camden, Maine

Down East Books

An imprint of The Globe Pequot Publishing Group, Inc.
64 South Main Street
Essex, CT 06426
www.globepequot.com

Distributed by NATIONAL BOOK NETWORK

British Library Cataloguing in Publication Information available

Library of Congress Cataloging-in-Publication Data Available
ISBN 978-1-68475-246-1 (paperback)
ISBN 978-1-68475-247-8 (ebook)

∞™ The paper used in this publication meets the minimum requirements of American National Standard for Information Sciences—Permanence of Paper for Printed Library Materials, ANSI/ NISO Z39.48-1992.

To Ree Miller and Jim Thompson for first giving me the opportunity to write sports when I didn't have a clue I could write.

To Peter Gammons, Bob Ryan, Ray Fitzgerald, and the Boston Globe *sports section of the 1970s for inspiring me as a teenager to be a better sportswriter.*

To all the sports editors and sportswriters I have worked with from Maine to Colorado to Illinois to California for helping me and believing in me.

To my Maine sisters Dianne and Donna, my brother-in-law Sam Lindsay, my niece Michelle and her husband Tim Huston, my wife Caroline, children Damianne, Drake, and Brock, son-in-law Chris Steward, and mother-in-law Gloria Hechim for supporting me on this book project.

To my late father, Earl, who instilled the value of hard work in me, and my late brother, Dick, the best athlete in the family who would have loved to have participated in this book.

To the 1975 Foxcroft Academy state championship boys basketball team for sharing their stories and rekindling memories and reconnecting me to my hometown and my home state and one of the best times of my life.

Contents

FOREWORD

As a native of Maine who played and coached high school and college basketball in the state for more than thirty years, I was delighted to hear about Dave Albee's *The Last One Out of Town Turn Out the Lights* as it brought back great memories for me.

I recruited a young Skip Hanson to coach at our "Super Week" summer basketball camp at the University of Maine. That's where, as head coach of the Black Bears, I first laid eyes on Kevin Nelson of Monson when he was fifteen years old and I wound up recruiting him to play at Maine. At that time, Kevin was the most sought-after schoolboy basketball player in Maine history. He followed a number of great players I recruited out of the backwoods of the Penquis League and Piscataquis County.

Two of my earliest recruits were Tony Hamlin from Milo and Dave Anderson from Dover-Foxcroft. Before Kevin, I recruited Wally Russell to Maine out of Penquis Valley High School, and the next big man I signed out of the Penquis League was Curtis Robertson, a 6-foot-10 center from Mattanawcook Academy in Lincoln.

In fact, my last team at Maine for the 1987–88 season included another Monson product, Dean Smith from Foxcroft Academy, and Todd Hanson, Skip's son, who started his high school basketball career at Piscataquis County High School (PCHS) in Guilford.

All these players, like Kevin Nelson, were shining stars in small-town communities. One of my best recruits, Rick Carlisle, came from tiny Lisbon, New York, and Worcester Academy. Rick played for me for two seasons shortly after Kevin graduated. Rick transferred to the University of Virginia, played with Ralph Sampson, and went to the Final Four in

1984. Rick was drafted by the Boston Celtics and has gone on to a successful career as a head coach in the NBA, lately with the Indiana Pacers. Jim Boylen, one of my players at Maine, is one of Rick's assistant coaches.

When I played at Maine, the Black Bears competed in the Yankee Conference when the University of Connecticut and the University of Massachusetts were conference members. The Pit—the nickname given to Maine's old memorial gymnasium—was packed for games featuring UConn and UMass with Julius Erving.

One of my teammates at Maine was Wayne Champeon, a terrific two-sport athlete from Greenville High School in Piscataquis County. He was All-Yankee Conference in both football and basketball, and we were teammates after college when we both played for Jack's Five, a renown semi-pro basketball team in the area.

Champ wound up coaching and teaching at Foxcroft Academy, which gave me the opportunity to reconnect with him whenever I visited Dover-Foxcroft and Piscataquis County to recruit Kevin Nelson.

Memories of these great days gone by were stirred by Dave Albee's book. It captures the essence of rural Maine high school basketball in the 1960s and '70s and the impact it had on civic pride through, first, the Monson Academy Slaters then a controversial school district consolidation that connected them with the Foxcroft Academy Ponies. That led to FA's remarkable one-and-only undefeated state championship run in 1975.

The book takes you on a journey from the driveways, barns, and quirky gyms where these Maine kids came to love the game of basketball to the lessons they learned, the team chemistry they developed, and the joy they brought to themselves and their community. The book reaches back to a time when small-town high school basketball was at its peak in popularity before consolidations and economics led to an erosion of excitement and participation for these rural high school basketball teams.

While the story is told mainly through the eyes of Kevin Nelson and Skip Hanson, *The Last One Out of Town Turn Out the Lights* features the memories and perspectives of many friends, foes, and fans who contributed to a special era of small-town high school basketball in Maine and throughout the country.

— Skip Chappelle

Thomas Nelson "Skip" Chappelle, the winningest coach in University of Maine basketball history, is a native of Old Town, Maine. In 1957 as a hot-shooting guard, Skip helped Old Town High School win the Maine State Basketball Championship, leading the Indians to the New England Championship in the Boston Garden where he scored 38 points. He was a three-time All-Yankee Conference player at the University of Maine, where he set twelve scoring records and, in 1961, was the first Black Bears player to be selected first team Little All-American. He also was the first player from the state of Maine to be drafted into the National Basketball Association by the NBA's St. Louis Hawks in 1962. He tried out for the Boston Celtics and roomed with future NBA Hall of Fame John Havlicek in training camp. Skip returned to his alma mater to coach the Black Bears for seventeen seasons from 1971 to 1988, winning a school-record 220 games.

PREFACE

When I was riding home to Dover-Foxcroft from Augusta inside the bus with the Foxcroft Academy Class B State Championship Boys Basketball Team on March 1, 1975, I had some idea what to expect miles ahead, but no idea I would be writing a book about it fifty years into the future.

It all changed at my fiftieth high school reunion in 2022.

The inspiration for this book was born out of a conversation with a Foxcroft Academy classmate, Duane "Dewey" Warren, who I hadn't seen or spoken to in more than forty-five years. Knowing I had been a long-time sportswriter, Dewey asked me to write a bio for him for his induction into the Foxcroft Academy Athletics Hall of Fame. Upon reading it, Dewey was impressed and asked why I had never written a book. Our subsequent late-night cross-country conversations concluded that I should write a book about the undefeated 1975 FA state championship boys basketball team.

I remember that team. I covered that team. And, at the time—when I was inexperienced, immature, and naive at my job—I actually felt like a member of that team. That was the impact that team had on so many people, not just me, as it made all of us feel like winners.

Over the years, I covered pro teams in Super Bowls, World Series, World Cup, and the NBA and NHL playoffs and college teams in football bowl games and NCAA basketball tournament games including the Final Four. But nothing compares to the feeling of your first championship team.

Hence, this book is important to me personally and professionally. It is in some ways my romanticizing it as Maine's version of *Hoosiers*.

It meant tracking down people through LinkedIn, Facebook, Google, and Foxcroft Academy alumni relations and asking them to remember events from fifty to sixty years ago when I have a hard enough time remembering things from fifty to sixty *minutes* ago. It offered the additional challenge of communicating with them three time zones and three thousand miles away from my home in California. I made two special trips back to Maine for research and face-to-face meetings, from Scarborough to Augusta to Boothbay Harbor to Orono to the Maine Basketball Hall of Fame in Bangor twice.

Yet with each in-person, phone, email, text, or DM interview I conducted for this book, I was moved by the myriad of emotions it revealed and the emotions it evoked in me and others. I laughed more than I have in years at the stories I was told and winced at some of the sad ones that got lost along the way. I rejoiced at the basketball tradition achieved at Monson Academy and was troubled by the misery the town felt when the high school closed because of a school district consolidation. I researched the basketball shortcomings at Foxcroft Academy and tried to examine and explain the purpose and process aimed at changing that. I rebooted the memories and sentiment I experienced in the years I followed the Ponies and the dozens of games I covered leading up to the state championship game.

There was one common theme, however, throughout this project. Everyone remembered the sign—THE LAST ONE OUT OF TOWN TURN OUT THE LIGHTS. It became to me the obvious title for the book, though it would be hard to squeeze it all onto the cover.

The book project became a full-time job once I retired in September 2023. I put all my heart into it, so much so that I joke that it was the cause of my mild heart attack in May 2024. The book was an absolute blessing. It rekindled friendships and created others. It uncovered stories and people willing to share them. And it reconnected me to my high school, my hometown, and my home state and how extremely proud I am of all three.

I hope this book impacts you reading it the way it impacted me writing it.

Ode to the Slaters

THE ELEVEN-YEAR-OLD WAS WIDE-EYED AND IN AWE. HE WAS TALL FOR his age, tall enough to see the spectacle in front of him yet not tall enough to see what the future held for him and his hometown.

The Monson Academy Slaters boys basketball team had just returned 140 miles from Portland after winning the 1968 Maine State Class S Boys Basketball Championship game that afternoon, and Kevin Nelson, then a 5-foot-10 fifth grader, was amazed at the sight of the celebration all around him in the school's jam-packed gymnasium. He was the protégé kid in the proverbial candy store. Everywhere he looked, there was something good to see that made him smile and wish for more.

This was Kevin's basketball fantasyland.

The town police and fire department, featuring a 1938 Ford fire truck, had greeted the state title team as Route 15 descended Tenney Hill Road. The motorcade grew to more than forty cars as it snaked around the lefthand curve past the town's only gas station onto Main Street. It was a nonstop parade, as Monson did not have a single traffic light to intercept it. The street was lined with flares, lighted signs, and oil-burning black smudge pots normally used as road hazard warnings but, in this case, signaling a championship party ahead. There were parked vehicles filled with fans, honking their car horns and beaming with pride for the hometown heroes' welcome in the normally sleepy town of six hundred people. All eyes were focused on the championship team—not sitting up high in a school bus, but riding behind it in two passenger cars driven by the coach and the school principal because the team's mighty roster consisted of only eight players.

It was a chilly winter's night on March 9, cold enough for locals to build a bonfire out of old tires on the shore of nearby Lake Hebron. Ordinarily on a Saturday evening most Monson residents would be home watching the Jackie Gleason or Lawrence Welk shows or *My Three Sons* on television. The only heroes they expected to see on Saturday night were TV's *Hogan's Heroes*.

But, on this incredible Saturday night, the shining light was on Monson Academy's Quonset hut of a gymnasium, the Madison Square Garden of the Upper Kennebec Valley League and the centerpiece for civic pride. To Monson, this was Maine basketball the way it should be.

This was a time when TikTok was the sound a grandfather clock made. When Rocky was a flying squirrel, not an underdog boxer. When *Avengers: Endgame* was wondering if and when the Beatles might break up.

Inside, Kevin Nelson, craning his neck, anxiously waited in the third and final row of wooden bleachers among a standing-room-only crowd of admirers as the state champion Slaters finally walked into the school's gymnasium for their coronation. They were hailed with music from an organ. "Happy Days Are Here Again" must have been on the play list.

Greg Lander—with the brilliant Gold Ball state championship trophy in his hands and a big fat cigar in his mouth—was the first player to arrive in the gym as if he was Mickey Mouse stepping onto Main Street in Disneyland. He was followed by Kevin's idol, 6-foot-5 star center Cyril "Buddy" Leavitt Jr.

Kevin, jumping for joy, was dreaming that he, too, could be a left-handed shooting big man like Buddy and someday lead Monson to another small school state championship and receive such a hero's welcome. Kevin's eyes followed each of the players like they were so many presents lined up under the tree on Christmas morning. He was soaking in the assembly of community gratification in front of him and the possibilities ahead. The kid was stoked.

This was his bliss.

Kevin Nelson had so much hope in his heart for the future that day. There was no doubt Kevin had the height to succeed as a basketball player—though his dad once thought he had polio, his older brother one time questioned his toughness, and Kevin had his own self-doubts about playing basketball. He was extraordinarily tall in his youth and in basketball, in that era, that equated to potentially being dominant in the sport.

Raised on a rural tree-lined country road in Southeast Monson with a population of fifty or so, Kevin was built to take the town to even greater heights. He was Monson's next Big Thing.

Yet Kevin never imagined at that moment in that gym in that tiny little town going absolutely berserk over its high school basketball team that his dominance would someday be for Foxcroft Academy in Dover-Foxcroft—a booming metropolis compared to Monson—twenty miles away. He would be bussed to a town with six times the population, twice as many traffic lights, a graduating class much larger than that of Monson Academy, and a basketball tradition far inferior to Monson's. Though born in Dover-Foxcroft, in some twisted way that town was the enemy to Kevin.

The thought of bringing Dover-Foxcroft its first and only state basketball championship as the Maine State Basketball Player of the Year in 1975 was not at all on Kevin's mind or in his conscience in 1968. Then, Kevin had a singular vision of someday bringing Monson another state title. He realized, even as a preteen, that there were obstacles ahead far more imposing than playing bigger local middle school teams with more talent, more depth, and more everything in Piscataquis County and elsewhere.

In the year that McDonald's introduced the Big Mac, Elvis Presley fathered a baby, and Mister Rogers evidently lived in the best neighborhood, Kevin Nelson was dreaming like David in a world of Goliaths even though in size he was one himself.

Anything, it seemed, was possible at his young age. Landing on the moon really wasn't so far-fetched.

"I knew at that point, as a fifth and sixth grade team, we weren't very good. We just weren't," Kevin said. "We were getting crushed by the Dover teams and Dexter teams and now, in 1968, we're thinking, 'Wow! We have a high school at Monson Academy that's a state championship team?!' At our level in fifth and sixth grade, we were scoring 4 or 5 points a game. However, our high school team at that time could have been the New York Knickerbockers or the Boston Celtics or any professional team and I couldn't have been more impressed. The town was in such a good mood."

Then came the dreaded C word. Consolidation. In Monson, it might as well have been the plague. It sucked the air of whatever ballyhoo basketball had to offer.

Consolidation was the notorious coal-black cloud hanging over Monson for years. Monson Academy students were slowly coming to grips with the likelihood that following the 1969 season—the Slaters' farewell season—that they were going to be lined up and bussed to Dover-Foxcroft, the shiretown of Piscataquis County, to join School Administrative District 68. SAD 68. The acronym was symbolic of their mood moving forward.

After years of angst and arguments, Monson reluctantly voted in the summer of 1968—mere months after the climax of winning a state basketball championship—that it was best for the town to ship its senior high school students to Dover-Foxcroft to further their secondary education. The town, bonded by its basketball team, was bitterly divided at the prospect of dismantling its school and basketball program and all the pain and sorrow that comes with that.

This was Kevin's basketball reality.

Monson was ground zero for consolidation implementation. Consolidation was Monson's Vietnam.

"Town meetings around the issue quickly descended into shouting, and more than once longtime rancor, most likely borne of a common helplessness, reared its head," Wendy Anderson wrote for William Sawtell's *Monson Academy Revisited 1847–1997*.

Consolidation was like the second coming of Frankenstein in Monson. The town was all up in arms.

Kevin Nelson's destiny was being decided by a show of hands. Many of them had the middle finger extended.

After his seventh-grade year in Monson, while Monson Academy's doors remained open for elementary school students only, Kevin would attend Dover Grammar School, newly named SeDoMoCha. Though the new junior high sounded like a lavish cup of hot chocolate, it was named to incorporate SAD 68's consolidation of Sebec, Dover, Monson, and Charleston.

There would be no turning back. The consolidation was going forward. The only miracle that was going to happen in the summer of 1969 was the Mets. Monson Academy was set to close as a high school that summer and eventually Kevin and his Monson classmates were to make the round-trip trek by bus every weekday for forty or so weeks out of the year every year until they graduated from Foxcroft Academy. This was not their idea of a freedom march.

Located along the final stretch of the Appalachian Trail—which extends 2,200 miles from Springer Mountain, Georgia, to Mount Katahdin, Maine—Monson and its dilemma seemed to have reached a dead end. It was the poor town stuck in the middle between the touristy town of Greenville and the Moosehead Lake Region to the north and the town of Guilford, which is on the way to Dover on Route 15, to the south.

The student-athletes of Monson felt more like pallbearers than ballplayers.

"The quickest way to kill a town is to send its school down the road," said Buddy Leavitt. "I realized it would have been extremely tough to continue at Monson Academy, but we had much industry back in the day between the slate quarry and the Moosehead mill. We were so dependent on tax dollars, but you kill a town when you send the school down the road."

It was arguably the darkest time in the history of Monson, a tight-knit small farming town founded in 1815 and named after Monson, Massachusetts. Among the earliest settlers in 1828 was Solomon Bray who had fourteen children—enough kids to play a game of basketball if the game had been invented by then.

When the Civil War happened, many of Monson's residents left Maine to fight for the Union. More than forty of them died, twenty-two were wounded. Crop farming suffered with their absence and Monson incurred financial hardships.

The saving grace for Monson was when slate mining became a major industry in town in 1870. The rich quarries provided a steady source of employment and income for Monson. It eventually furnished a suitable nickname for Monson Academy sports teams after the high school was built and opened in the summer in 1848. Slate was abundant and, as nicknames and mascots go, politically correct. Slate even made Monson a vacation destination.

By the early 1900s, Monson's population had more than doubled to over 1,200 residents when the Monson Narrow Gauge Railroad was linked to town. Families of Swedes, Finns, Welsh, and other Europeans began migrating from Canada and gravitating to Monson for jobs in the slate mines. They were hard-working, courageous, and particularly tall. Those genetic qualities undoubtedly contributed to Monson winning state basketball championships in 1909 with only five players on its roster and in 1932 with a coach, Salve Larson, who worked in the slate quarries. According to the 1932 *Pharetra*, Monson Academy's yearbook, the Slaters team that year had a 14–2 regular season record (the two losses were to college teams) then won all four of its county tournament games, then won all four of its games in the Bangor Y.M.C.A. State Tournament.

The 1932 team included Oswald "Cookie" Poole, the only non-Swede or Finn in the starting lineup, and team captain Oscar Suomi. Cookie told his son, Glenn Poole, now president of the Monson Historical Society, that Oscar developed a jump shot around the year 1930. The inventor of the jump shot in basketball is widely believed to have been Kenny Sailors, who developed it in high school in Wyoming in 1934. Oscar is not recognized as having invented the jump shot, but he could have been the original Big "O" ahead of college basketball and NBA Hall of Famer Oscar Robertson.

There is no debate about Monson's history of slate and its place in American history. The town was particularly proud of its black slate and nicknamed its high school sports teams the Slaters, wearing black and orange as its school colors. The slab of millstock that marks the gravesite of U.S. President John F. Kennedy in Arlington National Cemetery came from the Portland-Monson Slate Company. Buddy Leavitt's dad, Cyril "Bud" Leavitt Sr., a former Lance Corporal in the U.S. Marine Corps, supervised the cutting of the slate for John F. Kennedy's gravesite.

Slate to Monson was like antlers to a bull moose: a symbol of strength and stature. Slate mining was a profitable yet dangerous business in those days. Slate expands, and mine walls can collapse. According to the Monson Historical Society, the Monson Slate Quarry created its own burial site for miners who did not survive if a cave collapsed and they had no family around to claim victims. For them, slate determined their fate.

Monson's industry started shifting from slate to manufacturing beginning in 1945 after the Monson Maine Slate Company closed. Following a fire at Moosehead Woodcrafters in Greenville, the company relocated to Monson and resumed building rock maple wood furniture products out of a former slate company building. In 1947, it became known as Moosehead Manufacturing and eventually opened a sister plant in Dover-Foxcroft.

It was as if Monson was the Six Piece Dining Set Capital of the World.

Other than natural black slate and high quality furniture, the pride and joy of Monson was its continued success at basketball. Pete Gattrell, an instructor and coach, began teaching students the game and organizing basketball teams when they were in third grade. When most students were learning reading, writing, and arithmetic at that age, Monson kids were learning dribbling, shooting, and rebounding.

By the time these budding Monson basketball players reached high school, their progress was not only the talk of the town but literally chronicled in *The Annual Monson Town Report*. This would be akin to the president of the United States praising the Super Bowl champions in the State of the Union Address.

The ultimate goal for sports-minded kids growing up in Monson was to play basketball in Monson Academy's gymnasium. The townspeople had raised funds in the early 1940s to build it. It was a Quonset hut, a prefabricated structure inspired in Great Britain during World War I that became popular in World War II. As odd as it may have looked, it was home to Monson basketball, though no one ever took credit or attached a name to it.

"That might explain the stubborn pride of people in Monson," said Buddy Leavitt. "Maybe it's because the gym looked more like a military barracks, but that place would rock."

"The locker rooms downstairs were like a dungeon. The home team's locker room was like an oversized bathroom," said Shawn Nelson, Kevin's older brother. "But the atmosphere was phenomenal. The gym was packed for games. There was standing room only. This was for every game. And it got hot inside."

A wooden entry made from plywood was constructed outside for fans to wait in line for tickets to be sold before the game and a place for fans to huddle, cool off, and smoke at halftime. The basketball court a few steps away inside was regulation-sized and, once Monson added glass backboards, it became the cream of the crop among gymnasiums in the Upper Kennebec Valley League. The Quonset hut was the hip place to be.

"We used to play a lot of the larger Class M schools and we'd piss them off because we beat them about every year," said Steve Bray, a freshman on Monson's 1968 Class S State Championship team. "Some of them wanted to drop us right off their schedule, but we kept them on. They used to help us a lot on our Class S points."

Other antiquated gymnasiums in small towns within a sixty-mile radius in the deep woods of Maine couldn't measure up to Monson's. They were more makeshift than mainstream and had fan or half-moon shaped metal backboards.

In Hartland's gym, there was a bed mattress nailed to the stage at one end of the court to protect players from running into it. It had the look of a garage sale.

"If you came into that end on a driving layup then *wham!* You ran into the mattress," Leavitt said. "I guess we were lucky it wasn't a box spring."

There also was a large fishing-like net separating fans on the stage from the players on the floor.

"It was like playing inside an MMA cage match," Steve Bray said.

In Harmony's gym, the ceiling was so low that players had to change the trajectory of their field goal attempts. It was like shooting in a toll booth.

"If you were 4-foot-11, like me, and you shot with a lot of arc you could hit the ceiling and it would be ruled out of bounds and the ball would go to the other team," Bray said. "You had to learn to shoot line drives."

Monson and Harmony were bitter rivals. In Harmony's gym, to support one of its baskets, there were two cables or guide wires attached to a backboard that extended to the end of the bleachers within reach of the home team's fans. They would yank on the wires sometimes when a Slaters' player was shooting a foul shot.

"The Harmony fans would shake those cables when they got excited," Leavitt said. "It was like shooting at a moving target."

In Solon's gym, they had pot-bellied wood stove near the sideline to heat the building.

"If you ran too close to the stove, you'd get soot on your sneakers and kick it all over the court," Leavitt said.

Solon also had two white wooden backboards, one literally bolted into a wall. The backboards didn't even have a shooting square—the 2-inch white-taped rectangular block above and behind the rims to help players gauge their bank shots.

Shawn Nelson recalled playing in Solon as a freshman and noticed that there were silver thumb tacks pressed into the snowy white backboards so "their star player Terry Cahill knew taking certain shots if he hit a tack it was going to bank into the basket."

This game strategy put new meaning into the word "tactic."

In North New Portland, the gym was located upstairs in a building where there was a balcony hanging over the corners of a basketball court. There's one story, in fact, about a drunken fan who stumbled off the balcony and landed upside down stuck in one of the baskets.

The court in North New Portland was so small that the jump circles surrounding the two foul lines intersected and overlapped with the jump circle at mid-court. It also featured a concave square cast-iron grate on the floor under one of the baskets—basically a sprained ankle or worse waiting to happen.

"As an artist, it was kind of a wonderful sort of geometric abstraction," said Alan Bray, Steve's older brother, who became an artist and has exhibited his casein-on-panel landscape paintings from Maine to California.

Then there was the "gym" in Athens. It was located inside the town's fire station and, when basketball games were played, the town's two fire trucks were parked on ready inside in plain view about 8 feet from one of the baselines.

During Alan Bray's freshman year playing for the Slaters, there was one game in Athens that created a Bugs Bunny cartoon-like contest in the fire station. Someone was destined to get clobbered like Daffy Duck.

"It was a brutally cold night, and it had a tile floor, and the floor was sweating from the heat inside so there was like a skim of moisture on the floor," Bray said. "Everybody was slipping and sliding. It was like a skating rink."

Monson, led by 6-foot-7 Dick Wyman, had a superior team coached by Ken Perry, the school's principal. However, in the first quarter, Perry decided to bench his entire starting lineup. For safety reasons.

"When you were doing a layup in that gym you had to be careful not to hit a fire truck and, with the floor wet, Dick Wyman slipped and literally slid right under the truck," Bray explained. "Perry immediately took the first team out and put us subs in. The expendable guys."

Basketball was turning into Ice Capades. Eventually the game's referees called both coaches and teams together and changed the rules for one night.

"They stopped calling traveling," Bray said. "It was sort of like backyard basketball."

The Monson Slaters would play anyone anywhere any place. They played in bandbox gyms in small towns from Jackman, Maine—16 miles from the Canadian border—to Jonesport and Beals, located on an island in the Atlantic Ocean 200 miles from Jackman. When Monson traveled to the coast to compete in those games, they would play on Beals Island on a Friday then be paired up with Jonesport players and their host families and stay over on Friday night so to play Jonesport High on Saturday night. After that game, they would make the four-hour drive back to Monson, arriving there early on Sunday morning on a bus, usually driven by Alan and Steve Bray's dad, George, that left the players hot or cold, sweating or shivering. It had a heater in the back and a defroster in the front, but they didn't work at the same time.

On long road trips like that, the Slaters were at a distinct disadvantage. Their opponents had a home court—and hometown—advantage.

"No one ever beat Beals on Beals Island. They had like ten players named Beals on the team and two Faulkinghams, and the two refs were probably named Beals," Steve Bray said.

Buddy Leavitt recalls one night he and teammate Roy Taylor spent with a Jonesport family. After walking downstairs on Saturday morning, they came upon the father of the house. He was sitting and reading the morning newspaper about Monson's game against Beals across the bridge the previous night.

"He said, 'Boy, if I could find out who this Bob Leavitt and Royal Taylor are I would make sure they wouldn't get to the game tonight,'" Leavitt said. "Here I am a sixteen-year-old high school student in a stranger's house, and I had heard so much about these lobster fishermen who shot people who messed with their traps."

It sounded like the plot to a Stephen King horror movie. Leavitt was wondering when the father would put down the newspaper and pick up a knife.

"So, I'm nervous and I say, 'I'm not Bob Leavitt. I'm Bud Leavitt.' He said, 'Well, they have you in the paper as Bob, but I damn well know who you are.' He was just joking, but he scared the tar out of us."

Not much spooked Monson during the 1967–68 season. That Slaters team, in their Halloween-colored uniforms, surprised everyone. They were not burdened with the expectations of the 1961 Monson team that many thought was capable of winning a state championship, led by Wyman who went on to play at the University of Maine. The Slaters won a third consecutive Upper Kennebec Valley League championship in 1961 and compiled a two-year record of 27–3. They averaged 74 points a game while limiting opponents to an average of 48 points per game.

"How they managed not to win the state championship I have no idea," said Glenn Poole, who played varsity basketball for the Slaters from 1963 to 1966. "This was a team that everybody on the starting five was over 6 feet tall."

In 1961, the Slaters, with their superior reach, were blowing teams out left and right, including a 30-point Eastern Maine Class S Tournament semifinal game victory over Easton in the famed Bangor Auditorium. That gave Alan Bray, then a 4-foot-11 substitute freshman guard, a rare chance to play on the big stage. However, someone forgot to pack uniforms for him and several of his teammates. When Alan entered the game, Lauri Anderson, a three-time All-State player, took off his uniform top and handed it to Alan to wear.

One big problem. It was the basketball equivalent of a wardrobe malfunction.

Lauri stood 6-foot-4. Alan had to literally tuck Lauri's uniform top deep into his own trunks, which in turn blocked the view of the number on the jersey on the front and back. George Hale, the legendary Maine sports broadcaster, was doing the play-by-play of the game for WABI Radio. Hale—who also was the sportscaster for WABI-TV Channel 5, the CBS affiliate in Bangor—could not identify Alan Bray by number because, well, he couldn't see the number as half of the numerals were blocked by Bray's trunks. So, Hale started calling him "Cousy," a nod toward famed and diminutive Boston Celtics' NBA All-Star point guard Bob Cousy. Tickled by the sight of the little boy who could wear a big man's uniform, Hale was laughing hysterically on air when Alan Bray made a layup during his brief appearance late in the game.

The irony in 1961 is Monson lost its next game by a single point, 60–59, in the Eastern Maine Class S Tournament finals to Stonington, the eventual state champion. Stonington's star player that year, Gary Webb, became Monson's coach for the 1968 season. Webb lived in Ellsworth yet taught and coached during the week in Monson 90 miles away where he rented a room in a house on Tenney Hill. When the landlord decided to sell her house, Webb relocated to the Leavitts' house on South Main Street. He would teach school and coach Buddy by day and sleep in the guest bedroom at the Leavitts at night.

The Slaters started slowly during the 1967–68 season, going 4–4 in great part because Buddy Leavitt was academically ineligible for the first month for not getting good grades while playing on Monson's baseball team the previous spring. But the basketball team and the town didn't hold it against him.

"What was unique about going to a small school like Monson Academy—where we may have something like only seventy or eighty total kids in the school—was they were really strict about academics," Leavitt said. "They didn't care if you were 6–5 and 180 and could put the ball in the hole if you didn't pass Algebra."

Unfortunately, about the time Leavitt returned to the lineup, two of his teammates, Craig Erickson and Jimmy Crockett, were dismissed from the team because of poor grades. Fortunately, co-captains Dickie Woodard and Roy Taylor—a hockey-loving player out of Canada who never played basketball until he moved to Willimantic—elevated their games. Taylor, in fact, was named the Slaters' Most Valuable Player at season's end.

"We didn't really have a great shooting team, but we were physical," Steve Bray said. "And then when Buddy came back it was a whole different dynamic."

Bray also provided a different dynamic. He became a media star in the Eastern Maine Class S Tournament, thanks to George Hale, who may have remembered Alan Bray's freshman debut in the tournament in 1961. He became known as Little Stevie Bray.

"I was only 4–11, for God's sake," he joked. "The smallest kid in the tournament."

Monson, seeded No. 2, defeated its UKVL rival and No. 7 seeded Harmony 61–55 in the 1968 quarterfinals, No. 6 seeded Oakfield 64–47 in the semifinals, then, with Dick Woodard scoring 21 points, upset top-seeded powerhouse Mattawamkeag 68–58 in the Eastern Maine Class S championship game as Greg Lander shut down Keagers' star Dennis Libbey. Mattawamkeag had a reputation for having legendary basketball players. Anita Belanger still owns the state's girls high school single-game scoring record of 81 points set in 1955. She averaged 55.6 points a game in her career. Dennis Libbey went on to play shortstop at the University of Maine, where he eventually was inducted into UMO's Sports Hall of Fame. Libbey was the biggest stumbling block from keeping the Slaters from playing in the state championship game, and Lander was assigned to guard him.

"He guarded me when I was on *defense*," Libbey told Leavitt.

The Slaters suddenly were the darlings of the *Bangor Daily News*. During the semifinals, a *BDN* photographer snapped a photo of Shawn Nelson and his parents, Hollis and Rose, cheering in the bleachers at the Bangor Auditorium. Before the state championship game in Portland, a *BDN* photographer came to Monson for a behind-the-scenes photo journal feature on the Slaters to highlight the team and its hobbies away from the basketball court. He snapped photos on Lake Hebron of players snowmobiling and drilling holes in the ice and fishing as if it was a *National Geographic* special.

Steve Bray was photographed with a fishing pole in his hands. He looked as out of place as a rainbow trout in a bathtub.

"I never ice fished in my life," he said.

For the State Class S Championship game, Monson was paired against undefeated Casco High School, the Western Maine champion, in a Saturday afternoon tilt in the Portland Exposition Building. Opened in 1915, the Portland Expo is the second-oldest arena in continuous operation in the United States.

Gary Webb, the Slaters' coach, doubled as the team's chauffeur. He took half of the team to Portland in his 1967 Pontiac LeMans and the other half went with Monson Academy principal Antonio Paradis in his Ford Galaxie on Friday. It didn't make sense or cents to transport a team of only eight players and two managers to Portland in a big gas-guzzling school bus to stay overnight before the state title game.

"It was one of the few times I had ever stayed in a hotel room in my life," said Steve Bray. "I was fourteen years old. I stayed with Stuart Anderson and Jeff Greenleaf, and I was so wound up I kept them up all night."

The local newspapers didn't seem to give Monson Academy, with a school enrollment of sixty-seven students, much of a chance of beating Casco Bay, which had a record of 23–0 and had averaged 90 points a game in winning the Western Maine Class S Tournament. Yet the Slaters relished the underdog role.

"It was the right place at the right time," Bray said.

The rest of Monson, including the team's six cheerleaders, traveled to Portland the next morning. Among the Slaters fans were Judge Millard Emanuelson, Earl Brazier, and Oswald "Cookie" Poole, who were photographed for the *Portland Press Herald* newspaper. The three were teammates on the 1932 Monson Academy state championship team that brought the Gold Ball home.

The Monson crowd in Portland also included the Nelson family. "Nobody ever experienced anything like that," Shawn said. "Going to Portland back then for folks was like me going to Chicago now."

"I was going to Portland, Maine of all places," Kevin said. "I couldn't have gone to New York City and been any more impressed."

Almost as impressive as the surprising size of the Monson crowd in attendance in Portland. Slaters fans packed the Expo, which five years earlier hosted the first East Coast concert of the Beach Boys. Monson fans had good vibrations. It didn't matter that they had to drive almost three hours over frost-heaved roads to get there.

"We were playing a team that was undefeated and all five starters averaged double figures and they lived 24 miles from the Expo, and we put as many damn people in the gym as they did," said Buddy Leavitt. "It was crazy. It was just crazy. In Monson, if you weren't at the game people were asking why. If you were not a varsity player or a junior varsity player or a member of the girls' basketball team—and we obviously were not big enough to have a school band—you had fans. They were genuine fans, and they came out.

When we won the Eastern Maine championship in Bangor and went to the Portland Expo to represent Class S basketball, I saw people there from Monson that never went to a game in Monson. My grandmother went—my mother's mother who never got off Water Street—and she's saying, 'I don't know what the heck is going on here, but I know when that ball goes in the hole everyone goes crazy.'"

On this day, Buddy sent his grandmother into delirium. He helped the orange-and-black–clad Slaters forge to an early lead by scoring 14 points in the opening quarter and, when Casco Bay narrowed an 8-point halftime deficit to 3 points midway through the third quarter, Leavitt scored 6 consecutive Monson points.

Steve Bray, who committed two turnovers in the final 16 seconds of the first half, was almost praying he wouldn't have to play in the second half. He was the back-up point guard and he was feeling the pressure sitting on the bench.

"All I could hope in a game like that was that Greg Lander wouldn't foul out, but he got three fouls early on," Bray said. "Then in the second half when the game got tight and you're close to a state championship and I'm a 4–11 freshman all I'm thinking is, 'Lander! Do not foul!' Jesus Christ, please. I do not need that on my basketball resume.'"

Lander didn't foul out, but he did make two crucial foul shots—his only points in the game—with 1:14 to play that pushed Monson's lead to 62–57 shortly after Casco Bay had tied the game at 55–55 with three minutes left. Leavitt, who made a jump shot to give the Slaters the lead for good at 57–55, finished with a game-high 31 points and 15 rebounds. He also drew the fifth foul on Casco Bay star Dale Eldridge, who fouled out of the game with 20 points and 16 rebounds with 5:00 to go. Roy Taylor had a game-high 19 rebounds and four field goals, the last of which gave the Slaters their largest lead of the game, 47–38, with 2:38 remaining in the third quarter. Dickie Woodard netted 12 points, and teammate Ed Kronholm contributed nine rebounds and 11 points, including Monson's first 6 points of the second half.

"I got a lot of the accolades because I scored a lot of the points and that's what happens, but the biggest reason that we had success was those other kids—we only had eight on the varsity—and they all accepted their role and they played their role and you've got to do that to be success-ful," Leavitt said. "Everybody had a role and nobody tried to exceed it. Everybody stepped in, and everybody has a piece of that championship."

Before taking that coveted Gold Ball back to Monson, the team stopped at Valle's Steak House in Portland for dinner. Unbeknownst to them, one of the diners that night happened to be Boston Celtics star—and future NBA Hall of Famer—Sam Jones, who had watched a portion of their title game. Somehow news of Monson's state champion-ship drifted to Sam Jones, and he invited the team to his table to offer congratulations. Sam stopped and popped out his hand to Buddy and his teammates. Buddy grabbed a restaurant napkin and had Sam Jones autograph it.

However, the reception the Slaters received from the Celtics' star didn't compare to the wild one they received at home hours later. It was ticker tape–like without the tape and tall buildings.

"We had a rally when we came back to town after the state championship and there were people coming through our receiving line putting money in our hands. Honest to God," Leavitt said.

No one at the time was thinking about next year and the countdown to consolidation. Monson was reveling in its basketball prowess. The town had produced Susan Greenleaf—perhaps the greatest girls basketball player ever in Monson—and the Slaters' girls basketball team in 1968 won the Upper Kennebec Valley League, though there was no girls high school tournament in Maine until 1975. And the prospect of Monson Academy's boys basketball team winning its first state basketball championship in thirty-six years seemed as preposterous as astronaut Buzz Aldrin slicing a 6-iron on the moon.

The Slaters overachieved that season, and the town swelled with pride all the way around the world. Leavitt received a congratulatory letter from Vietnam from Jim Greenleaf, Monson Academy Class of 1966, who was serving there in the U.S. Air Force.

"The year they won it, they went way beyond expectations," Glenn Poole said. "Maybe reality set in a little bit in 1969."

That was Monson's last year of Monson Academy basketball. The consolidation was set to begin in the fall of 1969, so the spring of 1969 was Monson's last chance to play basketball as Slaters. Foxcroft Academy principal Tillson Thomas made a special trip to Monson to explain the process of the transition. Let's just say Richard Nixon at Woodstock would have received a warmer welcome than Tillson Thomas at Monson Academy.

"The whole student body walked in, all ninety of us," Leavitt said. "If we could have voted we would have swung the vote. The consolidation thing was a bitter issue. It tore the town apart because there were a lot of proud people. We have a bond. We were a tight-knit group. Everybody knew everybody's business."

The Slaters, defending state champions, had plenty enough basketball talent, but they were not old enough to be champions for their cause at the ballot box. They were helpless.

The final Monson Academy basketball season ended at the Eastern Maine Class S Tournament at the Bangor Auditorium. To get there, the Slaters had to pass by Foxcroft Academy and go through Dover-Foxcroft to stay on Route 15 to Bangor. Not a good omen.

The last Monson Academy basketball game was in the tournament semifinals, a 79–51 loss to the Island Falls Owls on a Friday afternoon on February 21, 1969. The Slaters were outscored 20–2 by the eventual state champions in the first quarter. Buddy Leavitt had a game-high 26 points, Steve Bray added 13 points, and Shawn Nelson, then a freshman, scored the final points in Monson Academy basketball history.

"If the Bangor Auditorium was still there, I could go and stand probably within a foot of where I made that last shot," Shawn said. "I own one distinction at Monson Academy that nobody has ever or will ever—ever!—hold or be able to hold. I scored the last 2 points for Monson Academy."

The town of Monson then prepared for the inevitable, fulfilling a prophecy. It was Shawn and Kevin Nelson's mother Rose who years earlier, deciphering the consequences of forming a school district, wrote in the *Annual Monson Town Report*, "This is the end of Monson Academy."

In retrospect, it was probably years in the making. In 1957, the State of Maine passed the Sinclair Act to restructure its educational system by consolidating Maine's many school districts into fewer, larger ones. It was considered a cost-cutting measure designed with the idea that larger school districts would offer more resources than smaller ones. The Sinclair Act resulted in a 40 percent drop in schools in Maine with the average size of existing schools doubling.

On April 14, 1966, the *Piscataquis Observer*'s lead story was about Monson holding a town meeting on April 18 to debate joining such a school district. The story featured a photo of Monson Academy with the caption "What Is the Future of Monson Schools?" and noted that the state would not subsidize any type of renovation or building of school facilities unless that school was part of a school district.

Foxcroft Academy was openly courting Monson Academy students and their parents. In October 1966, the Joint Board of Foxcroft Academy invited students and residents of Monson to attend a Foxcroft-Orono football game at Oakes Field, then tour Foxcroft and the FA gymnasium. The state-of-the-art gym, opened in 1962, had seating for more than a thousand fans in two retractable wooden bleachers on one side of the court and seating for the student body and Foxcroft Academy Band on a retractable wooden bleacher section on a large-raised stage on the opposite side. There were two glass backboard baskets on each end of the court and four retractable hoops on the sides. It was quintessential basketball heaven compared to their Quonset hut.

Monson was being backed into a corner in the county and dealing with real-world problems. The town's population and school enrollment were dwindling. From the time Monson won its first state championship in 1909 to its last one in 1968, its census had dramatically slipped from about 1,300 residents to less than 700, causing the town's tax revenue to drop. In the meantime, its two biggest sources of industry—slate mining and manufacturing—were fading like the color of leaves around town in December.

Monson's student population was facing a crisis. Teachers' salaries were rising, but enrollment was not. Kevin Nelson, at the time, was a student in Gary Webb's fourth- and fifth-grade combo class that had forty-three students packed tighter than Spam in a can. Teachers were not being paid extra for teaching double grades. The cost and quality of education was being compromised, and the townspeople were in a catch-22 situation.

Paul Allen, chairman of the School Department, noted in the 1966 Monson Town Report, "The people of Monson, in my opinion, are very concerned about what to do for the best secondary education for their children. At present there is a possibility of the Town of Monson joining into a School Administrative District with three areas, namely Dover-Foxcroft, Greenville, and Guilford." The State Master Plan for School Administrative Districting, Allen continued, places Monson with Greenville.

"The Monson Townspeople are in favor of keeping their children's education within the bounds of the town," Allen wrote. "It is my opinion that time is running out for secondary schools similar in size to Monson Academy, as they are unable to offer the comprehensive educational program to the students that is needed today."

In the 1967 Monson Town Report, Superintendent of Schools Norman W. Moulton explained why consolidation was needed, citing the long-range educational goals of Monson's children and rising costs, particularly to teachers' salaries.

"To compare the educational offering of today with the curriculum of thirty years ago is hardly different than comparing the Apollo Space program with Lindbergh's flight across the Atlantic," Moulton wrote.

Monson Academy, it would seem, was the *Titanic*, but with a better choice of lifeboats.

Consolidate with Greenville High School 17 miles to the north? Or go to Guilford, 11 miles to the south? Or go for broke and consolidate with Dover-Foxcroft? The townspeople were reluctant to send their children to Greenville, especially in the harsh Maine winters, and PCHS in Guilford was not ready to handle an influx of Monson students. Neither of those schools, however, offered educational resources, extracurricular activities, and the "Academy" moniker that Foxcroft Academy possessed.

The move to Dover-Foxcroft was endorsed by John Durham, one of the most influential people in Monson. He and his brother Telford helped turn a decaying slate-mining building into the Moosehead Manufacturing Company. In 1960, Moosehead Manufacturing opened a second plant in Dover-Foxcroft. The Durham family was pushing hard for consolidation at Foxcroft Academy. They got their wish and Monson Academy basketball buffs aimed their anger at John.

"I just don't understand the politics of it—how in the world would it benefit him—but he was always to blame. It was like Durham's crew against the rest of the town," said Buddy Leavitt, whose dad, Bud Sr., earned his diploma from Guilford High School. "There was joking that they had former employees wheeled into town in wheelchairs to vote. . . . That was a major political time back then. It split families. I couldn't for the life of me figure why anybody would want to get rid of our school, because I just loved it so."

On August 5, 1968, a special vote was taken in the towns of Dover-Foxcroft, Sebec, Charleston, and Monson on the formation of what was to become School Administrative District 68. The vote followed the recommendation of a study group of selectman and school board members who, after five meetings, presented a final proposed draft to the Maine State Department of Education. The draft noted that Monson Academy would remain open during the 1968–69 school year, then high school students would be transported to Dover-Foxcroft for the 1969–70 school year.

It was put up or shut up time, or, in Monson, shut down time.

All four towns voted in favor of the consolidation. According to the *Piscataquis Observer,* only seventy-eight people voted in Dover-Foxcroft, yet they voted unanimously in favor for SAD 68. Monson had by far the largest number of voters, and its vote was the closest, 77–58.

Thus the bus wheels were being set in motion. They would be steered toward Dover-Foxcroft no matter what anyone thought or cared.

"When you start talking tax dollars and how much a school that's got, what, sixty kids, depends on that then compare it to what you have to pay to send them to another school, it makes sense," Steve Bray said. "We were friends with a lot of the Greenville kids, and we talked among the basketball players. I think Greenville thought that would be a good consolidation there, but Greenville thought they got left out and then it's funny that we got bussed to Dover every day and we had to go right through Guilford. When it came to where we were going to go, I think the Durhams had more influence on that than anything."

Monson Academy students felt powerless. Though they were not old enough to vote on the matter, they could express their feelings. Some shared their private thoughts in words and poetry in the 1969 *Pharetra,* the Monson Academy yearbook.

Wrote Wanda Leavitt:

When I moved to this town, I thought it was great
Until our school was forced to consolidate
Foxcroft Academy is so far to go.
Especially in the freezing rain and snow.

We the kids, could have nothing to say,
But we are the ones who will have to pay.
The next town I move to I think I'll wait,
Before I decide and think it's so great.

Carol Mattson expressed fear and apprehension in a poem entitled "Good-Bye Old M.A."

We had a decision, a great one to make,
The out-come which made my old heart ache.
Old M.A. has been such a wonderful place,
Closing her doors will be hard to face.
All the joy has gone from her walls,
It's like a waterless Niagara Falls.
If I were older and lots of wealth,
I'd restore my old M.A. back to its health.
I'd make you bigger, and better than ever.
You'd outdo Dover or any other.

The Nelson family struggled with the final decision. Hollis, a logger man, was a Monson town selectman. Rose was working in Guilford at the time. One was a Democrat. The other a Republican. Yet, the Nelsons tried to be open-minded and forward-thinking.

"We were more focused on other things like, 'Who's doing the dishes tonight?'" Kevin said.

"Going to Greenville probably would have been the best for both towns—Monson and Greenville—and it would have boosted Greenville's enrollment numbers considerably," Shawn said. "Guilford overall in a sense for us might have been a happy medium. But, by the same token, I'm glad we didn't."

Instead of possibly building a basketball dynasty at home in Monson, Kevin Nelson, after his seventh-grade year, was going to be sent to Dover-Foxcroft, which had no distinguishable high school basketball tradition to speak of. The decision was out of his big hands.

"I was brought up to obey authority," Kevin said. "So, if these people in town made the decision to go where we are going who am I to question that? I was not brought up that way. The consolidation wasn't on my radar screen or any of the kids' radar screens unless you were inside the bubble of the decision makers. It was a goal and a motivation that we could win another state championship in Monson someday. In my seventh-grade year we had a good group of athletes and good players. In Class S if you had one or two really good players you stood a chance of running the table."

Kevin Nelson's idol felt the same way.

"One guy can carry a Class S team. It takes more in the bigger schools," Buddy Leavitt said. "One person with a decent supporting cast can win it all in a smaller school. The state championship team that I played on, everybody had a role and they accepted it and they were coachable kids and appreciative. Every one of those guys have as much a piece of that Gold Ball as I do."

That Gold Ball the Slaters won in 1968 now rests on top of a trophy case placed against the north wall on the top floor of the Monson Historical Society. The trophy case was removed from Monson Academy when it closed. Though Foxcroft Academy principal Tillson Thomas visited Monson Academy to address its students during the school's final year of operation as a high school, his words were hollow to most.

"The loss of a town's high school is a tough blow as many have pride and identify with the school. Citizens live vicariously through their schools and students," Glenn Poole wrote in *Monson Academy Revisited*.

"From the opening of the Quonset hut, the basketball program grew to be one of the very best in the state. Its departure from the scene was sorely felt."

The future of high school basketball in Monson would play out in Dover-Foxcroft. The anticipation of the seemingly inevitable closure of Monson Academy and other small schools was influential in a move in 1967 to reclassify high school basketball in the state of Maine to either add LLL to LL, L, and M and eliminate S or create new divisions A, B, C, and D.

"Monson Academy may be another of the SAD casualties with a move underway to have that school join Foxcroft Academy, bypassing Guilford and not going north to join ever closer Greenville. That would keep the S list dwindling," wrote *Bangor Daily News* sports columnist Owen Osborne.

For the 1969–70 season, the number of Class S basketball teams in Eastern Maine was down to thirteen and, following the 1970 season, Class S changed to Class D. In 2023, the Maine Principals' Association rejected a proposal to re-create a Class S for schools with enrollment under one hundred. It would have consisted of twenty-two schools state-wide, including Greenville, and would not have been split into regions. The MPA will continue to review school classifications.

Upper Kennebec Valley League schools from the 1960s consolidated with other school districts. Salon, North Anson, and North New Portland unified as Carrabec High School. Jackman morphed into Forest Hills High School. Bingham evolved as Upper Kennebec Valley High School. Harmony and Athens students went to Dexter High School. Hartland consolidated with Nokomis High School in Newport.

The final high school graduation ceremony in Monson was June 1969 with twenty-one seniors earning their diplomas. Monson Academy, a two-story wooden structure, was ultimately demolished in 1984, replaced by a bandstand. A block of black slate inscribed with the words "Site of Monson Academy 1884–1969" rests on a hillside next to the driveway leading to the former school.

"It was like this temple," Kevin Nelson said.

That shrine became a bus stop. It was the pick-up and drop-off location each school day to bus Monson students to and from Foxcroft Academy. Consolidation was being rubbed in their faces as they boarded the bus right next to Monson Academy whose doors were closed shut to them.

"I wanted to stay in Monson. That's where I grew up. That's where I went to school. That's where I was comfortable," Shawn Nelson said. "My freshman class was the biggest class that Monson Academy had ever had, and it had twenty-two kids in it. It was home. It was a shock going into a whole new world."

His younger brother concurred. Though his memories of growing up in Monson are frozen in time—watching the 1968 State Champion Slaters celebrate in the Monson Academy gym—Kevin Nelson's lifeline was always basketball. Going to Dover would extend that.

A huge custom-made orange-and-black sign was soon attached to the Monson town office on Main Street. The sign was shaped like a half-moon metal basketball backboard and read: "State Champions Class S." It was a memento, almost like a coat of arms, to commemorate the last homegrown team phenomenon in Monson.

Kevin drew inspiration from that sign as the school bus to Dover pulled out of the Monson Academy driveway each school day beginning in his eighth-grade year. The consolidation was crushing to the basketball-crazed town, yet Kevin tried to put a positive spin on it. He still had a place to go to play the game.

"I wasn't planning on anything, but I told myself I'm going to keep playing basketball," Kevin said. "It was the way it was."

And so it was. That's the way the basketball was bouncing for Kevin. He would be dribbling and passing and shooting it in a maroon-and-white Foxcroft Academy uniform away from home in a bigger town that had no basketball state championship sign to speak of nor proudly display for all to see.

Dover-Foxcroft, to Kevin Nelson at the time, was just another destination with a hoop. "That was the context about everything with me at that age: Where would I be playing basketball? That was most important to me. It wasn't the educational opportunities necessarily," he said. "I always had seen the teams from Dover come up to the Monson gym and play us. My reaction was I would be going to a place where I would be playing basketball with people I used to play against. The world was in front of me then. I didn't know what to expect."

Jump, Kevin, Jump!

THE YELLOW SCHOOL BUS PULLED UP ON MAYO STREET IN DOVER-Foxcroft for the first day of school for Kevin Nelson in 1970. It was his day one in the Consolidation Era. It was scary beyond belief.

From his vantage point, Dover Grammar School, newly named SeDoMoCha Middle School, looked like Alcatraz. If he had a basketball, one might have thought it was attached to a chain to lug to class.

"I remember stepping off that bus from Monson to Dover that September morning and it was almost like prisoners being brought to a prison. There was so much fear and nervousness," Kevin said. "It was palpable for all us Monson kids, but I think I had the advantage of having played against a bunch of Dover kids in my fifth- and sixth- and seventh-grade years. I remember John Danforth—who became my best friend—meeting me at the foot of the bus."

Other students gathered around Danforth, more naturally out of curiosity than anything. They were to be classmates, not inmates, and they wanted to get the first glimpse of these out-of-towners. Who was this new big kid from Monson stepping off the bus and onto their turf? Would he hit his head on the door jamb stepping out? If he did, who would break his fall?

"He was a monster compared to all of us," Scott Mountford said. "I'm sure he was intimidated by a new school, and we all were intimidated by his height. He was the new guy in town, so we didn't want him jumping on our girlfriends."

Whether he was a Prince Charming or a Wilt Chamberlain, Kevin Nelson certainly was making a big first impression. Kids were staring up at him. He was looking down on them. It was an awkward situation in more ways than one.

"My earliest memory of Kevin was in eighth grade when he and Valerie Mussy, who was 4-foot-2, tripped over each other in the hallway," said classmate Keith Chadbourne.

Kevin—tall, dark, and gangly—was more a threat at that point than a teammate. All the Dover kids knew about Kevin Nelson was that he was big. A big mystery. They knew little about his life before Dover. In Monson, Kevin could have lived an iconic Norman Rockwell existence, but, in Dover, he was a blank canvas.

The Dover kids didn't know that Kevin was crown bearer for the 25th Annual Monson Winter Carnival in 1962. They didn't know he received a Cub Scout wolf badge and had his first communion in Dover in 1965. They didn't know he circulated the guest book at his grandparents' golden wedding anniversary. And they for sure didn't know Kevin starred in Monson Elementary School's production of *Goldilocks and the Three Bears* in 1967.

"My future as a thespian was pretty bleak," Kevin quipped.

Nevertheless, Scott Mountford's first description of Kevin Nelson as a monster looked way off target and out of bounds. Monster? Kevin Nelson appeared to be more like an oversized Opie in Maine's version of *Mayberry RFD*. He had a sweet innocence about him. Polite. Sincere. Too good to be true.

"My first impression was he is tall! At the time I was only like 5-foot-6," Dick Hatt said. "I didn't really talk to him much then, but what I did notice was his humility. Really a humble guy for being so popular."

They suspected on that first day of school in 1970 that Kevin Nelson should, could, and would play basketball. A tall kid was as likely to be associated with playing basketball than a shy kid wearing glasses being stereotyped as a nerd. Kevin was made to play basketball, right?

In reality, his new classmates and teammates at Dover Grammar School had no idea of Kevin's journey. They did not know that Kevin came close to quitting basketball. He had his doubts. He had his challenges.

As a toddler growing up, Kevin was too often ill and was inexplicably losing weight. His parents, Rose and Hollis, finally decided to take him to a specialist. The doctor ended up taking a biopsy on his left calf. Kevin still has the scar on his leg.

"Back then polio was the rage, and I was just listless," Kevin said. "The only thing I would eat was eggnog. I just liked eggnog. My mother told me my dad would just rock me to make me feel better."

It turned out that Kevin did not have polio, but his father, years later in the final days of his life, insisted that Kevin had had "a touch of polio."

"I don't know how you get a touch of polio," Kevin said, "but I was born a very chubby little kid and I just got thin and didn't eat well for a long time."

Nevertheless, Kevin to this day believes the early age illness and polio scare is the reason he was always skinny. He was in the shape of an I to everyone else's W. He didn't spend as much time on the scales, as he did standing against a bathroom doorway in the Nelson house where his mother would measure his height. She would guide a pencil horizontally across the top of Kevin's head and mark the doorway behind him, then measure his height from that mark to the floor.

It never occurred to Rose that she might one day need a stepladder to do this.

Kevin was told he inherited his height from his father Hollis, who was 6-foot-4, but the lineage of tall Nelsons goes back to Kevin's paternal great-grandmother, Marcia Pennington. She and her husband, Samuel, married in Monson in 1886.

The Nelson homestead was off Steward Road, a 2½ mile straight and hilly backroad in Southeast Monson connecting the Willimantic Road and the North Guilford Road. There were no streetlights to speak of. Porch lights and the moon provided the best source of illumination on dark nights. At one time there was a small one-room schoolhouse off Steward Road, and today Turning Page Farm Brewery is the local attraction.

Southeast Monson is now designated by a bronzed sign off the Willimantic Road reading Vinton District. It's a tribute to the Hiram

Vinton family, who moved to Monson, Maine from Monson, Massachusetts to become one of the first families to settle in the area.

To get directions to the Nelson's childhood house in the pre–Google Maps days one needed a pen or pencil and a long notepad or about a dozen Post-it notes. It's not easy to get from here to there. The quickest way to drive from Dover-Foxcroft to Southeast Monson back then would be to drive out West Main Street past Mountain's Market, Butterfield's Ice Cream and Foxcroft Academy onto the Guilford Road, go past Low's Covered Bridge and Herring's Meat Market before taking a right on Guilford Center Road, past the cemetery and driving to a dead end at the T intersection of Blaine Avenue/Route 150. Veer right there then take a left onto North Guilford Road then take a right onto Steward Road. The Nelson house, with a gravel driveway and big barn, was on the right. You can miss it.

Road atlas maker Rand McNally needed a microscope to find Southeast Monson. Though Piscataquis County is Maine's second-largest county, it is the state's least populated. One might find more people in line at Dunkin' Donuts than people on Steward Road.

Living in Southeast Monson was considered to be living "out in the country," a term for someone who resides somewhere between "the middle of nowhere" and "Hicksville." It is where few snowplows venture. The closest body of water is Second Davis Pond, which is north of First Davis Pond and south of Third Davis Pond, literally proof of just how simplistic life can be in Maine.

Though only four miles away, to a kid growing up in Southeast Monson, downtown Monson seemed like light years from civilization. In some ways, Kevin lived a sheltered life, which was more a by-product of where he lived and not how he was raised. He and his older brother Shawn were three years apart in age, a gap that prevented them from being closer as siblings, thus they didn't share the same interests. With Rose and Hollis both working, their sons relied on their legs or their bicycles to get them from here to there. Mostly they had to stay here at home and improvise.

"We invented our own entertainment," Kevin said.

Kevin's closest friend and perhaps only friend on Steward Road growing up was Mike Sandberg, who lived with his family about three hundred yards down the road. In the wintertime, they would go sliding on hills in plastic saucers or dig and make their own snow caves from large snow drifts or mounds of snow created by snowplowing or by drifts caused by a nor'easter, New England slang for a blizzard.

In the summertime, they might build a tree house or play kids' games like cowboys and Indians and ride their bikes along Steward Road. In those days, kids collected baseball cards yet they would take some and attach them to the spokes of their bikes with wooden clothes pins to make a neat snapping noise. They placed as much value in the stick of bubble gum in the package than the stack of cards.

Kevin swears he may have used a Mickey Mantle card—Mantle's rookie card is now valued to be over a million dollars in some cases—on his bike.

"Can you imagine how much a Mickey Mantle baseball card would be now?" he said. "But, no, I had to go out and put it in the spokes of my bike to make a rubbing noise out of it."

Kevin's mother kept a close eye on him. Rose played the piano and sang at weddings and funerals. She belonged to an album club and would play Al Hirt, Andy Williams, Ray Conniff, and Herb Albert and the Tijuana Brass while cleaning house and cooking.

"She had an influence on us and we never gravitated toward it," Kevin said.

Rose also loved reading and passed that hobby onto Kevin. His parents bought a set of *World Book Encyclopedias* for the house.

"That was my internet back then. I just devoured it," said Kevin who, had he not become a state basketball champion, might have been a Jeopardy champion.

While Rose tended to the house, Hollis worked in the woods as a private contractor cutting and logging pulp. When he went to work, Rose would make him lunch and pack it in a metal lunch box. "He would come home and we would always go and open his lunch pail and he always made sure there were a couple of cookies left for us. That was important to him," Kevin said.

When home, Hollis would tend to his garden and make time for his kids. Kevin would grab his baseball glove and a rubber ball and play catch by himself by bouncing the ball off the side of the barn or off its roof. When twilight came, his dad would surprise him by coming out of the barn with a bat in hand. Wearing a baseball cap and his Dickies work boots, Hollis would hit pop flies to Kevin until it was too dark to see.

"That's how we really bonded," Kevin said. "My dad. This is why I am the way I am and always have been. My mother was the great communicator. I could talk to her about anything and everything. My dad, he wasn't like that. He lived by example."

The Nelsons rooted for the Boston Red Sox. Kevin had a poster of Carl Yastrzemski on his bedroom wall as Yaz was worshipped throughout New England beginning in 1967 with the Red Sox "Impossible Dream" team. Hollis would listen to Red Sox games on the radio. He would sit at the bar in the kitchen with a glass of milk, and Kevin would sit at the kitchen table. Kevin would be listening to the game, too, while reading his copy of *Who's Who in Baseball* to learn about each player.

"I wish I could have remembered chemistry and physics and biology that way, but I remembered all these baseball stats and I would tell my dad. I would recite the stuff to him," Kevin said. "I think he got the biggest kick out of that. I think I became his own personal color commentator."

Of course, the Nelson boys couldn't relax until their chores were done. They had to mow the lawn or hang laundry on the clothesline or fill the wood box as the house was heated by wood. They also did the dishes. One brother would wash and the other would dry, though Shawn claims Kevin would conveniently excuse himself to go to the bathroom to escape that chore.

One time Hollis and Rose, in an effort to escape their physically demanding jobs, decided to open a restaurant on Main Street in Monson called The Coffee Shop. They were proprietors for only one year.

"We as a family years later laughed about why they did that for only a year. They laughingly said, 'Because you two boys were getting into too much trouble while we were working in the city,'" Kevin said.

Kevin and Shawn knew better than to get in trouble. Their home life was Beaver Cleaver-like.

"I rarely if ever heard any profanity and there was no alcohol in the house," Kevin said. "My mother was the frontline person to say, 'Look, wait until your father gets home.' That was enough of a detriment for me personally. He was a big man. He never hurt us physically, but he was a presence. It was enough to say, 'I think I better wise up.'"

In the summers, Kevin and Shawn would join their dad in the woods, which was hard and grimy work. They learned to drive a tractor, use a chain saw, and help their dad log pulp. It was hot and humid, and there were black fleas, mosquitos, and other bugs and insects swarming around them.

It looked and sounded like an episode of *Naked and Afraid.*

To earn extra money, Kevin sold packets of vegetable and flowers seeds through the American Seed Company of Lancaster, Pennsylvania, from colorful ads he saw in comic books. He would sell the seeds and earn points to buy swell prizes from a catalog. One of his first purchases was a chemistry set with a Bunsen burner.

"Parents letting their kids have a chemistry set that had a Bunsen burner! What were they thinking?" Kevin joked. "We had it set up in the attic off my mother and father's closet. With a Bunsen burner there! We could have burned down the house! I don't know what they were thinking. I was thinking, 'Wow, this is pretty special. I have a chemistry set and no one is around to see what I'm doing and I'm mixing all these chemicals in all these test tubes and lighting them on fire.' This could have gone sideways real fast."

The best purchase Kevin made from selling seeds was buying his first basketball and basketball rim. He bought them from the *American Seed* catalog rather than a *Montgomery Ward* or *Sears Roebuck* catalog, which most adults preferred as there were few sporting goods stores. Basketball was becoming Kevin's go-to activity at home and his attention-getter at school.

It was obvious then that Kevin was tall, which made him the center of attraction in Monson Elementary School. He seemed as big as Mount Katahdin about 100 miles away and as ominous as Borestone Mountain about 10 miles up the Elliotsville Road. Fellow students in Monson were always looking up to him, including the girls. He was more focused on impressing them than shooting a basketball at that young age. "My interests were not big picture at that point in my life," Kevin said.

One day in fourth grade, Kevin, now the proverbial big man on campus, was taught a lesson in humility. He was playing kickball during recess when he cut in line. His new twenty-two-year-old fourth grade teacher, Carla Lund, was watching and she scolded him.

"She caught me and she went up one side of me and down the other and said, 'Who do you think you are getting in front of someone else? You're no more special than anyone else. Get back in line,'" Kevin said. "She put me in my place. . . . Incidences like that get lodged in your brain. This was about the time I started playing basketball. Who knows what kind of impact that had on me. I felt terrible."

Kevin has never forgotten that incident nor the fact Miss Lund gave him a kiss on the cheek on the last day of school. Apparently, all was forgiven.

"I thought, 'Holy crap! I'm not washing this kiss off my face!'" Kevin said.

About that time the success of the Slaters' boys basketball team also became the apple of Kevin's eye. He and his parents and brother would drive to Monson Academy and root for the Slaters, who were perennial contenders to win the Upper Kennebec Valley League championship and advance deep into the Eastern Maine Class S Tournament.

Kevin remembers walking into the Quonset hut gym and seeing Monson fan Agnes Ackley. She was multitasking with one eye on the game and the other on her needles.

"She sat in the bleachers on the left and she brought her knitting during the game," Kevin said. "The game was the only thing going on in town. That was it. It was something you looked forward to. That was pretty special. You would go there and see all these players you just revered."

The Slaters in any year were the talk of the town from the supper table to Cookie Poole's grocery store where any Monson basketball player could buy a Coke then receive a critique as they passed the cash register. Cookie, the town's sports fanatic, would give them his two cents in more ways than one.

Basketball was the heartbeat of the town, and Cookie was among many who checked the pulse. To the people of Monson, basketball wasn't just a game, it was like a religious revival.

"The only thing we did in Monson that meant anything was play basketball," Shawn Nelson said.

At the very least basketball got them through the winter. As comedian Jeff Foxworthy once said: You know you live in Maine if you know all four seasons: Almost Winter, Winter, Still Winter, and, of course, Road Construction.

To get around town, the bare necessities included a snow shovel to get to your car, an ice scraper to clear the windshield, and snow tires to back it out of the driveway.

In Monson, once the autumn leaves dropped to the ground and the trees became bare and winter played its first cards, entertainment options were limited, particularly in an era before cable TV, video stores, and video games. In a Maine winter, animals hibernate, birds migrate, and people spend most of their time indoors. There's a stillness and quiet outside that sets in like a fog.

The greatest distraction during winter was the sound of basketballs bouncing, sneakers squeaking, and fans cheering in the local gymnasium. High school basketball games broke up the monotony of winters in Maine from Thanksgiving until the leaves and green grass grew back and the red-breasted robins returned. Basketball helped people endure the dreariest days of the year, especially in a small town like Monson.

Kevin Nelson was drawn to basketball and the opportunity and excitement it brought. His first coach was Alva Crockett, who had two basketball-playing sons, Jimmy and Preston. Kevin's first idol was Buddy Leavitt. That's who Kevin longed to be in Monson. He identified with the Slaters' star center who, like Kevin, shot left-handed. Kevin became so enamored with Buddy that in elementary school Kevin drew a picture of Buddy on construction paper with crayons and scribbled a personal note: "You a real fine basketball player."

"He had me with stick figure legs about 10 feet taller than anyone else I was playing against," said Leavitt, who still has the picture.

Rose passed that picture onto Buddy's mom, Dorcas, whose husband, Bud, occasionally worked in the woods with Hollis.

"Buddy was everybody's idol. He was 6-foot-5. He was a good-looking guy, but what distinguished him was that his confidence level was like to the moon," Kevin said. "He had a high skill set. He could handle the ball. He could shoot the ball."

Kevin started playing organized basketball in fourth grade, and he tried to pattern his game after Buddy Leavitt and Jake Smith, another great Monson athlete who was so good that he played baseball on the Slaters' varsity high school team when he was in eighth grade. Jake at one time had a job as a janitor at Monson Academy and he would allow Kevin to come into the gym and shoot. If he had time, Jake would set aside his broom and help Kevin with his shooting and his defense in the Monson gym, which was located between the elementary school and high school buildings.

Jake Smith was like Mr. Miyagi to Kevin.

"He spent some time with me and helped me out on a lot of things. He was just a huge figure in Monson in terms of basketball for me," Kevin said. "He was this prototypical basketball player. Terrific athlete. He was one of those guys that if Monson Academy had a football team, he certainly would have been a football player. He was a confident guy and he had a big motor."

Though tiny in terms of enrollment, Monson played against larger junior high school teams like Dover's. However, to fill out its roster, Monson had to use fourth and fifth graders to play against Dover's "B" squad, which consisted of mostly sixth graders and some seventh graders. That discrepancy in age and experience led to many lopsided games. Kevin was 5–11 in sixth grade and still raw and undeveloped as a basketball player. He was being asked to play against eighth graders. It was a mismatch.

"My memory of that was thinking, 'That's the way the world is, Kevin.' These are the teams you get to play around here whether it's Greenville, Guilford, Dover, Dexter. These are the teams you play," he said. "These teams have good players. This is what we've got. We go out and lay it all on the court and if you lose 58–3 or 69–4 or whatever . . . it didn't feel good, but that's what it was."

The score of the games, however, did not reflect Kevin's upside. He just needed a more level playing field on which to compete.

"He was a big kid and he had a great attitude and a great family and he was smart," Steve Bray said. "You just knew he was going to turn into something special."

Kevin trudged on. One of his early coaches, Bill Clark, pushed him to improve his basketball ability. He realized Kevin, because of his height, would have a natural advantage on the basketball court. But Clark also realized that Kevin couldn't rely solely on his reach. During practices and even before games, Clark, raising his voice, would implore Kevin to leap and bound for the basketball.

JUMP, KEVIN, JUMP!

This became Clark's mantra, like Jenny repeatedly yelling to Forrest Gump, "Run, Forrest, Run!" Clark was trying to will Kevin to leave his feet and improve his vertical leap. This practice wore on Kevin.

"You need to sink or swim; either I could shrink up and not do what he says and shy away from it or I try to respond to it and use it as motivation," Kevin said. "I think, even though I was kind of a timid kid, I think I used that. I liked Mr. Clark."

However, between Clark's pleas and Monson's poundings on the basketball court, Kevin had serious doubts about continuing to play the game. The coach's instructions made sense and had a purpose, but the result was another disheartening loss at the end of the day. Kevin and his team didn't win a single game against grammar school competition in fourth and fifth grade.

"That's how I grew up. That's how I launched my whole basketball endeavor: Getting crushed every single game," Kevin said. "What did that do to me mentally or emotionally? I don't know, but I did step into a program that was beaten every year and I was an integral part of that program, which could have formed my character and my whole confidence level much different than it did. It wasn't demoralizing, because we just got to play. If you didn't like it, you could go up to Lake Hebron at night and ice skate or do something different."

Kevin did consider something different. *Anything* different. He questioned whether his passive personality was conducive to the competitiveness of basketball in a small town that thrived on the game. Kevin thought about quitting basketball but was talked out of it.

"What if it hadn't happened? I don't know if I would have kept playing basketball," Kevin says. "I was a very timid kid. That was my nature. I wasn't somebody who was aggressive. I almost didn't play my seventh-grade year."

It was at this juncture that Bill Clark, who also was a teacher in Monson, jumped in. He met with Kevin's parents and expressed his belief in Kevin's potential as a basketball player. Clark convinced the Nelsons to convince Kevin to keep playing.

"They were kind of leaning to me to play basketball," Kevin said. "I don't ever remember any sort of pressure. But the only thing offered in school was school sports. Up in Monson there wasn't a music program or a drama program or anything like that at that level. It was all about sports. As I grew taller . . . C'mon. What am I going to do? Am I going to play checkers or something? I got more interested in basketball. I went to Monson Academy basketball games as an elementary school kid and was just being wide-eyed. I was thinking, 'Wow, this is the coolest thing.' Eventually I thought I would be playing there and little did we know I would never be playing for Monson Academy. I'd be playing for Foxcroft."

The Nelson family was unified about playing basketball wherever it took them. Hollis had played basketball at Monson Academy, and Rose had been a student at Greenville High School before Wayne Champeon led the Lakers to a state basketball championship in 1954. They raised their kids with family values found in sports.

"If you did something wrong in our house, you were accountable for it," Kevin said.

Hard work and teamwork was the foundation of the family. The Nelsons pulled together and pooled their resources to make ends meet. Though they lived near Poverty Road, they were not poor. Hollis was a full-time woodsman, but he also worked part-time as a substitute postal carrier. When they weren't working with their dad in the woods, Kevin and Shawn on summer afternoons would bale hay with their dad's relatives living down the road. Thurley Knowles would rake the hay, Kevin and Shawn would bale and lift the hay onto a truck driven by Thurley's sister, Eloise (or "Weezie"), and her husband would load it into the barn on a conveyor belt. Then they would all celebrate by drinking a pitcher of Kool-Aid.

The Nelsons were sustained by the simple pleasures in life.

"We were a blue-collar family," Shawn said. "We didn't have a lot of luxurious things."

For fun, the biggest investment in time and money for the Nelsons was to go snowmobiling in the winter. They couldn't afford to buy a snowmobile, so they rented one for a couple of weekends. There were plenty of open fields and some snowmobile trails near them to explore in the Maine woods and they made the best of their snowmobile adventures.

Fortunately for Shawn and Kevin, they had basketball to pass their time all the time. Jimmy Ranta had a basketball hoop in his family's barn, and Jimmy and Preston Crockett had a basketball hoop upstairs in their barn. The Greenleafs and the Leavitts had basketball hoops and it didn't matter what time of the year they played basketball—from humid summer days to brutally cold winter nights.

"Sometimes the ball was so cold we couldn't bounce it, but we made believe we were bouncing it or we would be called for traveling," Buddy said.

"A lot of the kids after school many nights would go to one of those places and play ball until it got too dark to see," Shawn said.

Finally, as a sign of progress, the Town of Monson built an outdoor basketball court on blacktop outside Monson Academy. This became the most treasured destination when the kids got the urge to dribble and shoot before, during, or after school. Not even an overnight snowstorm would keep them from playing. They brought a shovel with their basketball.

A blacktopped basketball court being built in Monson was like a baseball diamond being built in the middle of a corn field in Iowa.

"That was a big day," Steve Bray said. "Everyone in school helped move the backboards around and fill up the dirt in the barrels behind them. That was big. We had those outside chains as nets. We used to love the sound of the ball coming through the chained nets."

"We wore that court out," Buddy Leavitt said. "We played hoops 24/7."

For the Nelson brothers, however, a trip to Monson usually required a school bus.

During school they would take the bus to town and that could be an adventure. One day, when Kevin was in elementary school, he and Shawn and other students who lived out in the country were being driven to class by "Super" Franny Jones, a school bus driver and dedicated sportsman. Suddenly, Jones spotted a partridge perched on the side of the road and veered the bus slightly off course. He killed the partridge in its tracks.

"He used the bus like a weapon," Kevin said. "He got out and picked the partridge up and went to the back bumper and snapped its neck. Then he put the bird under his driver's seat. When he got home, he must have plucked it or put it in the refrigerator to save for supper."

Years later, perhaps inspired by Franny Jones and others, a new restaurant called The Roadkill Cafe opened in Greenville.

Though they used more conventional weapons than the bumper of a school bus, Shawn and his dad were avid hunters and fishermen and, in Maine, hunting and fishing go together like the L.L. in Bean. Kevin found them boring. He did save up his money for a long time to buy a fishing pole in the hardware store in Monson, but he didn't get much use out of it.

"Back in those days in the sixties before the environmental movement, Lake Hebron was not clean at all," Kevin said. "It was just filthy. It had tires that were thrown in there. Bed frames. Broken glass. You didn't walk in that water because you didn't know what you'd step on. The only fish in there were sunfish."

Kevin found more joy playing basketball. He didn't need to be taken by the sport hook, line, and sinker. He and his brother had their very own basketball arena on their farm in the form of the family's barn. This was their Boston Garden.

In an adjoining shed there was a horse sleigh on the far wall, and its rudders formed a triangle. Shawn and Kevin would throw a small ball through the triangle and pretend it was a basketball hoop. In time, they had a real basketball hoop attached above the front door of the barn where they would play and shoot free throws day or night in rain, sleet, and snow. Eventually Shawn got creative.

"Then I got a little more adept with a handsaw and a hammer and I built a wooden backboard, almost a regulation-sized backboard, and we put it inside our barn at our house," Shawn said. "We hung it from a cross beam in the barn."

The barn, which smelled of hay and dust, was dimly lit at first, but Hollis placed a spotlight above the barn door inside facing the basket. The "court" was made of old rough-hewn boards with bumps and cracks that made it challenging to dribble. It was inside that barn that Shawn would invite Kevin to go one-on-one.

At first, the games were fun. Shawn pretended to be Bill Russell or Walt Bellamy or Nate Thurmond or Willis Reed, he said, "because I hated Wilt Chamberlain." Kevin pretended to be anyone but a Boston Celtics player. He didn't like the Celtics and felt that the sight of Boston coach Arnold "Red" Auerbach lighting a victory cigar after every win smelled of arrogance.

"I didn't like that as a feature or characteristic of anybody," Kevin said. "I can remember being in my mother and father's bedroom and going upstairs and in one corner I would put a small trash can and in the other corner I would put another small trash can and I would play simulated games with rolled-up socks. Oh my God. I would purposely throw the game if it was Celtics-Sixers game in favor of the Sixers."

It is perhaps the only time in his life Kevin can be accused of trash talking.

When the rolled-up socks were put back in the sock drawer, Kevin would shoot in the barn by himself. Occasionally he would play against Shawn. They played on the wooden floor in the barn, which, according to black numerals on one of its walls, was built in 1886. There wasn't much space above the wooden backboard. It was tight with not a lot of elbow room.

"If you shot with too much of an arc, it would hit the roof. It was a cathedral ceiling, but if you were facing the hoop like you were going to take a foul shot, the foul line would have been like only nine feet from the basket," Shawn said. "We didn't learn to shoot foul shots there."

Kevin, to his credit, developed a hook shot in that barn. He also developed an attitude.

"Most of the time it was one-on-one then we'd get to arguing and fighting and then it was one and nobody else," Shawn said.

Translation: Kevin would storm into the house.

"We had a love and hate relationship sometimes," Shawn said.

Kevin was known to have thrown rocks at Shawn as a kid and one time, when Shawn had been teasing Kevin and was running away from him into the shed, Kevin angrily picked up a lead pipe on the doorstep and hurled it at Shawn. It knocked him out.

"I won't deny that there were times that I hurled a few retaliatory projectiles at him, but he seems to have developed a case of amnesia or else he conveniently forgot to mention the time he threw a dart at me and stuck one in my temple," Kevin said. "Clearly, neither one of us was an angel."

As they got older, Shawn's child's play became more purposeful. He realized his younger brother had the height to be an exceptional basketball player so he would play rough in their one-on-one games. Shawn's strategy was to make Kevin a better basketball player in the long run. Kevin didn't buy it at the time.

"We were typical brothers. He was such an independent-minded person. Because I was as tall as I was, he wanted me to be as tough as he was. And I just wasn't," Kevin said. "I never saw him as being someone who was trying to make me a better player. I saw it as someone who was just trying to push me around. That's how I thought about it back then."

Kevin was naturally demure. Maybe it was the tender way in which he was nurtured and raised after his polio scare? Maybe the Miss Lund kickball episode at recess robbed him of his aggressiveness? Maybe years of being isolated on Steward Road prevented him from being more outgoing and assertive?

"I think a large part of it was the DNA implant in me—the Nelson side of my family," Kevin said. "We weren't very demonstrative. It just wasn't embedded in me."

Mentally, Kevin had some growing up to do to be the basketball player everyone else thought he could be. Physically, too, he was a work in progress. But Buddy Leavitt, his idol, started taking notice, assessing that Kevin was skinny yet worked hard, despite having problems with his footwork and his feet.

Kevin's feet might as well have been fitted for basketball like Fred Flintstone's were fitted for driving and braking.

"You think back to the type of footwear we had back then. We had nothing," Kevin said. "You might as well have been playing in sandals."

Indeed, Kevin was playing basketball with a degree of pain.

"He had a bone on the side of one foot that protruded so that he went through a ritual to put on his sneaker just to be comfortable. The poor kid suffered," Buddy said. "He grew in grade school like a son of a gun. If you look at old yearbook class pictures of him in the fifth grade or sixth grade, here's Kevin in the back and you're thinking, 'Who the hell is that kid?' He was head and shoulders taller than anyone else."

Kevin thought the same thing later in life when he looked through scrapbooks. In sixth grade, he was 5-foot-11. In seventh grade, he was 6–2. In eighth grade, he was 6-foot-5 and ¾. He grew almost six inches from sixth to eighth grade.

"He looked like Manute Bol playing with ants," Buddy said.

But could Kevin compete with the big boys? And not just at basketball? Kevin was raised to be well-rounded, equal parts athletics and encyclopedias.

In the spring of 1969, Rose drove her youngest son to the Dover Grammar School gym for a competition. It wasn't a basketball game, but a spelling contest. Kevin was a contestant in the annual Piscataquis County Spelling Bee.

"And I didn't last long," Kevin said, smiling.

He recalls getting through the first round and anticipated the second word would be just as easy. The word was "rough."

Kevin, feeling confident, spelled it R-U-F-F.

"I looked at the bee master like he had two heads, 'What do you mean I'm wrong? Of course, it's spelled R-U-F-F,'" Kevin said.

Then Kevin realized his mistake.

"I used to read the cartoons in the paper, and Dennis the Menace's dog was named Ruff," he explained.

Fortunately, the next important competition he had at the Dover Grammar School gym didn't involve spelling. He came to Dover Grammar having been the Most Valuable Player on the Monson Grammar School "A" squad team as a seventh grader. He received his MVP trophy and his "M" letter at a buffet supper in the Monson gymnasium in March 1970 from the school's principal Bill Clark, the coach who asked Kevin's parents to persuade him to keep playing basketball. It didn't hurt when Kevin's teams won a game every so often.

"I remember the elation of being able to win some games in sixth and seventh grade," Kevin said. "I think we beat Dexter my seventh-grade year and we could have beaten UCLA and not been any happier."

Coming to Dover Grammar was an awakening of sorts. Kevin and his new classmates and soon-to-be new teammates quickly developed a friendship during recess in a Miss Lund Free Zone. There were two standing baskets on the blacktop outside the school, a tether ball and pole, and, beyond that, a grass field large enough to play football. That was the breeding ground for their team chemistry.

Kevin also played on Dover Grammar's baseball team, which played and practiced on the diamond at the Piscataquis County Fairgrounds across town. His legs were so long that the school didn't have baseball pants that fit him, so he had to wear jeans with his uniform top. Kevin was a pitcher and evidently could throw a baseball so hard that it broke the middle finger of John Danforth, his catcher.

In fact, Kevin threw a no-hitter against Greenville.

"But there is a provider," Kevin said. "I think I walked like 15 batters. It was not a perfect game."

Though basketball was Kevin's first love, he also liked baseball. In seventh grade, he built a baseball diamond in a field next to the family's farmhouse on Stewart Road. Yes, Kevin had his own *Field of Dreams*.

"For some reason I kept hearing voices saying, 'If you build it, they will come,'" Kevin joked. "But unfortunately no one came."

His first homeroom teacher and baseball and basketball coach in Dover was Gary Larson. He had replaced Eben DeWitt, who ultimately became the superintendent of schools for SAD 68. At Dover Grammar, DeWitt was a highly successful basketball coach, but Larson was ready to make a change in philosophy. He had played basketball in high school for the Brownville Junction Railroaders and their Hall of Fame coach Carroll Conley.

"Eben was one of these coaches who liked big people and he always played a zone," Larson said. "And then he retired, and I took over and switched to the skills I had learned from Carroll Conley and played man-to-man defense because I thought it was better in the long run for the kids."

When Larson was promoted from "B" Squad to "A" squad coach at Dover Grammar, he soon came to realize that Kevin had the height and the passion to succeed at basketball. During that season, Kevin and his new teammates would knock on the door of Larson's apartment on High Street and beg him to open the Dover Grammar School gym close by so they could play.

"The kids would come over on a weekend and ask me if I could get them in the school's gymnasium and you could do that then and no one would say anything," Larson said. "My wife kept reminding me that Kevin would have to duck to get into our apartment."

Not only did Kevin and his teammates have the self-motivation to get better and the drive to be champions, they also helped Larson drive. There were times when they had to jump-start Larson's MG Midget, huddling around the coach's car.

"The kids at school did a lot of pushing because the distributor cap would not work correctly so they would come outside and give me a push to get started and I'd be on the way," Larson said.

Once the 1970–71 Dover Grammar School basketball season started, there was no stopping the Eagles, the nickname of Dover Grammar. The team's coach and the team were all adjusting nicely to Kevin and his height. He was a welcome sight.

"We were all so small and I remember our tallest player at the time was probably like 6-foot or 6–1 or 6–2 and he was a giant compared to the rest of us," Jeff Dunn said. "Then Kevin comes in."

Kevin was head over heels better than everyone on the team, so Larson had some of the Dover Grammar faculty practice against the "A" squad. One of them was a teacher, David Michaud.

"He was like the first big guy I ever played against," Kevin said. "I think he had a master's degree and he was like 6–4. I'm thinking, 'This guy is a man. I'm not a man. This is a man.'"

With Kevin being pushed at practice and getting acclimated to his new teammates, the Eagles were soaring. Kevin and Scott Mountford, who moved to Dover-Foxcroft from Millinocket in elementary school, became co-captains, fast friends, and kindred spirits.

"Scott was one of the most gregarious people on our team," Kevin said. "He was a likable guy. He was a tough guy, too. He was just out there. Nothing scared him. Nothing intimidated him. He was such a great personality to be around, and he was such a good athlete."

During their first season together at Dover Grammar, Scott was invited to Kevin's house in Southeast Monson for a birthday party. There had been a snowstorm and the snow had drifted so high they were able to step up from the shed and walk onto the roof of the barn. They pulled a toboggan behind them to the top and literally slid down the roof to the drifting snow below.

"You find entertainment where you can find it," Kevin said. "We'd climb up there to the top with the toboggan and as soon as we lifted our feet up you were flying down."

Mountford also was quite daring inside the house. He was a growing boy and took liberties at eating any snacks around the Nelson house during the birthday party.

"His mother eyeballed me because I ate all the clam dip," Scott said.

Rose Nelson may have given Scott Mountford an icy glare, but it didn't compare to the cold conditions he and his teammates faced after practices and games at Dover Grammar. The rectangular-shaped concrete gym, which had few windows, had four rows of wooden bleachers on one side of the court; the other side stepped up to a stage that served as the seating area for lunch at the school cafeteria where there was a kitchen in the corner. There were no lockers or dressing rooms in the gym. The basketball players had to change and shower in a dressing room in the basement of Mayo Street School next door where sixth graders attended class.

To get from the Dover Grammar gym to that dressing room in the Mayo Street School, the players—hot and sweaty after games or practices—would have to exit through a side door into the freezing cold on most evenings then turn left and scurry up a small, albeit slippery, hill about 30 feet to Mayo Street School. This was the definition of an Arctic blast before the *Weather Channel*.

However, Kevin and his Monson teammate Barry Church didn't have time to take a shower after practices. They had a SAD 68 activity bus to catch. On some winter nights after basketball practice, the activity bus would drop Kevin off at the corner of Steward Road and the North Guilford Road and then drive off. He would have to walk alone uphill the last mile to his house, even if it was pitch black and might be freezing cold and snowing or sleeting. There were nights when Kevin didn't get home until 8 or 8:30 to thaw out, have supper, then do his homework.

Most days Kevin had to board two busses each way to get him from Southeast Monson to Monson to Dover-Foxcroft and back. Those busses were on a tight schedule, making the commute a challenging experience for Monson students, particularly Barry who had challenges in daily life. He was deaf. Barry chose not to pursue playing basketball at Foxcroft Academy.

"Barry was hearing impaired in an era when kids with daunting disabilities were mainstreamed in the classroom," Kevin said. "He was an incredibly gifted all-around athlete. He was as strong as an ox and could run like a deer. I'm not sure why Barry didn't go any further in hoops when he got to FA. If Monson Academy had not closed in 1969, I'm sure he would have been a four-year basketball star for the Slaters."

In fact, Nelson believes Monson Academy would have won at least one more state championship.

"Monson Academy, we could have made some noise had we stayed in Class S. With Barry, Tommy Hall, and Galen Erickson's younger brother Darrell—who was a good player—and with me and Jeff Kelly," Kevin said. "In Class S if you had two or three really good players you could go deep into the tournament. You wonder what might have happened. Everybody kind of went their own way."

Other than Barry, Kevin hardly knew anyone at Dover Grammar when he arrived. He did know Kenny Burtchell, because their fathers sometimes worked in woods together and one time they all drove to Boston to watch the Red Sox play at Fenway Park. But soon Kevin met new teammates and that developed into friendships and something special came out of that. Instead of barely winning at all in Monson, Kevin landed on a team in Dover that didn't lose.

"At that point in time, it was like a switch had just turned. I went from hardly ever winning to going to a season where we went undefeated," Kevin said. "That just shows that the sport of basketball to me—I know, we all think of individuals but, no, it's a team sport—you have to have good players playing together to win and to go undefeated. One person doesn't get you through that. It just doesn't happen."

On the basketball court, they developed a team identity that would carry with them for years. SeDoMoCha easily won the annual Dexter Invitational Grammar School Tournament, beating Guilford by 20 points, 66–46, in the championship game as Kevin Nelson, wearing uniform No. 35, scored 16 points and Scott Mountford, John Danforth, and Kenny Burtchell each added 14 points.

The Eagles celebrated their junior high school championship at a banquet in Dover Grammar School with University of Maine football great John Huard as the guest speaker. Huard, then a linebacker with the Denver Broncos, was the first player from the University of Maine to be inducted into the College Football Hall of Fame in Atlanta. Huard was photographed with Kevin Nelson, Coach Larson, and Scott Mountford for the *Bangor Daily News*. For Kevin, this capped off a 14–0 season.

"Nobody could beat us because we had Kevin," Mountford said. "When we got to eighth grade, we felt like nobody was going to beat us anywhere and we were kind of cocky and arrogant about it. We had a 6–6 guy on our team. That allowed the rest of us to loosen up and take chances."

Kevin Nelson also allowed the team to dream. Even in eighth grade the expectations were growing. For him. For their future. There was an exceptional team on its way to Foxcroft Academy and its new head boys basketball coach, Arthur "Skip" Hanson.

"I knew that Kevin was going to be better than anything that Fox-croft had ever seen," Gary Larson said. "When we went up there for a scrimmage, I told Skip, 'Kevin is better than what you have right now.'"

Skip Hanson, Foxcroft Academy's new boys varsity basketball coach, was already onto Kevin Nelson. He could see it with his own eyes. He was scouting him. He was well aware of Kevin, his height, and his potential.

When Skip didn't have practices or games at Foxcroft during Kevin's eighth-grade year, he watched the Eagles' center play basketball at least a half dozen times. The Ponies' new coach would make special visits to the Dover Grammar School gym with his wife, Peg, and each time a rumor of Skip Hanson's imminent arrival in the Dover Grammar School gym and the anticipation of that would spread like wildfire. It was like Taylor Swift going to an NFL game.

Kevin was prepared to put on a show for Skip.

"You couldn't have had Adolph Rupp, John Wooden, or Red Auerbach walk in and I wouldn't have been more impressed," Kevin said. "He was the Foxcroft Academy basketball coach coming to see us play. That means something. Skip and Peg walked in together and I remember going through a layup line and he was coming in that side door to the gym by the baseline. I remember it was at that point that I had started trying to dunk the ball in practice. Back then, dunking the ball didn't have the same exuberance as it does now. But, when I saw Skip, I was thinking about doing it to impress him."

Kevin didn't need to. Skip was already impressed. Kevin Nelson was playing in the moment. Skip Hanson was thinking ahead to the future.

Skip-a-Dee-Doo-Dah Skip-a-Dee Day

It was Christmas morning and a teenage Arthur Lester "Skip" Hanson III was incredibly happy to find a new basketball under the tree. He was so delighted that he wanted to play with it right away, but not outside in the driveway.

Skip wanted to play ball inside Central Hall on the basketball court above the municipal offices.

On Christmas Day.

He picked up the telephone and called Johnny Ronco, the custodian for Central Hall, at his home on outer North Street. Skip asked Johnny if he could drive downtown and let him and some of his buddies rent the court and play a pick-up game with his new basketball.

On Christmas Day!

Well, Johnny be good and he got out of his pajamas and drove down to Central Hall on East Main Street and opened its doors. He was the real Santa Claus making a special delivery—the key to get in.

On Christmas Day! "Slow days. Snow days. Any days," Skip said. "We could make a call and get five, six, seven guys there in about two minutes and play basketball and Johnny Ronco was great. We'd say, 'Johnny, can we play ten more minutes?' and he'd say, 'OK. Throw the ball over there when you are done.' A couple times he came down and opened the doors for us. And you can imagine the noise that was downstairs while we were playing upstairs? No one ever complained. People were great. They probably wanted us playing basketball rather than being outside doing something else."

Convincing a janitor to come in to work on Christmas was an example of the power and persuasiveness that Skip Hanson, even at a young age, possessed when it came to basketball. It was evident then that Skip had a true passion for the game yet also the confidence and communication skills to turn what might seem like an impossible situation into a real possibility. Skip had a goal and saw it through.

Jean and Arthur's boy Skip was a native son. He was born and raised in Dover-Foxcroft, a town of about four thousand people that serves as the county seat, or shiretown, of Piscataquis County. Today it is best known as the site of the Maine Whoopie Pie Festival, an annual event that draws double the town's population each June to sample variations of the classic New England dessert traditionally made of two soft chocolate cake-like cookies sandwiched around a white creamy marshmallow filling.

Dover-Foxcroft, located geographically on a map almost directly in the center of the state of Maine, was originally two separate towns. They were mostly divided by the Piscataquis River, which became a source of power to lumber, grist, flour, and woolen mills that were built around it. The towns merged in 1922, making Dover-Foxcroft the only hyphenated township in Maine and one of a few in the country.

Though Foxcroft was incorporated first, most local people still refer to Dover-Foxcroft as "Dover" and drop the "Foxcroft." It's like leaving the "Las" out of Las Vegas. One goes on a trip to "Dover" like one goes on a trip to "Vegas," except some might say pretty much nothing happens or stays in Dover for long.

The official merge of Dover-Foxcroft was so significant that it was celebrated with a "marriage." It also was a precursor to the women's movement.

According to an article in the *Shiretown Conserver*'s spring 2022 issue written by Dover-Foxcroft Historical Society president Mary Annis, it wasn't until women were allowed to vote that the towns of Dover and Foxcroft finally agreed to consolidate after more than a century. Twice, a measure to merge the towns had been defeated by male voters during a five-year period filled with several postponements and plenty of posturing. Thus, 1921 was the final attempt to officially connect the communities unless another act of legislation was passed. Dover voters repeatedly rejected the merger because its agricultural people didn't trust the people of Foxcroft.

No, this was not a Stephen King-like *Children of the Corn* problem.

Finally, on March 14, 1921, a total of 665 people—311 more than ever before—came to Central Hall to at last vote in favor of the union of Dover and Foxcroft. The women, who previously had watched the vote from the balcony, participated for the first time on the main floor and swayed the vote.

On the eve of the official proclamation that the two towns become one, a mock wedding was staged at the Piscataquis Club at the Exchange Hotel in Monument Square. The "bride," Miss Dover, was Mrs. Charles (Maude) Stanhope and the "groom," Mr. Foxcroft, was R.C.D. Chandler.

The first town meeting of Dover-Foxcroft occurred at Central Hall on March 8, 1922. Of the ninety articles put up for vote that day, one was that the town agree to pay tuition charges to Foxcroft Academy for the town's high school students.

Foxcroft was originally purchased from Bowdoin College in 1800 by Joseph E. Foxcroft. A few years later, Dover was purchased by a pair of Boston merchants from the state of Massachusetts. In 1812 the town of Foxcroft was incorporated and a decade later was followed by the incorporation of Dover, the same year a lawyer, James Stuart Holmes, organized the town's first high school and became its first instructor. In 1883, the Maine Legislature granted the charter for it to become an academy—the first incorporated in the state.

In 1904, Dover closed its high school on Pleasant Street and Foxcroft Academy accepted its students into its high school across the bridge on West Main Street near Monument Square. Eventually, after the towns merged and the population grew, a new high school was needed. In 1941, Louis Oakes, a Foxcroft alumni and a player on FA's first football team, donated 56 acres of land that became the site of the present-day Foxcroft Academy. It opened in 1952. It's located on outer West Main Street off Maine State Route 15, which extends from Stonington on the Atlantic coast 180 miles northwest to Jackman near the Quebec border. The football field at Foxcroft is still named in Louis Oakes' honor.

According to longtime *Piscataquis Observer* sportswriter and historian Lou "Scoop" Stevens, Foxcroft Academy started playing football around 1893 and the town was so enamored with it that following a

0–0 tie against mighty Bangor High a celebration ensued at Central Hall. When the players—still coated in mud and dirt—returned from Bangor to the train station on Summer Street, they were ushered to an oyster stew supper in the Central Hall dining hall downstairs capped by ice cream and cake for dessert.

Basketball didn't have the same reverence in Dover-Foxcroft as football. Foxcroft Academy started playing basketball in 1903.

Stevens, in his DVD video "Memories of Central Hall" recorded in 2010, told of Central Hall evolving into the hub for entertainment in Dover-Foxcroft. There were minstrel shows, Halloween parties, and the popular "Uncle Tom's Cabin" that featured bloodhounds and small circus animals. Central Hall also was home to school plays, proms, and graduations plus choral performances, band rehearsals, and even Curly O'Brien, a local country-western singer who had his own television show on WABI in Bangor.

Then in 1940, the town manager of Dover-Foxcroft, who doubled as the town's building inspector, deemed that Central Hall—opened in 1883—be "condemned from public gathering." As Central Hall had no basement, dampness had caused the sills to rot. When large numbers of people came to watch FA boys' basketball games, the weight of fans in the balcony strained it to the point that it began to pull away from the walls.

Basketball games in Central Hall attracted capacity crowds. Spectators sat on the stage above the baseline on one end of the court or in three rows of bleachers courtside where the players sat. Fans in the bleachers hung their winter coats from wooden brackets above them that supported the bottom of the U-shaped balcony where more fans would either sit or stand during games.

The only home court edge Foxcroft owned was with the knowledge that the balcony curved over the corners of the south end of the court. That allowed the Ponies to prepare a trapping defense whereas they would attempt to surprise and force their opponents with the ball into those two corners. There, Foxcroft defenders could double team opposing ballhandlers who could not pass or shoot out of those corners because of the low ceiling beneath the balcony. Of course, that advantage only lasted two quarters after the teams switched sides at halftime.

Faced with the prospect of the balcony collapsing, the town of Dover-Foxcroft was presented with a proposal to build a new hall parallel to Central Hall at a then pricey cost of $15,000. Albeit, voters chose the alternative—approving $5,000 to repair and renovate Central Hall. Yet, by 1954, visiting high school teams started refusing to play games in Central Hall. There were constant problems, including a malfunctioning scoreboard. Lou Stevens, who was the FA basketball team's manager for two years, was handed a whistle which he used to alert the referees whenever the scoreboard froze. Once the refs stopped play, Lou would climb under the scorer's table and run to the scoreboard on the stage and poke his pencil through a hole to cause numbers to advance on a rotating wheel to project the actual score.

In John Glover's *A History of Foxcroft Academy,* FA had been trying to build a new high school gymnasium since 1952 after the new Foxcroft Academy opened. FA trustee Maynard H. Beal signed a check for $1,000 to initiate fundraising for a new gym. Original plans called for a separate building to be built to house a new gym midway between the existing Foxcroft Academy building and the football field. But Louis Oakes thought construction costs were too high. Plans were changed to attach the new gymnasium to the west wing of FA. There was funding for $115,000, but FA requested a gift of $100,000. When the request was increased to a $200,000 gift to complete the gym sooner, the proposal was voted down by Dover-Foxcroft on June 18, 1960. It took an impassioned speech by Athletic Director Ernest "Lap" Lary to get the project back on track and finally, on January 12, 1961, a contract to build the new gym was awarded. Construction began in spring 1961 with the intention of opening the new gym by January 1962.

In the meantime, all Foxcroft Academy boys basketball games were played at Dover Grammar School. That did not stop players from continuing to play pick-up games in Central Hall. It was still the place to go for kids of all ages to play basketball on snowy, rainy, cold, freezing days—even on Christmas Day. Lionel Bishop, one of Skip Hanson's lifelong friends, called Central Hall "the Dover-Foxcroft mecca of basketball."

The municipal town offices and police chief's office were located on the ground floor, directly below the basketball court upstairs. The town employees would hear above them the constant sound of kids running and the thumping of a basketball being dribbled.

Somewhere in Central Hall was Johnny Ronco, who was more the kids' guardian than the building's custodian. He was a short man with a broom in hand, keys jingling from his belt, and a shovel in arm's reach to put coal in the stove in the basement. Upstairs, he collected the kids' nickels, dimes, and quarters to rent the basketball court for as little as a dollar an hour and kept track of it in a little black notebook.

Skip Hanson was one of his regular customers. He was a fixture at Central Hall, and also quite foxy. Skip was known to sneak up the fire escape stairs outside the building, slip through a window, and pop down onto the Central Hall court.

"I think Johnny did it on purpose. He'd leave the window unlocked," Skip said. "A couple of times he'd come and just sit down and watch us. The police would come in, too, and watch us every once in a while. All Johnny would say is, 'Lock up afterwards.'"

If something went awry, they knew where they could find Skip and lock him up. He grew up on Grove Street, down the street and around the corner from Lionel Bishop's house on Pleasant Street. Skip was four years old when he got his nickname from his father Arthur Sr. His father had to go to Eastern Maine Medical Center in Bangor with a mysterious infection or ailment in his left eye for a couple days. Doctors decided the eye needed to be removed and Arthur would need to wear a glass eye for the rest of his life. The glass eyes would arrive by mail in a package of eight.

"I know that I was called Skip in that moment when he came home and the eye was running," Skip said. "He was really in pain, but I remember him calling me 'Skip.' I can visualize the whole thing."

Skip was infatuated with basketball. In 1954, after his parents bought him a cool new bicycle with a bike horn attached to the handlebars, Skip was mesmerized following a fleet-footed, hot-shooting 5-foot-7 guard named Wayne Champeon leading the Greenville High School Lakers on a championship run. They were the best basketball team in Piscataquis County at the time.

"That was one of the first times they had high school tournament games on TV. I was sitting on my bike in the living room and every time Greenville would score, I'd honk the horn, having no consideration for my father who was trying to sleep," Skip said. "I remember watching Champ when I was 10 years old saying, 'Holy Christ can he play!' I saw him play later when he was at the University of Maine. He was phenomenal. He was unbelievable."

Champ was a local legend who inspired Skip and others to play basketball. And Skip was playing basketball all the time, anywhere he could.

"He developed a real passion and a love for the game of basketball at a very young age," Lionel Bishop said. "Around his middle school years when we started playing competitive for the first time on 'A' and 'B' squads, that was the first real taste of competition."

Growing up, Central Hall was the home base to Foxcroft Academy basketball for Skip. When they were working summertime jobs, Skip and Mike Weymouth and their friends would get together and shoot hoops.

"Every single night after work we'd go down to Central Hall and meet and split the rental fee and play basketball," Skip said.

Central Hall today is known as Central Hall Commons, a community center that has been undergoing renovations since 2015. The upstairs' stage, balcony, and floor have been upgraded and beautifully restored, but the basketball court, backboards, and rims are gone. The building is rented out for weddings and large meetings.

A plaque honoring Johnny Ronco hangs on the wall on the flight of steps leading from the ground floor to the second floor. That's about the last semblance of basketball memories in Central Hall.

But Skip and his friends in their era also had another favorite place to play basketball in Dover-Foxcroft on days and nights when the weather was nice enough to play outside. They would hop on their bikes and congregate and invite themselves to play in the asphalt driveway at the house of Dr. Linus Stitham off West Main Street. It had a bright floodlight above the garage door so the kids could play for hours on end.

Susan Stitham, one of Linus' five children, said, "Dad hot-topped the driveway and put up the basket and the floodlights for me, possibly—although probably not—anticipating my eventual induction into the FA Athletic Hall of Fame, which he might have found more significant than a Kiwanis award."

Susan, who graduated in 1961, starred on Foxcroft's girls varsity basketball team when women's basketball rules dictated that teams play six players a side—three on the offensive end of the court and three on the defensive end. Women's rules were transitioning to men's full-court five-on-five rules when Susan became the girls basketball coach at FA in 1965. The women's rules allowed two players on each team—called *rovers*—to dribble or run past the mid-court line and play on both sides of the court. Susan coached the Ponies to a 12–4 record her first season and the next season coached FA to an undefeated record (16–0) to win the Penquis League led by Karen Blodgett, who once scored 50 points in a game.

Unfortunately, the Maine Principals' Association did not sanction girls high school basketball tournaments in the state until 1975.

Growing up at 50 West Main Street, Susan apparently had dibs on playing basketball in the Stitham family driveway, but Skip Hanson and his friends always seemed to have designs on playing ball at the Stithams'. They would invite Susan to play with them.

"When it started to get a little dark and Doc came home for supper, we'd step aside and he'd drive his car into the garage," Skip said. "We continued to play with the lights on while the family sat there and had supper. After dinner he'd sit in the chair by the window and watch us. We were outside the window playing basketball and they never said a word."

Until years later.

Susan's brother Kevin, who graduated in 1970, said, "They'd play all hours. They got more use of our driveway than Central Hall because it was free."

The priceless Stitham hoop, however, accumulated some sentimental value as well. Once his kids grew up, Dr. Stitham gave the basketball backboard and hoop to Jim Thompson, editor of the *Piscataquis Observer*, to put on his garage on Lincoln Street. Years later, Jim gave it back to

Kevin Stitham. Kevin took a piece of the backboard and made a plaque out of it to give to Susan to commemorate the basketball-playing experience that spanned the life of the five Stitham siblings growing up. Their driveway became a freeway for pick-up basketball games.

"We always had four, five, six, seven of us playing basketball. It was a love for all of us," Skip said. "I never thought about coaching back then. It was far beyond my dreams."

Basketball was Skip's first love, yet he was a standout multisport athlete. He was converted from an offensive tackle to an end in the 1960 season, the year Lionel Bishop, a running back, was named the FA football team's Most Valuable Player. The next year the Ponies, with a senior-laden team, won the Penquis League football championship in the final game of the season, upsetting Dexter 14–6 in front of an overflow crowd at Oakes Field. It was on the same day that Foxcroft laid the cornerstone for its new gymnasium to be built on the west side of the high school.

Football was king in Dover-Foxcroft, and each player on that FA team was given maroon-and-white jackets by Maine Leathers tannery in town. Skip was named first team All-Penquis League as an end and second team All Eastern Maine.

The basketball season began a couple weeks later, and Skip went on the offensive. He scored 29 points in a road game in East Millinocket against Schenck High School. He had a game-high 17 points in a 75–50 win over Piscataquis Community High School in Guilford and a game-high 19 points in a 56–45 win at Dexter. But the Ponies had problems winning at home because the new FA gym was not quite ready. Skip believes that delay cost Foxcroft a chance of qualifying for the Eastern Maine Class L Tournament at the Bangor Auditorium. The best Foxcroft could do was play in the DeMolay Tournament in Bangor weeks later.

Since the 1949–50 season, the Maine Principals' Association, the sanctioning body for the state's high school sports, has used the fair yet complicated Heal Point System to determine what teams qualify for its postseason tournaments. The Heal Point System was designed by Durwood Heal, then principal at Schenck High School, to fairly project placement of teams that too often played weaker schedules to qualify for the tournament. The computation formula seems as difficult to solve as Rubik's Cube. Basically, its intent is to select teams for tournament play on the basis of athletic strength as demonstrated through the regular season schedule.

The athletic strength of a team is determined by a two-step process: (1) a preliminary index whereas each school is assigned a point value based on which classification it competes in, and (2) a tournament index determined by adding the preliminary indices of each school it defeats with that total divided by the number of games played on the schedule. The top eight teams qualify for the Eastern and Western Maine tournaments. Foxcroft finished ninth in Skip's senior year.

"We missed the Class L tournament in 1962 by fractions of a point and, because the new FA gymnasium wasn't going to be finished by January, we played our first nine games of the season away," said Skip, the Ponies' co-captain. "Then, of course, it wasn't finished on time, so we played nine home games down at the Dover Grammar School gymnasium and that really screwed us up. We would have made the tournament that year, particularly if we didn't have to play so many away games at a time."

The Ponies didn't have much of a home court advantage because the seating capacity was limited. The Dover Grammar gym was dark, and with just four rows of bleachers on one side of the court, it was nearly impossible to separate fans from opposing towns. That led to bickering inside the gym and pushing, shoving, and fist fights outside in the parking lot. The heated words even spilled over to the dressing rooms next door in Mayo School, because the rival teams after the game had to share a small shower room, which had only six shower heads. Needless to say, a hot shower didn't guarantee that tempers would cool down.

"The Ponies played their games packed into the Dover Grammar gym. I just remember that team being unselfish with John Ireland, Barry Thomas, Dickie Albee, Tom Zilinsky, and Skip," said Jim Harvey, an ardent FA fan from the Class of 1966. "Skip was more a shooting forward with finesse, not a banging forward."

Originally, the Ponies were supposed to be able to play in their new FA gym after New Year's in 1962. But, because of material and shipping snafus, the team didn't play a single game against a high school opponent at FA during Skip's senior year. The new gym—which included an attached lobby with classrooms, locker rooms and a huge band room downstairs—cost approximately $297,000 plus $50,000 for gym equipment.

When Foxcroft Academy finally staged an open house in its new gymnasium on Saturday, March 17, an estimated three thousand spectators walked through the gym. That night, the first two games ever played on the new FA court were contested, but the honor of the first one was given to the Dover Grammar School "A" squad and the FA freshman team. The first basket scored in the new gym was by a freshman, Ernie Lary, Lap Lary's son.

"We walked in and we were star-struck because they had the glass backboards and we had never played with glass backboards in grammar school," Jeff Weatherbee said. "We were pretty cocky. We won all kinds of accolades around here with the eighth-grade team. But to walk in there . . . I can remember I kept saying, 'Holy crap, what a huge gym!'"

The second game was a contest between the Foxcroft faculty and Skip's varsity team. The Ponies' varsity won on two foul shots by Skip with two seconds left in the game. As memorable as that moment was, it didn't top a high school game he played against Milo High School whose gymnasium was located in Milo's Central Hall–like municipal building.

"The best game I ever had was at Milo," Skip said. "I think I scored 36 points. It was just one of those nights where no matter what I threw up it just went in. Everybody was coming up to me afterwards saying, 'Geez, I'm shocked.' And I said, 'So am I.'"

Skip played on the varsity team for three seasons in his four years at Foxcroft Academy, yet never played in the Bangor Auditorium, site of the Eastern Maine Class L tournament. In Skip's mind, had the Ponies had a taller player it would have made a huge difference.

"We weren't particularly successful in high school as a team, but I was virtually all the way through the tallest starter, and I was 6-foot-1," Skip said. "We never had much height."

Case in point: When the Ponies played Mattanawcook Academy from Lincoln in a crucial home game at Dover Grammar they couldn't contain 6-foot-10 Lynx center Bob Teehan and blew a 13-point lead. Three FA players, including Skip, fouled out of the game trying to defend the clumsy big man. They tried everything but a strait jacket to stop him.

"Teehan was tall, but he wasn't particularly good, and he was rugged. He'd shoot it up, wouldn't make it, but he'd get the rebound and shoot again and put it in," Skip said. "He scored about 40 points of us in that game and we lost that game, but we only lost by about 2 points. But that kept us out of the tournament."

In Skip's four years at Foxcroft, the Ponies never once qualified for the Eastern Maine Class L tournament. That irked him. Making the tournament and playing in the Bangor Auditorium was the consummate reward for months of hard work and dedication.

Bangor was the major destination, as it was in the 1965 Roger Miller country hit song "King of the Road." Skip wanted to be king of the court.

"His attitude about the game, whether it was down at Central Hall or at the Academy playing games—he wanted to win," Lionel Bishop said. "He played the game hard and fair and square and played the game the way it should be played and wanted to win."

With the backing of Ponies football coach Skip Sutherland, Lionel and Skip were considering continuing their athletic careers in college by playing football at Maine Maritime Academy in Castine on the shore of Penobscot Bay. Going to Maine Maritime would have required a two-year commitment to the Merchant Marines upon graduation.

Then, one day, Foxcroft Academy principal Tillson D. Thomas called Skip and Lionel and two of their teammates, Dick Albee and Leone Wellington, into his office. Till, who hailed from Mexico, Maine, had been FA's principal since 1947 after replacing Theodore Blaich, who accepted a position as guidance director at Fryeburg Academy.

Till Thomas had earned a reputation as a strong disciplinarian, so Skip Hanson was freaked out when he and his friends were called to the principal's office. "Jesus, what did we do to get in trouble?" Skip thought.

But, as it turned out, Till wanted to inquire about their plans for college. He knew they were interested in being physical education teachers. They had expressed a desire to attend Aroostook State Teachers College but had not received any response from its Admissions office.

"Till said, 'I hear you guys are all athletes and probably want to continue playing ball, but I understand you want to teach, too. Do you want to go to Aroostook State Teachers College?'" Skip recalled.

"And Till says, Aroostook State has got a terrific physical education program, which we knew. What we didn't know was he had gotten applications for us to go there. He called the school the next day and said, 'I want these guys to be admitted.' He just wanted to make sure that we were set in what he thought we should do. That's how we ended up there. He made it happen without question. Until that conversation, we were scared to death of Till."

In Foxcroft Academy's 1962 Yearbook, the *Review,* Skip's senior classmates listed "Phys. Ed teacher" under his "Ambition." Of course, as a gag, they posted "Janitor at Central Hall" under the category of "Will Probably Be."

Aroostook State Teachers College, now the University of Maine Presque Isle, is about 160 miles from Dover-Foxcroft in Aroostook County, the northern-most county in Maine. It's Maine potato country up there. Much closer to Canada than the Maine coast. The state of Maine dubs itself "Vacationland," but Aroostook County, which is vast and landlocked, was rarely considered a vacation destination. It is the largest county in Maine and the second-largest county in area in the United States.

At Aroostook State, the P.E. instructor also was the coach of the college's fledging soccer team, as the Owls did not have a football program. The coach invited the boys from Foxcroft to come to a practice one day and give soccer a whirl. They all wound up playing soccer for four years.

"We'd always done something in the fall and that was kind of a void. What the heck are we going to do now?" Lionel Bishop said. "We went out and we played and we kind of struggled at first. We played soccer a little like we played football. We played the man first then the ball. But we kind of enjoyed it. It was a social thing."

Then basketball season started, and it got real serious. Lionel and Skip both made the Aroostook State varsity team as freshmen.

"Our first game, we went to Orono to play the University of Maine freshmen, and that was an eye opener," Lionel said. "We were sitting there on the bench, wanting to know if these guys from UMO were freaks or were they really human."

Aroostook State also had an annual preseason game in Limestone against the basketball team at Loring Air Force Base, which, at the time, was one of the largest bases of the U.S. Air Force's Strategic Air Command. The base was deactivated in 1994.

"When we first went on that base, my eyes were as big as saucers," Skip said. "There were 20,000 people on base. I said, 'This isn't a friggin' base. This is a community.' It was unbelievable."

Loring Air Force Base's basketball players came to Limestone from all over the country. They were generally big and fast and more skilled in basketball than the players at Aroostook State. That didn't seem to faze Skip, as he led the Owls to victory.

"He was undersized compared to them, but he held his own inside both offensively and defensively," Lionel said. "He always played the game hard regardless of what the competition was. He always wanted to win."

"To every man, they were better than we were," Skip said. "But they were very individual getting the ball and keeping it. They weren't a team."

During his sophomore year, Skip was attending a hootenanny one night in the college's auditorium. He was taken by a pretty blond sitting in front of him. Margaret "Peggy" Lahey was an eighteen-year-old freshman from Lewiston, Maine, who was attending Aroostook State to become a teacher.

"They had songs and they encouraged everyone to sing, and I could hear him because he was sitting right behind me," Peg said. "I turned around and made a comment and of course he teases all the time. That's how it all began."

Skip wound up asking Peg on a date thanks to Lionel. Money was tight and Lionel was dating his future wife, Gail. Gail had a friend who lent a dime to Lionel who gave it to Skip, who apparently couldn't rub two nickels together. Skip put the dime in a pay phone and called Peg and asked her to lunch.

"If it hadn't been for someone lending me a dime, he would never had made it," Lionel joked. "The best 10-cent investment I ever made."

Skip and Peg started dating regularly—also called "going steady"—and Peg shared this news with her family in Lewiston. From her excitement over the phone and in letters she mailed home, they were anxious to meet Skip. As it turned out, they were coming to Presque Isle for a visit at the same time that Peg's brother, Bob, a star basketball player for St. Mary's College in Canada, was coming to Presque Isle to play Skip and Aroostook State.

Perfect timing. The Lahey family made the six-hour trip north to see Bob play then planned to meet Skip for the first time afterward.

It was the day after President John F. Kennedy had been assassinated, but the prearranged trip and postgame meeting seemed like the ideal opportunity for Peg to introduce her mom and her brothers to the apple of her eye, her knight in shining armor, her Mr. Right.

Wrong. During the hotly contested basketball game with the Lahey family in attendance, there was skirmish for a rebound. Tempers flared and a fight broke out on the court after Skip and Bob, Peg's brother, got tangled going for the ball, which set off a spark.

"My brother was very competitive and so was Skip and they got into it under the boards," Peg said.

Skip and Bob didn't actually fight each other, but they were suddenly sworn enemies and defended their teammates. Skip and Bob were too busy breaking up the fight. Skip claimed he was trying to play the role of peacemaker and was trying to pull a St. Mary's player away from one of his teammates. But the referees saw it differently.

Skip was kicked out of a game.

The planned meet-the-parents postgame introduction with hugs, kisses and warm handshakes plus smiles, pleasantries, and kumbaya was going sideways. What was intended to be a matter of convenience turned almost criminal.

Picture Peg saying, "Mom, Bob. This is my new boyfriend. The guy who was thrown out of the game for fighting, cursing, and who knows what."

There was all kinds of awkwardness in the air.

"I don't think Skip knew before the game which player my brother was. It was very uncomfortable for a while," Peg said. "But they laughed it off."

Peg's younger brother, Tommy, with his wit and sense of humor, defused the postgame get together. He served as justice of the peace after Skip, one might say, literally had to fight to get into the family.

"It was little awkward, except for Tommy," Skip said. "He teased me saying, 'What are you doing picking on my brother?'"

It turns out they had a lot more in common than just Peg. Basketball bonded them. With Bob—who for the longest time held the single-game Canadian college basketball scoring record of 60 points—Tommy and Skip formed a three-man team years later whenever there was a Lahey family reunion at their camp in Winthrop. They were competing against teams from, in Skip's words, "the younger generation" in an impromptu community basketball tournament for fun. Allegedly.

"You talk about knockdown, drag out, pushing and shoving," Skip said. "Those games had it."

In spite of getting kicked out of a game at the most inopportune time, Skip went on to have a terrific basketball career at Aroostook State. The next season, he was joined on the team by Gary Larson, a talented guard out of Brownville Junction High School in Piscataquis County. Larson quickly understood what his role was going to be on the Aroostook State team. Pass the ball and get out of the way.

"There was Skip and three other starters who liked to score, and then there was me," Larson said. "Skip was a very good basketball player, and he'd like to score, which most of them do."

"Gary undersold himself," Skip said. "He was not only a good scorer, but he could get the ball inside a lot. He was the best defensive player we had on the floor all the time, because he played for Carroll Conley in high school."

In a game at Maine Maritime Academy in Castine in Skip's final season at Aroostook State, Larson scored a team-high 21 points and Skip added 20 in a 120–90 win by the Owls. About a month later, Skip had 23 points in a loss to Husson College, which held the Owls to 76 points and then, a week after that, Skip had a game-high 26 points in an 87–78 win against the University of New Brunswick in Fredericton. The Owls finished Skip's final season with a 9–8 regular season record. He averaged more than 20 points a game for a team that averaged 88.3 points per game.

With his best high school and college basketball-playing years behind him, Skip started to focus on coaching basketball. He closely watched high school coaches in the Penquis League such as Carroll Conley at Brownsville Junction. He followed and admired college coaches such as Dean Smith at North Carolina.

But, personally, the biggest influences on Skip becoming a coach were Al Hackett, who was his coach at Foxcroft for three of his four years, and Frank McGraff, his basketball coach at Aroostook State.

"Frank wasn't real knowledgeable about basketball, but he always treated us like men, even when we didn't deserve it," Skip said. "He was a big inspiration."

After graduating from Aroostook State, Skip and Peg moved to Kittery, where the only basketball he was involved with was playing in an adult league across the Piscataqua River in Portsmouth, New Hampshire. Skip was offered a coaching job at Traip Academy, but he wanted to focus on being a solid teacher his first year out of college. He accepted a job as P.E. and health instructor and social studies teacher at Brisbee Junior High School, where Peg completed her student teaching. They married in 1967.

That year Skip learned of an opportunity to coach plus get closer to home. There was an opening to teach P.E., history, and social studies at Higgins Classical Institute (HCI) in Charleston, a town of about nine hundred people in Penobscot County, about 13 miles from Dover-Foxcroft. Charleston was better known for a U.S. Air Force aircraft control and warning station on top of Bull Hill, aka Charleston Hill, one of twenty-eight stations built as part of the second segment of the permanent Air Defense Command national radar network. Today it is the site of the Mountain View Correctional Institution, a medium-security state prison.

Higgins, a former college preparatory boarding school, was founded by the Reverend John Higgins in 1837. In 1893, it was deeded to Colby

College in Waterville, the last preparatory school that Colby would acquire. Higgins closed in 1975, and today the building houses Faith Bible College International.

Skip became the assistant coach for new HCI football coach Bob Stolt for a team that had fewer than twenty players on its roster. Following football season, Skip coached the Black Knights' basketball team. He inherited a squad that had lost eleven players off its twelve-man roster through graduation after HCI went 13–7 and was co-champion of the Central Maine League the previous year.

Higgins became home for the Hansons.

"We lived in the dormitory," Peg said. "It was like 24/7 and they thought I was the nurse. I was already teaching at the elementary school, and Skip was on duty all the time, putting the postgraduates to bed. He looked younger than some of those kids, honestly."

Skip had an easier time getting his basketball players to follow his instructions on the court than the postgraduates in the dorm. There were supposed to be four adult advisors assigned to the dormitory, but only two showed up. Skip had more trouble getting students to observe curfew and get in their rooms at night. It was like trying to herd raccoons.

"I remember telling Peg it's going to be them or me. I'd be goddamned if it's going to be me," Skip said. "I went on a rampage for three weeks. I told them, 'This is your time you have to be in your room, and you have to be getting ready to go to bed.' It's funny because I won more friendships out of that than trying to be a nice guy to them. It worked out great."

In fact, some of those students would leave their dorm rooms on the weekends to go home to the coast. Sometimes, when they returned, they would knock on Skip's door and leave fresh live Maine lobster.

On the basketball court, Skip had a harder time feasting on the competition. Though his teams were more inexperienced than him, Skip somehow managed to win half of his games at Higgins. His record was 18–18 after two seasons. HCI was a classic case of Skip simply getting coaching experience with a side of lobster.

"He started to have some success then, and he was very passionate about coaching, and he enjoyed it more and got more confidence," said

Lionel, who was coaching basketball at Central High School in nearby East Corinth.

Skip continued to play basketball as well. He joined Lionel's East Corinth Educators semi-pro team and scored 40 points in a 108–106 overtime win against the Monson Miners. He had 37 points in 141–110 loss to Bartlett's Five in East Millinocket. He had 39 points in an 86–85 win over Milo-Brownville A.A. in Charleston, and he had 30 points in a 104–100 win over Bangor A.A. He also played for the HCI faculty in an exhibition game against the Harlem Stars comedian basketball team.

Skip earned a reputation as a fierce competitor who hated to lose. His will to win was obvious. One time he played in a game at HCI against a town team from Milo that included a hot-shot teenager named Tony Hamlin—who went onto play basketball at the University of Maine then later was inducted into the Maine Basketball Hall of Fame as a player and coach and served as its chair of the board of directors until 2023.

Hamlin said, "We were beating him and his team. I was probably jaw-boning him a little bit, and he pushed me up against a wall by the baseline and put his hand on my throat and he was inches away from just throttling me and then he caught himself and thought more of it."

Much like his first meeting with Bob Lahey at Aroostook State, Skip's nicer side shined through as he got to know Hamlin off the court. Basketball Coaching Skip is more reflective of Skip than Basketball Playing Skip.

"Skip was always a sweet guy, a super guy and very humble. I have respected him for almost 60 years," Hamlin said. "I have never heard anyone speak ill of him. He's just one of those guys who goes about his business and is class about it."

The next order of business in Skip's business at HCI was the business of becoming the new boys basketball coach at Foxcroft Academy. It was totally unexpected based on a random meeting over a carton of milk.

Ron Marks, after only one season at Foxcroft, left in 1969 to coach Schenck High School in East Millinocket, home at the time of the Great Northern Paper Company in a thriving community. Coaches and teachers at Schenck and Stearns High School in Millinocket were paid well and their teams traveled well. Schenck would pull into the Foxcroft Academy parking lot for a basketball game in a roomy, comfortable chartered bus for its three-hour round-trip drive to Dover. Marks, it appeared, had bolted for greener pastures and better potential.

"He thought Schenck was a powerhouse," Skip Hanson said.

John Giffin had been the coach at Schenck, but he took the head coaching job at Orono High School and Marks replaced him, leaving Skip Hanson an opportunity to replace Marks. The coaching carousal left a spot for Skip to jump on the ride with the Ponies.

However, Skip wasn't initially aware of the coaching vacancy at Foxcroft Academy. He found out about the opening at FA when he went to buy milk and happened to bump into Lap Lary at Merrick Square Market in Dover-Foxcroft, now a hardware store. When they ran into each other at the market, Lap encouraged Skip to apply for the vacant job at Foxcroft.

Skip wasn't sure if he was ready. At Higgins, he'd been more successful disciplining postgraduate students than coaching basketball players.

"It may have been daunting with him only having a couple of years' experience at an even smaller school than Foxcroft and then going back to Foxcroft, having played there himself for four years, and playing against Dexter and Guilford and Milo and Orono, who played pretty good basketball," Lionel said. "He may have been thinking, 'I don't have the confidence yet and I don't want to go back to my hometown and be a flop.' I think anybody would be a little bit hesitant. That was a step up in competition and expectations in front of your family and all the people in the community that you knew."

Peg wasn't sure if Skip was ready either.

"I was a little hesitant," she said. "Going back to your hometown is kind of hard. I wanted him to think about it, but the coaching lured him. He loved the coaching aspect. As it turned out, we loved it. It's a great community and it was wonderful place for our kids to grow up."

Plus, Dover-Foxcroft had at least two of everything: grocery stores, drug stores, hardware stores, gas stations, banks, churches, restaurants, car dealerships, policemen, and traffic lights. It had a clothing store

(Koritsky's), a furniture store (P.E. Wards), and an appliance store (Gellerson's).

Skip, in the end, threw caution to the wind. The lure of coming home to coach was too great to pass up.

"So I went up and met with Lap and met with Tillson, and the rest is history," he said.

Till, after going through three head varsity basketball coaches in three years and five in nine years, wanted a coach who wanted to stick around for a while. Skip, a native son of Dover-Foxcroft, fit the bill. On May 29, 1969, Tillson Thomas announced that Skip Hanson would become the new boys' varsity basketball coach at Foxcroft Academy. Whatever apprehension Skip first felt had melted away.

"The person who was really great was Lap Lary," Skip said. "Lap was genuine with everybody, and I remember him telling me, 'Don't worry about it, Skip. I know it might be nerve-racking, but we've got your back.' Lap did. Till did. They did that for everybody they hired."

In the fall, Skip started at FA as its new P.E. teacher. In late November, Foxcroft hosted the annual round robin basketball tournament in the FA gym. It was a preseason tune-up event for the regular season when fans in nearby towns would come to Dover-Foxcroft, which had the largest gymnasium by far, to watch their high school boys basketball teams play frantic 12-minute quarters against each of the other high school teams. The Ponies lost to Schenck and Mattanawcook Academy of Lincoln in the eight-team round robin played in front of sellout crowd of an estimated 1,400 fans.

"The more the gym got packed, Tillson would come up to people and ask them to move over to make more space for other fans coming in," Skip said. "I got kind of defensive and asked him, 'What are you doing?' He said, 'This is money for the Penquis League. We've got to get people in.' Till was a good inspiration for me and, fortunately, he became one of my best friends when I came back to coach. He liked to golf. Good competitor. Good guy."

The traditional Penquis League round robin was a tipoff event for the basketball season and, ready or not, Skip Hanson was set to coach his first game at his alma mater. He won his first contest with a surprising and thrilling double overtime win at home against Lincoln. However, his first stiff test came the next night on the road against the Orono Red Riots, the defending Eastern Maine Class L champions. It was played on Pearl Harbor Day.

"Same result," Skip quipped.

The Red Riots ousted the Ponies. Orono had been Foxcroft's long-time arch-enemy in basketball and football. The only thing they had in common was the same ultimate goal. They wanted to win state championships. Orono was just a few months from winning another one. Foxcroft had spent decades trying to win its first and it appeared it might be a few more years to get even close.

For better or worse, Skip Hanson was locked and loaded and looking forward to the challenge at Foxcroft.

"I just felt lucky," he said. "I felt blessed to be there."

Quest for Winning Culture

Sometimes it's about going there, not getting there. Sometimes it's the journey that teaches you a lot about your destination.

THESE ARE THE INSPIRATIONAL WORDS OF DRAKE—NOT THE RENOWN English world explorer but the world-famous Canadian rapper—that would best serve Arthur "Skip" Hanson III well as he began his basketball coaching career at Foxcroft Academy. He had a lot of learning ahead of him. There were many gut-wrenching decisions to make. He was to encounter some enemies along the way.

This is the journey that Skip chose, and the destination started with a dilemma. There were ominous signs of consternation everywhere he looked. With minimal coaching experience Skip, at the age of twenty-seven, came back to his hometown to coach the local high school boys basketball team in a community that had grown to be skeptical and impatient year after year of falling short of expectations. He followed a long line of basketball coaches at Foxcroft Academy who had no sustained or remarkable success before him, replacing a head coach who stuck around for just one year before skedaddling out of town.

Prior to Skip's first year of coaching at FA, the Ponies' record in the previous ten years in the '60s was a mediocre 93–87 with only one Eastern Maine Tournament win.

Hence, Skip inherited a basketball program void of a winning tradition that seemed to be merely a bridge between football and baseball seasons. His lofty goal as a high school basketball coach was to lead his team to the Eastern Maine Tournament, a goal that eluded him during his four years as a high school basketball player.

As an avid golfer on the side, Skip seemed to be teeing himself up for failure at Foxcroft Academy.

All of these concerns were compounded at a high school undergoing a stressful and emotional transition brought on by a school district consolidation in an already turbulent and rebellious time. His basketball tryouts at Foxcroft started about the time 250,000 Vietnam War protesters gathered in Washington, D.C. His teams were picked around the time the military draft lottery was reinstituted after twenty-seven years. His first season opened with the United States and the USSR conducting nuclear tests like layup drills in the post-Oppenheimer era.

And the promise of a brighter future in Foxcroft Academy basketball, Kevin Nelson, was only in seventh grade in Monson.

Seriously? Hello? Did this leap of faith come with a parachute? Did Skip Hanson really know what he was getting himself into?

"I did," Skip said. "I knew the one issue that I probably would have, because I hadn't been away from Foxcroft for too long, was cutting players and them not making the team and knowing all their parents. And they weren't shy about telling me how they felt, which is fine. I could understand what they were saying."

Which is to say, Skip Hanson had a plan and a purpose. His basketball coaching career at FA began against a full-court press. He faced the prospect of trying to please dozens of players and their parents in at least two different towns and that was going to be a no-win situation no matter how hard he tried. He also realized that the first person he had to answer to was the person who hired him.

"After Tillson Thomas offered me the job I talked to my parents and some other people I respected in town. As everyone was in my era, I was intimated by Till Thomas. He ran such a tight ship when I was in high school," Skip said. "Early on, regardless of the outcome of games, he thought I got out of control a little bit with screaming or hollering, and he'd call me into his office, 'Skip, we don't need that.' Having him as a high school principal meant double so there was pressure."

Thus, there was a ton of tension surrounding Skip and the Foxcroft Academy basketball program for the 1969–70 season. There were a lot of moving pieces and more questions than answers. While Skip was laser-focused on building a winning program, his players were wandering the hallways just trying to find their way to their school lockers and their homerooms. Foxcroft Academy was a long, picturesque high school built of red velour bricks three stories tall from basement to roof. To incoming Monson students, it might as well have been a medieval castle.

"I was scared and awed and trying to figure out where my classes were," Steve Bray said. "At Monson, all you'd have to do is move about 15 feet and you were in your next class down the hallway. At Foxcroft, you'd have to walk upstairs to another floor. We were just trying not to look like hayseeds. Trying to fit in. Wondering what the Dover kids were thinking about us. I found everybody to be pretty welcoming. Of course, I was an athlete so that makes a little bit of a difference. . . . I was a little mouthy, so I fit right in."

For the basketball players, there was pressure to win on top of peer pressure.

Shawn Nelson walked off the bus from Monson on his first day of school at Foxcroft and headed to the main office where he met Phyllis Sweetser, one of FA's two secretaries. She was his GPS, his Siri, helping him map out his inaugural trip to FA.

"We Monson students didn't know what to do. She told me to go to Room 14 and gave me directions to where it was. No one told me. I don't know how I found it," said Shawn, as his younger brother stayed back in Monson to complete seventh grade. "I was really nervous. I looked around and noticed I'm the only one from Monson in that room. I found an empty chair and went and sat."

This was the reality in the world of school district consolidation. Monson students couldn't ask Scotty to beam them up to the comfort of the Starship Enterprise.

The Dover-Foxcroft students seemed equally indecisive and unprepared for the moment. They were not as keenly aware of the school district consolidation as their Monson counterparts.

"I didn't realize the whole thing until the first day of school when Shawn Nelson in Lap Lary's biology class came up to me and kind of like latched onto me," Duane Warren said. "That came with such a breath of fresh air, because Shawn was so positive and kind and always went out of his way to help you. But as far as knowing anything about the consolidation, I didn't know."

To some Dover-Foxcroft students familiar with mathematics it didn't make sense. The equation for the shortest distance between two points didn't compute. The "D" in D = √ apparently stood for Dover.

"We were trying to figure out why all these Monson students were being shipped all the way past Guilford's high school all the way down to us when they could be going to a school half the distance from theirs," Kevin Saunders said.

"I heard it was going to happen and it happened, and we all wondered why they didn't stop at Guilford," Bill Patterson said. "Nevertheless, they came to Foxcroft, and Rachel Brown caught a lot of guys' attention. She turned a lot of heads the first few days."

The consolidation, for better or worse, was going to have some advantages, one being the opportunity to make new friends that might blossom into more serious friendships. The pool for potential boyfriends and girlfriends was deepening. There was face-to-face communication, which helped, yet no FaceTime. No cell phones. No email. No escape.

"But I have to say after a few days—and it's a feeling-out period—I met some good friends," Shawn Nelson said. "Growing up in Monson, my social life probably wouldn't have blossomed the way it did in Dover."

This was a time when something called the internet was just being invented. Who knew what was going to become of this delicate Monson-Dover merger? This was *not* a story about a lovely lady and a man named Brady filling up nine squares on a TV screen.

"I knew the consolidation was inevitable. What can I do about it? Then I started thinking instead of having five girls in my class, I'd probably have about fifty at Foxcroft. That was a bonus," Steve Bray said. "Unfortunately, some of the kids from Monson came in with an attitude that they didn't have to get along. They were just going to put up with what happened."

Fortunately, Steve Bray and Shawn Nelson and other Monson student-athletes naturally made friends as they met their new teammates. There was some commonality between them. But it came with a sacrifice and a tight schedule. SAD 68 provided special "activity" busses to transport Monson students home from Dover-Foxcroft if they participated in extracurricular activities at FA, such as sports, band, or chorus. This was sometimes nerve-racking and a race against the clock for the Monson students to get to their activity bus on time and make it home by supper.

"If you weren't outside there, they wouldn't be sticking around," Kevin Nelson said. "I think there were times when some kids were left behind. We had to be so responsible. You didn't have time to linger. If you wanted to get home, you had to get on that bus."

While student-athletes from Dover-Foxcroft could simply drive home, walk home, or get a ride home from their parents or friends, it took a coordinated effort for athletes from Monson to get home if they didn't have their own car. That made for long, tedious, tiresome days. To participate in extracurricular activities at Foxcroft Academy, students from Monson were expected to be ready to be transported to FA by 7 a.m. and some did not expect to be home until after 7 p.m.

Vikki and Val Leavitt, Buddy's sisters from Monson, were cheerleaders for the Ponies their first year in Dover-Foxcroft, but Val also wanted to continue to play basketball at Foxcroft Academy. She was the Slaters' leading scorer, averaging 15 points a game as a freshman on Monson Academy's last girls basketball team that won the Upper Kennebec Valley League. The team was coached by Dick Wyman, Monson legend and Athens fire truck survivor.

"I regret more than anything not playing at Foxcroft, but the distance and my studies was basically the reason," Val said. "I just wish I had made it work somehow."

One of the Monson students who chose to play girls basketball at FA was Annalee Korsman, and it had a big impact on her life. It helped her meet Mike Libby of Dover-Foxcroft, who also was playing basketball at Foxcroft. They didn't have to swipe right to meet. They started dating in 1972 when Annalee was on the Ponies' varsity girls basketball team and

Mike was on the Ponies' junior varsity team. They have been married for half a century.

While some Monson students managed to make the best of a precarious situation, others never felt comfortable. Some referred to their new school as "Hogs Trot." All of their teachers were complete strangers, except for beloved English teacher Constance McPherson, the only Monson Academy teacher to join the FA faculty. Many Monson students carried with them the remorse of Monson Academy closing and the resentment of having to come to Foxcroft Academy.

"I knew there was a lot of tension there. You could just sense it. Not just from the sports end of it—because they had a pretty rich history of basketball up there of their own and there was a lot of resentment there—but there was a lot of resentment from the fact they were being taken out of their school and being put into this situation," Jere White said. "To this day it probably hasn't gone completely away."

Students from Monson Academy, because of its multiple state championships and perennial success at basketball, rightfully came to Dover-Foxcroft with a chip on their shoulders. That was a source of pride.

Basketball at Foxcroft Academy was more like a cow chip on the shoulder. Foxcroft Academy's limited basketball success paled in comparison to the winning tradition in Monson and other neighboring towns as well. The Ponies' basketball program needed some giddyup against its local competition.

Greenville High School qualified for seven consecutive Eastern Maine tournaments from 1953 to 1959. The Lakers won the state Class M championship with the legendary Wayne Champeon in 1954. The Milo High School Panthers won the state Class M championship in 1952. The PCHS Pirates of Guilford were the No. 1 seed in the 1953 Eastern Maine Class M tournament. The Mattanawcook Academy Lynx from Lincoln won the Eastern Maine Class M tournament title in 1956. The Brownsville Junction High School Railroaders won the Eastern Maine Class M tournament championship in 1959.

In 1950, Foxcroft was the No. 1 seed in the Eastern Maine Class M Tournament, losing to Milo High School in the finals. The next year, the Ponies lost in the tourney quarterfinals to Washburn. However, from

1952 to 1963, Foxcroft Academy's boys varsity basketball teams failed to make even one Eastern Maine Class M or L tournament.

In that same twelve-year span, Monson Academy appeared in five Eastern Maine Class S tournaments, three times as a No. 3 seed. The Slaters even beat Schenck one year.

"Foxcroft Academy was a football school," said Jim Harvey, class of 1966. "If we just got to the basketball tournament it was considered a great year."

"I remember Foxcroft as being athletic as hell—like with Dickie Annis and Trey Anderson and David Anderson—but it was a football town," said Tony Hamlin, a Milo basketball great who went on to become executive director of the Maine Basketball Hall of Fame. "Basketball-wise, Foxcroft was always competitive, but we didn't have any other options like playing football in places like Milo, Brownville, and Monson. So we grew up with a driveway, a basketball, and a hoop."

The Ponies ended their Eastern Maine Basketball Tournament drought in 1964 and 1965 yet both times lost in the quarterfinals. In 1966 and 1967, Foxcroft Academy just missed qualifying for the eight-team tournament by finishing ninth in the Heal Point System rankings, which in Maine determines what teams qualify for the tournament and how they are seeded. Monson, in 1967, made the EM Class S Tournament for the third consecutive year, losing to Class S big wheel Jonesport High School three years in a row.

Skip Hanson was well aware of Monson's basketball pedigree, however. He was slayed and swayed by the Slaters. They were the down-a-classification up-the-road albatross around the Ponies' neck.

"When I was in high school Al Hackett's brother, Don, was principal of Monson Academy, and I think he was the basketball coach at that time, and we used to scrimmage them in high school virtually every year," Skip said. "They were big and they used to clean our clocks. They would have continued and won multiple state championships."

In their final two seasons at Monson Academy, the Slaters won a state championship in 1968 and lost to the eventual state champion Island Falls in the semifinals of the EM Class S Tournament in 1969. Foxcroft, in those two years, qualified for the EM Class L Tournament as a No.

4 seed. The Ponies beat PCHS in the quarterfinals—Foxcroft Academy's first tournament win in eighteen years—but lost to Orono 81–56 in the semifinals in 1968 and, in 1969, lost to fifth-seeded Schenck as the No. 4 seed. Foxcroft Academy's natural rival across the county line, Dexter—as the No. 6 seed—played its way to the championship game in 1969.

Foxcroft basketball fans were at a loss for an explanation. It was if the Ponies looked the part as dancers but they were hardly ever invited to the prom.

What was most frustrating and maddening to Foxcroft Academy basketball fans was the success at the junior high school level was not translating to the high school level. During the 1960s, Dover Grammar School's "A" squad, coached by Eben DeWitt, amassed a seventy-seven-game winning streak. They were as dominant in junior high in that decade as the Boston Celtics were in the playoffs and the Beatles were in the world.

"We knew when we played Dover, we were going to get fried," said Shawn Nelson, who recalled losing a junior high school game to Dover in Monson by the score of 49–3. "Dover was the perennial powerhouse."

Steve Bray said, "That was a tough time if you were a Monson player. We couldn't play schools our own size. We had to play Guilford and Greenville and Dover. They were all bigger than us. I can remember some Dover games when the final score was like 70–6. And Eben wouldn't be kind either. I got to hate him because I thought he ran up the score on us."

So now comes the *$64,000 Question*: What in God's name happened to Dover Grammar basketball players when they became Foxcroft Academy basketball players and the winning tradition didn't follow them? It was basketball conundrum in Dover-Foxcroft. Why was the local team so good in junior high school, yet never good enough in high school with the same athletes?

There were three theories as to why:

The Fred Brawn Theory. At Dover Grammar School, Dover's teams, nicknamed the Eagles, were traditionally taller than their opponents, so they had a huge height advantage. However, for whatever reason, when the Dover boys got to Foxcroft Academy they seemingly stopped growing and developing as basketball players. The epitome of this theory was Fred Brawn, who was tall, rugged, and intimidating at Dover Grammar.

"I remember the first time I met Fred Brawn when I was playing basketball in Monson, and he was at Dover Grammar," said Steve Bray. "Christ, it looked like he was about thirty-five years old. Looked like he hadn't shaved and had a five-day beard. And I'm thinking, 'OK, yeah, here we go. Play basketball against *him*?!'"

"Fred could actually throw the ball from one end to the other and he rifled it," said Kevin Stitham, FA Class of 1970, who played football with Fred. "He didn't have to put any arc on it. It went straight as an arrow. And, of course, everyone in town knew he was literally eleven years old when he did this. When we'd go someplace else to play, opposing fans would yell, 'Why don't you go back to high school?'"

To their point, as a fifteen-year-old freshman, Fred Brawn had to fly standby as a minor to ride as a passenger on an airplane from Bangor International Airport to go see relatives in West Texas. However, the flight attendants wouldn't let him on the plane. They didn't believe he was fifteen. They told him he needed to present a birth certificate.

"It was a week later before I could get to West Texas," Fred said.

At Foxcroft Academy, Fred Brawn didn't get much taller and neither did his Dover Grammar teammates. He said he was 5-foot-11 in eighth grade but managed to get as tall as 6–2. "It's only three inches, but the other thing that goes with that is you gain three inches, and you also gain 20 pounds," Fred said. "It gets a little harder to jump."

Thus, the trend of its players not getting much taller or better was diminishing the odds of Foxcroft Academy winning at the high school level. Honey, we shrunk the Ponies.

"It was that way back to the '50s. Guys like Bob White, Tom Snow, George Harmon, and Dennis Smith just never got taller," Jim Harvey said.

"When they got to Foxcroft, they never grew too much," Skip Hanson said. "Even if they didn't have a lot of talent back in grammar school, they were big enough to dominate."

The Schenck/Orono Theory. Dover Grammar never played games against Orono and Schenck in junior high school, and those two programs, more than any other, became the main tormenters to Foxcroft Academy. For eight consecutive years, from 1967 to 1974, either Schenck or Orono played in the state championship game. If Foxcroft was considering contests with Schenck and Orono as measuring-stick games, the Ponies were on the short end. The Wolverines and Red Riots were the hammer, and Foxcroft was the nail in those rivalries. At one point, the Ponies lost 34 of 35 games to Orono High School and lost 11 consecutive games to Schenck High School by an average of 23 points a game.

To Foxcroft, facing Schenck and Orono was like live lobsters facing a boiling pot of water. The Ponies didn't stand much of a chance of coming out with a win.

Basically, Dover Grammar beat up on the smaller junior high schools in the area, including Monson, but when those players graduated to high school, Foxcroft had to play with the big boys in Class L or Class B.

Orono is near Bangor, the major population area in Eastern Maine. Orono is also a college town for the University of Maine. The sons and daughters of a number of university coaches, faculty, and administrators attended Orono High School.

Schenck High School is located in East Millinocket and, along with Stearns High School in Millinocket, benefited from the economic success and impact of the Great Northern Paper Company, a massive pulp and paper manufacture that thrived in the '60s and '70s. Stearns had a sixty-two-game winning streak in the '60s and won the New England Boys Basketball Championship in 1963. Schenck won back-to-back Maine Class B championships in 1971–72.

Both Schenck, named for Great Northern Paper President Garrett Bush Schenck, and Orono churned out long and lean standout athletes like the Maine woods did logs.

"My only memory of Schenck was in the tournament when I got in for some garbage time," said Bill Patterson, a hot-shooting guard at Dover Grammar. "They still had Mark Rosebush and Mike Paoletti in the game so I can remember seeing Rosebush's beltline up above my eyes and going up and putting the ball in the hoop."

The sight of Schenck and Orono players seemingly leaping tall buildings for a single rebound became commonplace when Foxcroft traveled outside Piscataquis County. The Ponies found themselves often outmatched when they played bigger schools in larger towns.

"That still exists," said Ernie Clark, a 1977 Foxcroft Academy graduate who became an award-winning sportswriter at the *Bangor Daily News* and in 2023 was inducted into the FA Athletics Hall of Fame. "What happened is when Dover Grammar became SeDoMoCha they were still playing a bunch of schools that are smaller—like Class C schools such as Guilford, Dexter, Milo—and then when you get to high school you are playing bigger teams. Class B teams. Teams from the Bangor area, Ellsworth, Orono. They go 14-0, 15-1 every winter now in junior high and they play these teams in an area of ten little towns and the only town nearby that they lose to every once in a while is Newport. Then they get to the Eastern Maine Tournament, and they can't beat Herman. They can't beat Ellsworth. They can't beat Old Town. It's the exact same thing going on now."

The Sweet Georgia Brown Theory. While Eben DeWitt's teams were building a seventy-seven-game winning streak at Dover Grammar School with its "A" squads with one man as coach, Foxcroft Academy went through four different head coaches for its boys high school varsity basketball program. DeWitt was a stickler for fundamentals beginning from day one of tryouts each year when players got in shape by jumping rope, a simple practice Eben learned as an outstanding basketball player at Milo High School. To start practices, Eben oftentimes had the Harlem Globetrotter's signature song of "Sweet Georgia Brown" blaring from a record player. He would have his players run around the jump circle at mid-court while he would stand in the middle with a ball and randomly throw blistering chest and bounce passes to them and ask them to do the same back to him. Eben—who started teaching at Dover Grammar in 1959, became its principal in 1961, and eventually became school superintendent in 1973—concluded the half-court drill by reciting the history of the Boston Celtics, who had built a dynasty in the NBA in his time.

This was like Yoda as a point guard describing the way of the Jedi.

With Eben DeWitt, the Dover Grammar School Eagles had the aura—and perhaps arrogance—of the Harlem Globetrotters. They expected to win every game.

"I remember people telling me that Eben would be a great high school coach and I would always say he would because of his success," Skip said. "He was very competitive."

Hence, when Dover Grammar's seventy-seven-game winning streak was stopped by Greenville Junior High in Greenville in December 1967, some players expected Eben to be angry. They thought there would be curse words and chair throwing. He was a short, bald man with a bold and intimidating demeanor.

"We were just scared to death of him coming unglued," said Eric Annis, who was on the "B" Squad at the time.

When the defeated team boarded the bus back to Dover-Foxcroft, Eben saw the long faces and heard the silence. There was some sobbing. As the bus was turning right on Moosehead Lake Road to leave Greenville, Eben addressed the players.

"He put his hand on the driver's shoulder and asked him to stop the bus," Annis said. "Eben gets up, turns around, and he says to us, 'Boys, even the Boston Celtics lose somedays.' I have so respected him all my life for that."

Eben commanded respect. He was serious about winning, as Skip Hanson found out in high school when he was asked as a teenager to referee a faculty scrimmage. Eben took Skip to task for some of his calls. Eben, it seems, had a keen eye and was as good at judging referees as he was evaluating players.

"I thought Eben was one of the best coaches," said Duane Warren. "We had to jump rope. That developed your core. That developed your balance."

Eben, however, admitted that jump rope and basketball fundamentals could only carry a team so far. He needed a Secretariat or two.

"You can't win without the horses, and we had some real good players over the years," Eben recalled at the age of ninety-one. "I also stressed basics. If you can't make a layup, you shouldn't be outside trying to make a long shot."

The astounding basketball success at Dover Grammar School became a curse for coaches at Foxcroft Academy. Some townspeople were so miffed at Foxcroft Academy's inability to continue the ritual of winning from Dover Grammar that they suggested Eben DeWitt be hired to coach the Ponies.

"I had a lot of fans that suggested it, but nobody in the school system ever came up to me," Eben said. "I wouldn't have gone either. I was happy where I was."

Eben also knew better. Expectations for winning basketball titles at Foxcroft rose with the success of its football team. Coached by Walt "Rock" Beaulieu, the Ponies football team from 1962 to 1967 compiled a record of 39–9 and won two state titles beating the likes of teams from Orono and Stearns. Schenck did not have a football program at the time.

In that same six-year time frame, the Ponies varsity basketball team had a record of 52–56 playing with essentially the same athletes who excelled on the football team. In 1962 and 1963, Foxcroft Academy handily beat Greenville High School on the football field yet lost twice each year to the Lakers on the basketball court.

Why is it that Foxcroft's basketball teams were not as prosperous and strong as its football teams?

Short answer:

"Shitty coaching," said Jeff Weatherbee who scored 20 of his 35 points in the final quarter of a win at PCHS as a starter in his junior year yet found himself on the bench his senior year.

Long answer:

"The continuity of coaching, or lack thereof, had so much turn-over," said Dave "Hawk" Anderson, the star quarterback of the Ponies' 1967 State Class C football championship team who had three head coaches in four years of playing varsity basketball at FA. "Stearns High School with coach George Wentworth had a run in basketball that was phenomenal, but if you look back to that era their feeder program was incredible. They had those kids playing the same way from a very young age and they wanted to be Stearns Minutemen. I think the absolute key was the coaching. Eben did a really good job with the fundamentals, but I don't think there was a strong link of communication because of the turnover at the high school level. I don't think that communication was a priority. I think that coaching aspect is absolutely critical."

So, when Skip Hanson became the boys varsity basketball coach at Foxcroft he had all these factors—real or imaginable—working against him. The bottom line is there was not a winning culture of basketball at Foxcroft Academy, and he was determined to change that. He wanted his players to be as competitive, as committed, and as focused as he was about basketball.

"As a coach we knew he would instill Pony Pride," said Foxcroft Academy alum Jim Harvey.

It wasn't going to be easy. All Skip knew about the Ponies was what Ron Marks, his predecessor, passed onto him before Marks left to be head coach at Schenck High School.

"He sent me probably three pages, listing each player, their strengths and weaknesses and stuff like that," Skip said. "He mentioned Jere. Jere White is going to be a good one. Good athlete."

In Skip's first season as the Ponies coach, three Monson players made the FA varsity team—seniors Jim Crockett and Craig Anderson and Steve Bray, a junior, who was quite a celebrity when he played at Monson Academy. George Hale, a Maine sports broadcasting icon, singled him out for his size and spunk during the Eastern Maine Class S Tournament in 1968 when Steve was a 4-foot-11 freshman. When Steve came to Foxcroft Academy to play, his body may have been in Dover, but his head was still in Monson thinking about what might have been in the 1969–70 season had Monson Academy remained open and the Slaters continued to play basketball.

"The only player we were losing that season would have been Buddy Leavitt," Steve Bray said. "Jimmy Crockett and I, Craig Erickson, Galen Erickson . . . we were all coming back. I was going to be in pretty good position as a starter for the next couple of years and suddenly I'm thinking, 'I've got to go compete with a lot of people at Foxcroft.'"

They all competed together, just not well enough. Skip Hanson was trying to instill pride and discipline and he established some team rules. One of them was that all team members were required to wear dress shirts, ties, and slacks for away games. "I always felt that since we were representing FA the teams should appear presentable," Hanson said.

In addition to a team dress code, Hanson established a team curfew the night before games. He would call each player at their home to make sure they were getting their rest and not out partying. He caught a few players missing curfew and benched them. In fact, there was one game during the 1970–71 season when Skip Hanson because of curfew violations was forced to play Steve Bray, a senior, and Tom Largay, a sophomore, as his starting backcourt.

One of the Foxcroft Academy players who was disciplined for missing curfew that game was Shawn Nelson.

"I was a victim of Johnny Warren getting us home late and I still had to drive to Monson," Shawn said. "When I walked into the house, I was about twenty minutes late and had to call Coach Hanson. Totally my fault. I always respected him for doing the right thing."

However, Rose Nelson, Shawn's mother, was not happy that Skip didn't cut her oldest son some slack. That led to an icy confrontation between Rose and Skip before the opening tip the next night.

"She marched across the floor and glared at me just before the game was going to start and said to Shawn, 'You don't have to sit here if you don't want to. You can come sit in the stands with me,'" Skip Hanson said. "I didn't say a word other than asking Shawn, 'Do what you think is best.' And she glared at me. It must have been five minutes before she walked away."

Let's just say, it wasn't the clam dip glare Rose gave Scott Mountford. This one had atomic missiles shooting out of her eyes.

"My mom was a high-energy person when it came to her kids," Kevin Nelson said. "My mom and dad were different personality types. Both of them were fiercely supportive of us, but they carried out their support in different ways."

"Yes, my mother was high energy in many ways," said Shawn Nelson. "But she also was the most kind and thoughtful person I ever knew."

One night, that team curfew rule led to an awkward moment when Skip called the home of one of his co-captains, Fred Brawn. Fred was married in high school and had to take a job at a local gas station to support his family while also going to school and playing basketball. When

Skip called to make sure his co-captain was home in bed, Fred's wife answered the phone. There may have been romance in the air.

"Mrs. Brawn, how are you? This is Coach Hanson. Is Fred there?" Skip recounted. "And she said, 'Yes, he is, and we are having such a great time and, Coach, you interrupted us.'"

Though the Ponies managed to upset Orono in a varsity basketball game for the first time in more than fifteen years, their record in Skip Hanson's first season at Foxcroft was 9–9. Dexter, Schenck, and Orono were the top three seeds for the Eastern Maine Tournament followed by Mattanawcook Academy and the new Penquis High School Patriots, a consolidation of Milo and Brownsville. In 1959, Milo and Brownville Junction actually played each other in the Eastern Maine Class M Tournament championship game in Bangor though the schools were less than eight miles apart.

Foxcroft finished tenth in the Heal Point rankings during the 1969–70 season and did not make the tournament. The Ponies' roster included a pair of 6-foot-5 players, Jay Nutter and Tom Sands.

"I always liked Skip. I thought he was fair. I thought he was a good coach. I think there were times he would get very frustrated, and it would show. Of course, when you have two guys who are 6–5 and can't jump but three inches off the floor, that's frustrating," Steve Bray said. "I was always treated fairly. I knew my junior year I'd probably have to sit quite a bit, and I did. And then I expected my senior year that I'd either be a starter or be the first player coming off the bench, and that happened. I do think my junior year I was surprised that Craig Erickson made varsity. That might have upset some people."

Skip's ideal player at Foxcroft was someone who was well-rounded. He, too, like Eben DeWitt, was a stickler for fundamentals and he wanted his players to be versatile and multiskilled.

"Skip didn't want anybody to be really dominant at one thing. He wanted everybody to be able to pass and score and rebound. Everybody did the best they could wherever they were placed," Fred Brawn said. "All of his decisions were toward the future. He was looking down the road for what was going to happen next year and the year after. He was trying to bring in the younger players to fill in where he thought he was going to need help and create some competition to see which players came out on top."

Year One of the Skip Hanson Era was basically a get-acquainted season. The players—both from Dover-Foxcroft and Monson—were getting to know their new coach as they were getting to know each other. Skip, to improve camaraderie and cohesiveness, created a summer basketball team at Foxcroft after his first season as the Ponies' coach. One hot summer night in 1970 that led to a heated basketball brawl with arch-rival Dexter during a game on Dexter's municipal tennis courts. Foxcroft Academy's Johnny Warren and Dexter's Dickie Kimball got into a fistfight, Skip and Dexter coach Ed Guiski got into a shouting match, and the game was called and never completed.

"It was a rough one and, I believe, the last one," Steve Bray said.

The Monson-Dover factor continued in Year Two. Class L became Class B, but the results didn't change too much, though Skip added a new assistant coach, twenty-four-year-old Dennis Kiah, to replace Joe Roop. Kiah, fresh out of the University of Maine, dropped in at Foxcroft Academy and introduced himself to Tillson Thomas while his wife Betty Ellen was interviewing for an elementary school teaching position in Monson. Kiah's timing was perfect. Tillson Thomas hired him on the spot to be the new lead assistant coach for head football coach Dewaine Craig and the assistant and JV coach for Skip Hanson, though Kiah had very little experience coaching basketball growing up in Brewer. What Kiah knew about coaching basketball he read in books.

"I didn't know Dennis personally, but I knew of him by his reputation. I knew a lot of people at Brewer and some at Maine," Skip said. "Dennis' greatest asset always was as a motivator. I knew he didn't know a lot about basketball because he was a football and baseball coach basically, but you could tell he was a great guy. He could coach any sport. He could certainly motivate kids in other sports even though you may not know the sport that well. Dennis was like that."

Kiah also brought some championship know-how to Foxcroft. He was an assistant coach on the Brewer High School 1970 state championship football team and played on a state football championship team in 1964 at John Bapst High School in Bangor.

Like the players, it took Kiah some time to get accustomed to Skip's coaching philosophy. He studied to become a better basketball coach as if he was cramming for a calculous test.

"After about two weeks, I remember Skip coming to me and saying we're changing the offense. And I said, 'Skip, I just learned *this* offense,'" Kiah said. "There were times when he would get upset, but the way he handled things was a lot different than what I certainly was used to. We hit it off really well."

The Ponies were an improved team for the 1970–71 season and thought in mid-season they might be on the verge of a major upset to push them higher in the Heal Point standings. Schenck—with former Foxcroft Academy coach Ron Marks returning to the FA gym—decided to discipline his top two players, Mark Rosebush and Mike Paoletti, before a game at Foxcroft. They dressed in uniform for the game, but they were sitting at the end of the bench in their warmups, perhaps figuring they might spend the entire game there.

Foxcroft quickly jumped to a 10–0 lead as Jay Nutter couldn't miss from the corner. Marks frantically called timeout, and immediately inserted Rosebush and Paoletti into the game. They played the rest of the way. Schenck won by 25 points.

"Schenck always cleaned our clock with Rosebush and Paoletti," Skip said. "I remember turning to Dennis and saying, 'Jesus. That's some tough punishment Marks gave to those two guys.'"

Skip tried his best not to make such irrational or judgmental decisions. He was more a big-picture coach. Though the Ponies made the Eastern Maine Tournament with Skip as their coach for the first time that season, they ran into Schenck in the quarterfinals for the third time in four years and lost to the Wolverines for the third time in the 1971–72 season, this time by 30 points, 93–63. Schenck went on to win the State Class B championship, lending further validation to Ron Marks' decision to leave Foxcroft.

To add insult to injury so to speak, Steve Bray was somehow named to the Honorable Mention list on the All Eastern Maine Class B Tournament Team.

"George Hale got me in trouble. My senior year at Foxcroft, when we were playing Schenck in the Eastern Maine quarterfinals, we all played horribly. I think I only had like 3 points," Steve Bray said. "The next week the *Bangor Daily News* lists its all-tournament team and I'm listed as Honorable Mention. I knew it had to come from Hale. I took so much ribbing from Jere White and Johnny Warren. 'How the hell did you get Honorable Mention?!' I don't know. Maybe they threw darts at a dartboard, because none of us played very well."

Skip Hanson was head scratching and trying to figure things out, too. He was learning to coach on the fly and oftentimes would lean on Athletic Director Ernest "Lap" Lary and basketball whiz Wayne Champeon, a mathematics teacher at Foxcroft Academy, for their support. Champ, who was a legend in high school in Greenville, was the first-ever All-Yankee Conference football *and* basketball player at the University of Maine though he was only 5-foot-7. He came to Foxcroft Academy to coach and teach. He coached boys varsity basketball for four seasons, and he taught math for thirty-one years, from 1963 to 1994.

"I just respected him so much and his advice was always good, but he never took credit for anything," Skip said.

The Foxcroft coach also got acquainted with Champ's University of Maine teammate Skip Chappelle, who was coaching the Black Bears' men's basketball team. The UMO coach each year would rent a university van and take a half dozen or so high school coaches with him to basketball coaching conventions. Skip Hanson was in basketball coaching utopia. He had opportunities to meet college coaching icons John Wooden and Al McGwire, and he was absolutely enamored with University of North Carolina coach Dean Smith. He listened to Coach Smith lecture about how he evaluated his Tar Heel players and how they might fit— or not fit—into his system of playing. Skip was amazed at how Coach Smith organized his practices and how discipline figured into the team structure.

One day at a convention, Skip Hanson bumped into Coach Smith in a hotel elevator and could not resist striking up a conversation.

"Coach, I need to thank you so much, and he looked at me and said, 'You've heard me talk?' I said, 'Yes, many times. Love your four corners.

Love your timeout strategy.' And he says, 'Thank you so much.' I was in a daze until two days afterward."

When Skip Hanson started coaching at Foxcroft Academy in 1969, Dean Smith had coached the Tar Heels to the NCAA tournament Final Four for three consecutive years. Skip was a sponge trying to learn how to coach, and he was immersed in Dean Smith's philosophy.

"We all were," said Skip Chappelle, a Little All-American basketball player at the University of Maine in 1961 who coached the Black Bears from 1971 to 1988 and won 220 games.

"He was top dog coming up in the coaching circles. He was the innovator with the game. The four corners offense. I think he came up with the idea that players should acknowledge teammates who made a great play or great pass by pointing to them on their way back on defense."

However, in that era, college basketball wasn't on television often, except for the occasional game of the week on Saturday afternoons. That changed in 1968 when syndicated TVS televised the so-called Game of the Century from the Houston Astrodome featuring Lew Alcindor and UCLA versus Elvin Hayes and the Houston Cougars. Dick Enberg called that game—a 71–69 Houston win—and then the next year became the voice for NBC's coverage of the NCAA men's basketball tournament when the field had only thirty-two teams.

This was before CBS acquired the TV broadcast rights to the NCAA men's tournament, before Brent Musburger coined the term "March Madness" and before "One Shining Moment."

Inspired in great part by Dean Smith, Skip Hanson was determined to create a winning culture at Foxcroft. Yet, it was hard to teach and coach that as it was hard to see winning cultures in Maine. There were only three television stations in Bangor, and the only time a championship high school basketball game appeared on TV was when the Class LL or Class A Eastern Maine Tournament finals or state finals were played on a Saturday night. Otherwise, the *Bangor Daily News* sports section and George Hale's nightly sportscast on WABI-TV were the go-to source for high school basketball information in Eastern Maine.

The results and box scores of Ponies' games were called into the *BDN,* and George Hale would mention Foxcroft in his big reveal each week when the latest Heal Point System rankings were released. To best follow Ponies' basketball, one had to attend games in person and Foxcroft didn't have enough success to stir much excitement or hope. Foxcroft Academy didn't have enough talent.

Skip Hanson was searching for the right formula to crack the code for a winning basketball program at FA. By Skip's third year, his master plan for Foxcroft Academy basketball was starting to take shape.

Kevin Nelson was graduating from grammar school. The basketball savior from Monson was finally coming through the door at Foxcroft Academy.

Cuts, Conflict, and Controversy

While disco was dribbling into mainstream America with vibrant music, freeform dancing, and the pants that flare from below the knee, a major cultural shift was about to take place in Foxcroft Academy basketball that had nothing to do with the Bee Gees.

The Ponies were treading toward a revolutionary time of roundball in the school's history. It was more a calculation than a craze, more a strategy than a swivel.

For years Skip Hanson had been hearing about the saga of Southeast Monson's Kevin Nelson, a Paul Bunyanesque basketball player destined for Foxcroft Academy. A schoolboy with the size proportionate to a redwood tree flourishing in the middle of the Pine Tree State. A tall, talented kid who could be a difference maker, providing the reach needed to get from ordinary team to extraordinary.

The so-called savior from the territory of Slaters.

Finally, in 1971, the Foxcroft basketball coach would at last get his chance to coach the prodigal son from Monson. Skip Hanson would be able to shape and mold a team with Kevin Nelson as its center and centerpiece. The Ponies would assuredly have the potential to chase a championship.

In due time.

That was a big deal in Dover-Foxcroft. But, building a team around Kevin Nelson was going to be an ordeal, complicated by agonizing decisions dotted with would haves, could haves, and should haves.

There would be revolt or two to go with rebounding.

Skip Hanson's toughest decision with regard to Kevin Nelson was simple enough. It was Shakespearean: To play or not to play varsity.

"I used to go down prior to or after our practices and watch how Dover Grammar practiced and Kevin was 6-foot-5," Skip said. "I watched him all through his eighth-grade year, but thought he would never start as a freshman because he had some things to work on. So, by the time he's a freshman, he's now 6–6, 6–7. The reason I said that in eighth grade is he didn't jump very well. Then I remembered that he was 6–5 and he didn't need to jump because everyone else on the court was like 5–7."

Skip Hanson came to his senses. It didn't take him long to realize the error of his assessment of Kevin Nelson as an eighth-grade basketball player.

"After the first practice his freshman year I turned to my assistant coaches and said, 'Don't ever let me take him out of a game.'"

Skip Hanson's eyes were not deceiving him. He was no dummy. Six-foot-seven as a freshman is easy to coach with a little patience.

The hard part was going to be figuring out how to pick and play the chess pieces around Kevin Nelson. Hanson had his lighthouse. He now needed some ships to come to port. The Foxcroft Academy coach had his own vision for creating a winning culture, and a player's commitment and dedication were equally as important as his ability to shoot field goals and free throws.

Skip Hanson's blueprint for the Ponies was going to rely more on promise and potential than past dribbles and discretions. Kevin Nelson was entering the mix, and the meshing with new teammates was going to require a delicate selection process. Some Sunshine Band to go with his K.C. Some Miracles to go with his Smokey Robinson, if you will.

With his youthful exuberance and eagerness, introducing Kevin Nelson to his new teammates was simple. He had them at hello. Several seniors on the Foxcroft Academy varsity basketball team were acutely aware of his arrival from the start and accepting of it. They couldn't miss him. They just couldn't get his height quite right.

"Once he came to Foxcroft, he was walking about school and everyone was saying, 'Who the heck is this tall kid who looks like he's 7-foot-2?" Duane Warren said.

"I heard tales about the kid," Jere White said. "I saw him walking around school. He was 6–6 as a freshman. He wasn't gangly. He wasn't all over the place. He was kind of graceful. He looked like physically he's got it together."

"We were seniors seeing a fourteen-year-old who was about 6-foot-5, and I didn't know anything about his basketball ability," Bill Patterson said. "I came out of junior high school thinking that I was going to have a good career at Foxcroft because I was like third in scoring in my eighth-grade year behind Jere and Duane. I got a big reality check in high school, especially my senior year when Kevin walked in. I got a few facials served to me by that freshman. You think you're going to shoot over him, but you're not."

Skip Hanson wanted Kevin, with his shot-blocking and rebounding ability, to be on the varsity team, yet he did not want to overwhelm him as a freshman. Skip didn't want to automatically give into temptation. He had a little trepidation. He called Kevin into his office with JV coach Dennis Kiah for a summit meeting of mindsets.

"Skip said, 'We will leave the decision up to you,'" Kevin said. "Here I am around senior and experienced players like Duane Warren and Jere White and Jon Weatherbee. I opted to play varsity. I could have said, 'I'm not ready and have played on the freshmen team. That was probably a pivotal moment for me. My world was so friggin' small. I could have gone to UCLA and been no more impressed than I was at Foxcroft Academy."

Much to the delight of Rose and Hollis Nelson, Shawn Nelson, their oldest son, also was chosen to be on the varsity squad with his "little" brother. After playing football at Foxcroft Academy as a junior, Shawn ran cross-country for the Ponies in the fall of his senior year to get in tip-top shape for basketball.

Shawn and Kevin were on different paths, however. One was less traveled.

"Kevin and I didn't associate a lot. It was fun to be on the same team and I didn't feel any competition with him. I had my own agenda," Shawn said. "My senior year I made it a point I wanted to be on the varsity and I knew I was going to have a lot of competition to make the team."

Aside from family pride, having siblings on the same team didn't have perks. For example, though Shawn bought a 1964 Ford Falcon for $500 from a family relative, he rarely gave Kevin a ride to school or a ride home from practice.

That didn't seem to bother Kevin.

"I never even realized it. We were in such different places Shawn and I. Isn't that wild? I do not have a memory of ever sort of saying, 'Geez. Why can't I go home with you? Or why can't you pick me up?'"

Kevin—after he rode the school's activity bus and got home—ate supper and went straight upstairs to his bedroom to do his homework. He was the bookworm in the family. Shawn was simply booking it.

"I had no idea what was going through his head. All I knew was that my brother had a girlfriend and he was driving a car. I was just in a completely different world. I got thrust into this, 'OK. You can play on the varsity and if you want to start, we'll start you' situation. That's wow," Kevin Nelson said. "We were living in different orbits. He was a senior and I was a freshman."

About the only thing they had in common other than basketball was they both had long hair. Not rock band or hippie long, but long enough to get in their eyes and catch their coach's attention. If one wanted to play for Skip Hanson, one had to have sheer will and a willingness to be sheared.

"One of my biggest concerns was making sure my hair was short and my pants were long enough for me. Skip put an end to that," Kevin Nelson said. "Right before the first game everybody got a haircut. Everybody made sure they had their hair cut above the ears and there was no negotiation."

Skip Hanson favored a crew cut when he was in high school so long hair was never an issue when he played. As haircuts go, Skip leaned toward a military look, not Led Zeppelin.

With barber shop quality, the clean-cut Brylcreem Ponies were prepared for the season. Shawn Nelson—along with fellow seniors Duane Warren, Bill Patterson, and Jere White—were all in step and on the same page with Kevin Nelson being on the varsity as a freshman. Indeed Jere White himself had played on varsity as a freshman at Foxcroft Academy and one night scored 42 points—22 in the JV game and 20 in the varsity game afterward.

"When I think of the prototypical three-sport star in high school, the first person that comes to my mind is Jere," Kevin Nelson said. "At no point ever, ever, during my freshmen season did he make me feel like I was a freshman. He was always supportive. He would offer suggestions. I always appreciated that."

As with the previous season, Skip Hanson's team included four seniors on the varsity roster. But he also decided for the 1971–72 season to have two sophomores on the varsity squad; Kevin Saunders and Eric Annis. Skip saw their capabilities and the opportunity to groom them in the big scope of things.

That decision upset several seniors who were cut, namely Angus Mountain, Kenny Kelley, and Steve Lamontagne. They fell in line with other youth of their age in rebellious times versus the establishment, angered by the fact that, though they were old enough to be drafted into military service for Vietnam, they were not deemed old enough to vote.

So the seniors who were cut protested in their own way. They had a four-lettered word in mind for their coach and it wasn't Skip.

Skip Hanson accepted that when he took the job coaching high school basketball in his hometown that this was going to be a point of contention. Being judicious didn't mean he was heartless.

"The hardest part of coaching is cutting players," he said.

"I know Skip always took things personal with cuts or discipline," said Dennis Kiah. "A lot of thought went into it. It wasn't just spur of the moment. I learned from Skip that it didn't matter where they were from. If they were the best players they were going to be on the team and play. I thought we had a very close-knit group with that team. It was like the Three Musketeers. One for all and all for one. It was awesome."

Not so awesome for the players who were cut, the enraged amigos. Angus, at least outwardly, was the angriest and most outspoken. His goal had been to play on varsity with his best friend, Jon Weatherbee. Angus soon after voiced his displeasure by yelling "Hanson sucks!" so loud and so often from the bleachers on the stage behind the Foxcroft Academy bench at home games that Lap Lary had to go into the crowd and calm him down.

"Being a captain, I had to go to bat for Angus because, if the shoe had been on the other foot and I got cut, I would have expected the captain to go to bat for me," said Duane Warren, who also was senior class president in 1972. "But Skip was adamant and, as time moved on, he obviously made the right decision."

Lamontagne, who grew up in the basketball hotbed of Brownville Junction, was the only one of the three seniors who were cut to ask Skip Hanson for a private meeting. He wanted an explanation ala Ricky Ricardo from Lucy.

"I remember him coming into my office and I felt so badly about it," Skip said. "I don't think Steve ever forgave me, and I don't blame him. Getting cut is a big thing. But I was looking to the future, and I knew he wouldn't play too much."

Lamontagne, a half century later, still harbors bitterness about that decision.

"I recall sitting alone in Skip's office after he cut all but four senior players from the varsity squad our senior year," Lamontagne said. "I expressed to him that he had wiped out our dreams of playing together as seniors on the varsity. We had grown up playing together since grade school. We knew each other, we hustled, and although we may not have been the best in the state, this was our senior year and we had looked forward to representing FA at the varsity level all our lives."

What happened next is either urban legend or forever lore.

Some of the players who were cut along with some of their buddies approached Lap Lary and asked if he could arrange for them a scrimmage against the varsity team in the Foxcroft Academy gym one day. They wanted to prove to Skip Hanson that he had made the wrong choices. They plotted their revenge.

"We did put a team together. Honestly, I cannot remember everyone who was on that rag-tag team. We traveled around and played against guys at Charleston Air Force Base and a few different teams. All year long," Lamontagne said. "Angus and I kept after Lap, good ole Lap Lary, to get us a scrimmage game against the varsity. He finally did manage to talk Skip into letting us scrimmage against the varsity. All I remember is that we were playing by ones until one team got to 15. The score was something like 13–5 and Skip stepped in and said, 'That's enough!' Our rag-tag group had trounced our varsity squad. It was good enough for all of us to say, 'Up yours, Skip.'"

Rick Pembroke, Lamontagne's classmate and another standout athlete who had played JV basketball at Foxcroft Academy as a junior, confirms that such a scrimmage happened. As does Paul McKusick, a football player who had been a co-captain with Lamontagne on the JV basketball team as sophomores but decided to ski rather than play basketball as a senior.

Pembroke's recollection of the scrimmage is it ended with bumps and bruised egos.

"It got a little rough. The way it was going, it was so rough that I was only making every other layup. I was either so excited that somebody was going to take me out or I got taken out," Pembroke said. "Angus was having a heyday with those skinny guys. They didn't have much meat on them."

Now comes the rub. Or the rebuttal.

Skip Hanson, albeit, does not recall that scrimmage ever happening. Nor do Jere White, Duane Warren, Bill Patterson, or Shawn Nelson, the four seniors who made varsity. It's possible the scrimmage was more impromptu than organized, more fiction than fact.

"I have no recollection of that game, none at all," Skip said. "I'm sure if they went to Lap, Lap would have come to me and said, 'What do you think?' It would be odd for me to approve something like that, to give the players that you cut and you know intuitively that it would turn physical. I can't recall that."

It's possible that there was some sort of scrimmage or pick-up game, but it may not have involved all members of the varsity team. Pembroke said the scrimmage was against "the newbies" meaning the younger members of the varsity team.

There is no Zapruder-like film to examine and debate this. Johnny Warren had graduated so there was no *Warren Report* to provide evidence or answers.

"There is a little neuron connection for some reason to my brain about that. I can see Rick and I can see Angus. If it was me and I was on the side of that ledger I would remember that," Kevin Nelson said. "They were more invested in the game. I don't remember it, but it could have happened. Here I am this deer-in-the-headlights kid, and I'm going to get pounded if I go onto the court and, if that's the case, OK great. Physicality-wise those guys were like men to me. They were like men."

Nevertheless, what is known is those disenchanted seniors never took out their frustrations at Kevin Nelson's expense away from the court. They didn't turn into "Mean Guys" at school. They left him alone. They focused on more important things. Like the 26th amendment, which finally gave American citizens at the age of eighteen the right to vote.

"At no point and time did they ever treat me like a dweeb," Kevin said. "I never got any hallway retribution from any seniors who didn't make the cut."

Whatever transpired or didn't transpire as a result of the cuts, the message was indeed crystal clear. Skip Hanson had his eye on the future with the purpose of building a winning program. That was going to require some tough choices. So be it.

"That's the rationale for that. I thought Skip was a very progressive coach. He took in a lot of theories," Kevin Nelson said. "I think a mentor of his was Dean Smith at North Carolina. He liked his practice strategy. Our practices were very closely orchestrated and very organized. I can see Skip making difficult decisions on personnel like that. When you think of Kevin Saunders and Eric Annis and me, you're kind of looking to the future. Maybe he said, 'I'm going to fish and cut bait. I'm going to fly with these guys, and I know I'm pissing some people off.' And he did."

Regardless of the hurt and disappointment those cuts caused, the foundation for the future of Foxcroft Academy basketball laid with Kevin Nelson and the other Kevin—Saunders—who was up and coming real fast.

"Realistically I'm thinking, 'What are you going to do when you've got two long-bodied kids there who were a freshman and a sophomore who needed to play?' Really the only seniors who were going to play a lot were Jere and Duane," Bill Patterson said. "It was always going to be built around Kevin."

It didn't get off on the right foot. Kevin Nelson's debut on varsity was impacted because he needed minor surgery with a scalpel to have blood blisters removed from the balls of his feet before his first game at Foxcroft. Kevin, who had high arches and hammer toes, didn't start the season-opening game at Orono High School, a loss despite a 23-point performance by junior guard Tom Largay. That was the only game Kevin Nelson didn't start in his eighty-two-game career at Foxcroft Academy.

Lap Lary, the team's athletic trainer, came to the rescue. With Kevin already wearing two pairs of socks, Lap devised a makeshift orthopedic wrap using athletic lube and ace bandages that reduced the friction with Nelson's feet in his sneakers before every practice and game that allowed Nelson to play. Throughout his career at Foxcroft Academy, Nelson always took a lap around the training table to stop and get ready for action.

Seeking a new identity, the Ponies also debuted new uniforms with their individual names on the back. They became the fashion kings of the Penquis League and the basketball court became their runway. Kevin Nelson was given No. 20 for no particular reason other than it fit him. The new jerseys, which included the last name of each player on their back *under* the number on their jersey, were similar to the unusual jerseys popularized in the seventies by the NBA's Atlanta Hawks and Kansas City Kings.

Foxcroft continued to wear the traditional short basketball shorts of that era with the trunks above the knees before Michael Jordan helped change the culture and the length of shorts in the 1980s. By then, of course, everyone wanted to be like Mike.

With Skip Hanson beginning to coach more by instinct than by the book, the Ponies won four of their first five games in the 1971–72 season but then suffered another psychological setback. During the Christmas holiday break, Bill Patterson, who lived near Branns Mills Pond about a 10-mile drive from Foxcroft Academy, decided the effort he was making to get to practice wasn't translating into more action on the court.

"It was too difficult and to not get any playing time, I just hung it up," Patterson said. "I'm not proud of it."

"I was crushed," Duane Warren said. "When he left, our season plummeted. We were never the same team."

The Ponies lost their first four games in the new year, including an ugly 81–57 loss at Bucksport on a Saturday night in January. Skip Hanson, who had been simmering over repeated defeats for a week, had reached a boiling point.

"Before we got off the bus back at Foxcroft, Skip gets up and says, 'We will have practice tomorrow at noon with no balls and come with your hair cut,'" Eric Annis said.

The Ponies spent the next day—a Sunday—running around in the gymnasium. Basketball practice was basically a steady 5K race. The only time the players may have gotten down on their knees in praying mode that Sunday was in front of a commode.

"Skip was sending a message and it got delivered," Kevin Nelson said.

Yet, after a 105–75 loss at Schenck to extend their losing streak to four games, the Ponies eventually rebounded. They avenged their 24-point road loss to Bucksport by beating the Golden Bucks 79–74 at home as Kevin Nelson scored 27 points.

"How I did that I don't know," he said. "That was the highlight of my freshman year until Duane scored 40."

Though there was no shot clock or 3-point line at that time in high school, the Ponies scored a whopping 111 points—40 of them by Duane Warren—in a 58-point win over Mattanawcook Academy. That sparked a four-game win streak that helped Foxcroft sneak into the Eastern Maine Class B Tournament, as the No. 7 seed with a 10–8 record. Once again, the Ponies met Schenck in the quarterfinals and once again got blown out by the Wolverines, this time by 34 points, 84–50. Once again Schenck went on to win the state championship.

Still Foxcroft, with its young corps and some strong upperclassmen, was making progress and showing promise.

All along, Skip Hanson was trying to make Kevin Nelson tougher. There were some occasions when Skip asked members of the Foxcroft Academy faculty to scrimmage against his varsity players in practice.

Dewaine Craig, FA's football coach and history teacher, would occasionally guard Kevin Nelson tightly and tenaciously, so Kevin was getting used to rough play. That was a pattern for him, beginning with his brother Shawn, who tried to toughen him up by playing basketball in their barn at home. Now Skip was trying to do the same playing basketball in the gym at school.

Kevin was getting the picture by the end of his freshman year.

"The most I learned was how much I had to learn. I wasn't an aggressive person by nature. The biggest thing I learned is I needed to become more aggressive to leverage whatever size advantage I had," Kevin Nelson said. "It seems everything changed when I went to that summer camp after my freshman year."

Foxcroft has Tillson Thomas to thank for that. After the 1972 basketball season, the retiring FA principal called Kevin Nelson into his office. He asked if the freshman center had ever considered attending a summer basketball camp and suggested he go to "Super Week" on the University of Maine campus in Orono. Kevin was hesitant, as it would be a big expense for him and his family. Then Tillson said he would pay for it.

"That changed everything for me," Kevin Nelson said.

Thus, one of Tillson Thomas' final acts as principal for twenty-five years at Foxcroft Academy was to help a fifteen-year-old kid from Monson improve his game. It was an investment in the future of Foxcroft Academy basketball, and it paid off. On August 16, 1972, Nelson appeared in a *Bangor Daily News* photograph at the UMO basketball clinic with Maine coach Skip Chappelle and five other players, including Scott McKay of Orono High School.

"That was one of our tools for recruiting. Getting players in and have them playing head-to-head," said Chappelle, who got his first glimpse of Kevin Nelson in action.

Skip Hanson was an instructor at that summer camp at Maine, and he wasn't the only person who saw measurable improvement in Kevin Nelson's game.

"Everybody was talking to me about Kevin and having him for three more years," Skip said. "We all agreed that he would have to toughen up, but in time he would. Kevin was the type of kid eager to learn and all the coaches there and all the players really made an effort to help him. They did a great job with him."

"I started to learn the fundamentals of the game instead of just being thrust into the fire," Kevin said of his UMO summer basketball camp experience. "I started to play against kids who are just as good as I am and go to instructional sessions to learn how to properly pass and dribble and shoot. All those things. That was the turning point."

It appeared the Foxcroft Academy boys basketball program was about to turn a corner with him. Prospects were bright for the 1972–73 season, but there was another hard lesson for the Ponies to learn. Skip was going to be put on the spot again making a traumatic judgment call.

"Skip was an excellent coach. He wanted to get the most out of us, but he was fair," said Eric Annis. "I always thought he was very fair, but I know there are a lot of guys who didn't. I know he had some tough decisions and, as you look back at it, he did the right thing. But it probably cost him a lot of wins. Losing Largay and Saunders was a big blow."

Early in that season, the team's two senior co-captains, Tom Largay and Steve Saunders, were suddenly pushed into the center of a controversy. They were both tremendous multi-sport athletes. They were best friends. They led Foxcroft to a 2–1 record, including a win at Dexter on December 5 when the popular pair combined for 31 points behind Kevin Saunders' team-high 22 points.

The Christmas holiday break was approaching. It was a long-standing tradition at Foxcroft Academy for a group of seniors to go into the Maine woods and chop down a few Christmas trees, primarily for use in Foxcroft Academy's annual Santa Claus and reindeer display erected on the school's front lawn. Tom Largay and Steve Saunders were on the Christmas tree committee that met at Gary Grant's house on the Board Eddy Road about five miles out of town. On the way, Largay stopped at a general store and purchased some beer.

"Back then you could buy beer when you were eighteen, but we were the two captains of that ballclub and stupidity took hold," Largay said. "We were just being dumb kids."

The trees got cut—and so did Largay and Saunders soon after. They left to go to basketball practice in the Foxcroft Academy gym, but, unbeknownst to them, Skip Hanson had set up a scrimmage for the Ponies varsity team to practice against some members of the FA faculty.

The two co-captains showed up for practice with the smell of alcohol on their breaths. That was obvious as they huffed and puffed and ran up and down the court. They may have been able to keep the beer drinking a secret from their teammates, but they could not fool the teachers.

The faculty players/human breathalyzers quietly passed on their findings to Skip Hanson. It was an incident that could not be covered up if inevitably word leaked out of the teachers' lounge to the principal's office.

Make no mistake, under the Foxcroft Academy athletics policy drinking alcohol during the season was a clear violation of in-season team rules, calling for an automatic dismissal from the team. Nowadays, it may result in a one or two-game suspension.

"I don't think Skip would have made such a big deal out of it if the faculty hadn't known it," Steve Saunders said.

After practice, Largay and Saunders were in the boys' P.E. locker room downstairs below the gym when they were summoned by Skip Hanson to a private meeting in the teachers' lounge. They hurriedly tried to cover any residue smell of alcohol. There was no gum or breath mints available to hide the scent.

"We were gargling a bar of soap, chewing it," Steve Saunders said. "It was a little late for that at that time."

Inside the teacher's lounge, the FA coach confronted his two co-captains and asked if they had been drinking beer before practice. They denied it at first.

"Skip got pretty excited. He threw his clipboard and stormed out of the room," Steve Saunders said. "Then he came back."

The interrogation continued. Pressured some more, Largay and then Saunders confessed to drinking beer before practice. Hanson kicked them off the team.

"Skip had so much remorse for that," Duane Warren said.

"I've never gotten over that," Skip said. "That was my lowest of lows as I truly thought the world of both."

"It broke Skip's heart. It really did," said Dennis Kiah, who is Tom Largay's uncle. "I wasn't involved in the decision at all, and I think Skip did that on purpose. I knew that decision bothered him, and it does to this day. It was the right thing to do."

Eric Annis and Kevin Saunders were in Steve Saunders' Camaro in the parking lot, waiting for Steve to take them home from practice that winter day. They never imagined it was to be the last basketball practice for Steve and Tom Largay at Foxcroft.

"Steve was our driver, and he came out and told us they had been kicked off," Annis said. "They were worried about having to tell their parents."

It was a messy, maniacal situation. The players weren't quite ready to come to terms with the decision and the consequences that came with it, which included coming clean with their parents. They already felt punished by their coach.

"That was kind of dramatic for my family," Kevin Saunders said. "I think it was part of Skip's master plan to flush out—let me put this delicately—some of the older, marginal talents off those teams in favor of younger, more athletic and perhaps easier to coach-type players. That would be my take on things. I don't think either Steve or Tommy were the un-coachable type. Would we have been a better team with them? Certainly. There would have been more team depth. I think Skip may have been backed into a corner and he had no choice."

For about a week, the dismissal was kept under wraps. Largay and Saunders were hoping Skip Hanson might let the incident blow over and ask them to rejoin the team, just not as co-captains.

They acted like nothing had happened.

"I went a whole week pretending I was going to practice," Largay said. "I didn't dare to tell my parents."

"We were thinking maybe Skip will let us back on the team so we prolonged the agony of telling our parents as long as we could," Steve Saunders said. "I packed my duffel bag just like I was going to practice. Then, of course, the word was getting around town."

The *Piscataquis Observer*, in its December 14 issue, had a story written by editor Jim Thompson, who sat on the Joint Board at Foxcroft

Academy. The story was placed at the top and middle of page 3 with a bold headline that read: "Two Foxcroft seniors banned from cage squad for season." The word was now out on the streets and it wasn't long after that Largay's and Saunders' fathers confronted Skip. He stood his ground.

Steve Saunders, who was working part-time at the weekly newspaper at the time, never saw the headline or story before it hit the presses.

"I didn't stay there too long after it was printed," he said. "That event changed our whole lives. It was a big thing around town. I don't know if it would be in this day and age. It was almost a battle in town and people took different sides in high school."

Five days after the *Piscataquis Observer* article about Largay and Saunders was published, the Ponies were trailing at halftime against Penquis in Milo. Skip Hanson felt he needed to light a fire under his team. The Ponies were still in a funk after losing their co-captains. The Foxcroft Academy coach sensed something dramatic needed to be said to get the team to snap out of it at halftime.

"He said, 'I want to go to that other locker room. I want to coach those guys because they have heart' and he slammed the door and left and never came back," Kevin Saunders said. "We sort of had a players-only meeting at that point and we went back out and played a very impressive second half. That outburst made a big impression on me. I was so pissed at Skip at the time, but he got exactly the results he was looking for. A bunch of pissed off players who went out and played the way they should have in the first half."

Foxcroft rallied to win the game in Milo then came home and hosted the Foxcroft Academy Christmas holiday tournament. The undermanned Ponies surprisingly won their own tourney by beating Hampden, then rival Dexter in the championship game. Skip Hanson's message to the team in Milo had a carryover effect. Skip recalls Jim Thompson of the *Piscataquis Observer* writing a positive story addressing "the doomsayers" in town.

However, when school resumed in January following the holiday break, the Tom Largay/Steve Saunders drama was far from over. There was still great debate up and down the hallways about their dismissal from the team. It culminated when the Foxcroft Academy Key Club held a fundraising event in the gymnasium where faculty and students volunteered to appear onstage individually to be put up for auction. Faculty and students would verbally bid on these subjects then the winning bidder would assign the subject a silly task to perform. It was all done in the name of fun and fundraising.

Somehow Tom Largay, who was named MVP of the FA football team in November, and Steve Saunders, who was the senior class president, found themselves together on stage, being offered up for auction in view of everyone. The fundraiser suddenly turned frantic. It was as if a brand-new Atari Pong video game was suddenly being auctioned off.

"It was out of control," Largay said.

"There was one set of teachers bidding—Skip and coaches—and there was another set of teachers, led by my French teacher Virginia Bradford—she loved me—and her crew who were for us and the student body was bidding," Steve Saunders said. "They stopped that auction two or three times so that the kids could go back to their lockers and get more money. They ended up buying us and didn't make us do anything. They just wanted to rub it in the coaches' faces."

Nevertheless, Saunders and Largay still held onto hope that their nightmare would end and Skip Hanson would wake up. But the Ponies' coach stood firm in his conviction. He felt he had little choice but to put his foot down once and for all to get everyone in line with the program and its expectations. A rule is a rule for a reason. It's in black and white.

"We thought Skip could replace us with Eric Annis and Junior Bradbury in the starting lineup and not lose too much, set an example, invite us back, and build for the next year," Steve Saunders said. "But that wasn't the case."

The whole calamity took its toll on the former co-captains. It was embarrassing. It was enigmatic. It was awful and sad.

"It was my own fault. I don't have anybody to blame. Am I bitter? Am I still today? You betcha," Largay said. "To be brutally honest I think I lost my way for a couple of years because it was my life."

Steve Saunders wanted to get away and hide, too.

"It really affected us adversely. I joined the Air Force before I graduated from high school just to get out of Dover," he said. "The Saunders name was tarnished. My parents were upset. They were really big on public perception. I got the hell out of Dodge."

Best buddies Saunders and Largay went their separate ways. Largay to this day has great regret. About twenty-five years passed before he, by chance, ran into Steve Saunders and his wife, Elaine, in a restaurant in Dover-Foxcroft. They made eye contact, stood up from their tables, met in the middle of the restaurant, and spoke to each other at length for the first time since the incident.

"That's the first thing that came up," Steve Saunders said.

"I said, 'I owe you an apology,' and he said, 'You don't owe me anything. It's just something that happened,'" Largay said. "I realized what happened was totally my fault, but I do harbor some ill feelings because back then it's not the same as things evolved over the years."

After the excruciating decision to dismiss his co-captains from the team, Skip Hanson again found himself in a bind. He had a team with a lot of potential—one that was gaining on Schenck—but he also had a set of rules and principles for his team to follow and uphold. He carried the burden of all his decisions related to discipline and defeats home with him.

"Skip set the tone for the players," said Peg Hanson. "He did have high expectations because he knew they were capable, but you also know with seventeen- and eighteen-years-olds, they don't always make the right choices. That was hard. . . . Skip didn't take losses well. He wouldn't fuss about it, but he was quiet about it, and you knew he was just miserable. He didn't talk about it so much, but he wore his feelings on his sleeve. Every loss he took terribly. He would clam right up. And it was very hard on him having to discipline the kids because he knew he just had to, but he got a lot of flak from some of the parents. He just felt so firm in his beliefs and how important it was to hold them accountable."

Dennis Kiah, still learning to coach basketball, also was learning how to coach boys into men. Skip's decisions, however dubious they may have seemed, had a positive impact on his assistant coach.

"I learned so much from those situations. How Schenck handled their situations and how we handled ours. I've been that way ever since," Kiah said. "If you do something wrong, this is what the rule is. I followed that as a coach and assistant principal. I've always felt bad about it, but never as bad as whether it was the right decision."

The Ponies, to their credit, regrouped after the loss of their co-captains and their coach's subsequent tongue-lashing in Milo. They won four of their next five games, including an 82–40 win over PCHS in Guilford as Kevin Nelson had 23 points, Kevin Saunders added 15 points, and Jeff Howard and Bob Kelsey of Monson chipped in with 14 and 10 points, respectively, for a balanced Foxcroft Academy attack. Without Largay and Steve Saunders, Foxcroft put together a winning streak that included a number of close wins and a tough overtime loss at home to Penquis.

"We certainly missed them. That was a pretty devastating blow to a young team, but I was surprised how we rebounded," Annis said. "Until we ran up against Tony Cioviello at Schenck. That was a hard trip."

Incredibly, Foxcroft finished with a regular season record of 13–5—its best regular season record since 1949. The Ponies' only losses were to Schenck and Orono twice plus the OT defeat to Penquis. Unfortunately, on the eve of the Eastern Maine Class B Tournament, the ghosts of the Largay and Steve Saunders dismissal resurfaced. In a pretournament preview story, their names appeared in print in a *Bangor Daily News* article praising Kevin Nelson, saying, "he has been supported all year by Kevin Saunders, Steve Saunders, and Tom Largay." It was like a scab had been ripped off a wound. The latter two were at the tournament in spirit only, having been kicked off the team two months earlier.

The Ponies were seeded third in the EM Tournament, their highest seed in twenty-three years. In the quarterfinals, Kevin Nelson and Kevin Saunders scored the Ponies' first 19 points of the game and wound up combining for 55 points in an 81–56 victory over Hampden. That meant Foxcroft Academy would play Schenck for the fourth time in five years and the third year in a row in the tournament. The second-seeded Wolverines had beaten the Ponies by 19 points, 72–53, when Schenck played in Dover-Foxcroft twenty days earlier after beating FA by 25 points in East Millinocket earlier in the season.

This time the determined Ponies were on the brink of a monumental upset. Jon Weatherbee, Kevin Saunders, and Kevin Nelson scored consecutive baskets to open the final quarter as Foxcroft Academy surged ahead and seized the momentum to take a 50–46 lead on Schenck. However, with 2:09 remaining, Kevin Nelson fouled out of the game with a game-high 27 points and 19 rebounds. The Wolverines rallied and escaped with a 61–58 win, the first time in the ten games they had played Foxcroft that they didn't win by double digits. The next night, Schenck lost in the Eastern Maine Tournament finals to Orono, who went on to win the state championship.

With Largay and Steve Saunders, the tourney outcome might have been different. The Ponies' overall record, counting the holiday tournament wins, was 16–5—their best mark in twenty-four years.

"I honestly think we had a shot to win the state that year," Largay said, "No doubt in my mind."

"The real bitter pill was they were co-captains," Kevin Nelson said. "Skip was making tough decisions, as he did the previous year. He made some tough decisions and I think he should be remembered in the long term in the history books for making those tough decisions to ultimately get it to a program that accomplished some big things."

And big things were coming. Skip Hanson and the Ponies were gravitating like disco and ABBA. There was some momentum building and more optimism about the Ponies' championship chances in the future. There were telling signs, including one Peg Hanson remembers in her husband's office at Foxcroft Academy. That sign served as a reminder to the Foxcroft coach not to settle and stay the course, even though there wasn't enough joy so far in the journey and the destination wasn't a given.

The sign read: ALWAYS DO MORE THAN WHAT IS EXPECTED.

Reflecting on the sign's significance, Skip said, "So many people go through life doing what they have to do. Others go through life trying to do more than what people expect out of them to excel even more. We all have expectations for ourselves. Some people feel—particularly if they're good athletes—that if they get what they expect out of themselves that's good enough. If you can do more than what you expect out of yourself and what people think you expect out of yourself, you will take that extra step and it makes such a difference."

Skip Hanson and the Foxcroft Academy Ponies were on the verge of taking that extra step in this journey. Their expectations were about to change.

FA Band of Brothers

UNTIL SKIP HANSON, EVEN AT A YOUNG AGE, KEVIN NELSON, AND THE Ponies basketball team came along, the biggest attraction at night in Dover-Foxcroft in the wintertime was a fake Santa, a fixed Rudolph, and some bobbing reindeer.

People would come from all over Piscataquis County and beyond to see the annual Christmas display erected on the front lawn at Foxcroft Academy. Handmade with Celastic in 1953 and powered by a washing machine motor, the iconic decoration featured a mechanically operated Santa Claus and nine reindeer led by Rudolph, who had a blinking red light for a nose—a virtual beacon for holiday trimmings virtuosos. The reindeer, with flashing white eyes, would rock back and forth while, at the rear in Santa's roomy sleigh, Santa's right arm would ring a bell like a town crier to the sound of sleigh bells.

It was a sensational sight on any silent night. A life-sized snow globe.

The traditional display, which stretched about 40 yards, was born in the boiler room at Foxcroft Academy and survived multiple acts of vandalism. It was originally molded with Celastic and connected to a runner system (now made of old wood from the gym's bleachers). Flanked by a wooden snow fence and brightly decorated Christmas trees and floodlights, it became a must-visit holiday fascination, especially during or following a light snowfall. Cars filled with smiling passengers of all ages would slowly parade along the Foxcroft Academy driveway, pausing for a few minutes to take in the splendor of the yuletide scene, a picture-perfect postcard setting from Ponyville.

A glimpse of the Santa exhibit at Foxcroft Academy was as heart-warming as the ending of a Hallmark Christmas movie. It provided a feel-good moment in the monotony of winter.

Basketball at Foxcroft Academy always took a back seat to this classic spectacle. It was Dover-Foxcroft's Rockefeller Center.

But, with the 1973–74 boys high school basketball season approaching, people finally had another reason to stop and gawk at Foxcroft Academy. Instead of turning left on the Foxcroft Academy driveway loop to go home, more people were suddenly turning right into the gym's parking lot and sticking around for a spell to ogle at the basketball team.

By Christmas Eve, Foxcroft fans were spellbound by the sight of the Ponies taking flight and they, along with Skip Hanson, were singing a different tune about the basketball players.

They whistled and shouted and called them by name
Now Nelson! Now Saunders!
Now, Annis and Junior!
On, Joyce. On, Jerome!
On Timmy and Libby!
To the top of the league!
To the top of the tournament!
Now dash away! Dash away!
Dash away all!

Unlike Santa, Rudolph, and the galloping reindeer, the Ponies were for real. They were making huge strides and winning games. They were the hottest ticket in town for an evening of entertainment.

What were the alternatives for amusement? There was no such thing as cable television or Blockbuster video. Home Box Office? HBO could have stood for Home By Ourselves. A Foxcroft varsity boys basketball game became the go-to, must-watch, get-your-popcorn-ready event.

The Center Theatre in Dover-Foxcroft—with its one giant screen, double features, and Jujubes—had closed in 1971. Its Main Street marquee was torn down three years later. Rocket Lanes, the 12-lane candlepin bowling alley on the Milo Road, was still trying to rebound from a fire that destroyed it in 1967.

And the Bingo games upstairs in the American Legion Hall above the town's coin-operated laundromat? They couldn't match the winning pace and excitement of basketball games at Foxcroft Academy.

Unless one wanted to drive an hour to Bangor to the shopping malls, the cinemas, or the closest McDonald's within miles, the Ponies had become the biggest and best wintertime diversion in Dover-Foxcroft at night.

Kevin Nelson was starting to get attention from big-time college recruiters, including Notre Dame coach Digger Phelps. Rising star Kevin Saunders, now 6-foot-3, was coming into his own as a formidable force for Foxcroft. And Skip Hanson had developed and crafted a skillful team that for the first time in decades had legitimate championship aspirations.

The Ponies also had a secret weapon—the Foxcroft Academy Band. To hear the Foxcroft players, the FA Band's music was more inspirational than the Beatles. Imagine that.

"The real dynasty at FA was the FA Band," said Steve Lamontagne who, after he was cut from the Foxcroft varsity basketball team in 1971, rejoined the band's percussion section.

Remarkably—and rather surreptitiously—the band's "dynasty" at Foxcroft Academy started at a striptease club in Waterville. A nudie bar was the launching pad for a musical revolution in Dover-Foxcroft.

That's where strait-laced music supervisor Lilla "Lil" Atherton, then a sixty-two-year-old widow, interviewed a young man named Bob Thorne. He had been discharged from the U.S. Army after a three-year hitch. To support his wife and son, Bob took a job playing saxophone in the orchestra pit band at The Chez Paree where Lil, on a recommendation, tracked him down.

Bob Thorne was talked into assisting Lil and taking on the task of rebuilding the much-maligned music program at Foxcroft Academy rather than playing David Rose's Stripper Song ("Take It Off") for a living. In 1959, Foxcroft had only twenty-four band members and failed to perform at the annual Christmas concert.

Upset by the apathy surrounding the Foxcroft Academy Band, principal Tillson Thomas directed Lil Atherton to become the academy's new music supervisor. But Lil had a better idea. She convinced Bob Thorne to be part of an inconceivable tandem with her to turn the Foxcroft Academy Band's fortunes around.

"Lil was a superstar at Foxcroft and she tells Bob, 'I'm going to change your life,'" said Kevin Stitham. "The furthest thing from his mind was teaching music."

In the book *We All Assemble,* Stitham, now a retired district court judge, researched and wrote a chapter entitled "The Bob Thorne Era: 1960–79."* It chronicles the musical history of Dover-Foxcroft from its beginning with Lil laying the foundation and culminates with Bob Thorne building the school's K-12 music program and taking it to its apex. By the 1971–72 school year, the FA Band had ninety-seven members—23 percent of the student population.

Upon his hire, Thorne first started visiting elementary schools with his assortment of shiny instruments to pique students' interest. Once hooked, students were buying into his music program. They became so dedicated and practiced so often that lazy summer evenings in Dover-Foxcroft soon morphed into solo concerts. For example, residents in the Cherry Street neighborhood were serenaded by the constant sound and echo of Darrell Buzzell playing his trumpet with the window opened in his upstairs bedroom.

Bob Thorne became the pied piper of the Ponies.

"He created a music empire at Foxcroft Academy," Lamontagne said. "All other extracurricular activities that occurred at Foxcroft Academy do not hold a candle next to the musical dynasty that Mr. Bob Thorne created. It is by far the singular event that helped shape the lives of so many FA students. One quarter of the students of our high school were in the band. It did not happen overnight just because a group of good athletes happened to be playing at the same time. Mr. Thorne had a passion for knowledge and for teaching, something that he loved so much. He brought out the best in kids by being patient, encouraging, and, at times,

*From Ryan, Jeffrey H., and Peter C. Ingraham, *We All Assemble: A Celebration of Foxcroft Academy's Bicentennial* (Indie Author books, 2022).

pushing us to excel. Mr. Thorne's passions were music and kids and, for that, anyone who he took under his wing will be eternally grateful."

The Foxcroft Academy boys basketball team was grateful, too. As there was no taped or recorded tunes played before, during or after games, the Foxcroft Academy Band was the only source of music in the gym, other than squeaking sneakers. They would fire up the toe-tapping home crowd by playing fan favorites and the school song—"Oh Foxcroft, We All Assemble"—which concludes with FA fans loudly and proudly spelling out F-o-x-c-r-o-f-t and yelling "Foxcroft! Foxcroft! Foxcroft! The Best!"

The FA Band provided the playlist—or the soundtrack—of Ponies' basketball. They were instrumental in pumping up the team on the court with their tunes and school spirit.

"You would have to have been absolutely in a coma to not be inspired by the FA Band's rendition of the National Anthem. My good gosh," Kevin Nelson said. "Let's not underestimate the band's involvement with our basketball team."

The Foxcroft Academy Band became a huge source of encouragement for the Ponies and a source of aggravation for opposing teams—and visiting referees.

"I remember one game at home when the band was playing so loud you couldn't even hear the whistle. The referees threatened to throw the whole band out," said Jeff Weatherbee, the Ponies' leading scorer during the 1964–65 season.

Throw the Foxcroft Academy Band out of a game? Bob Thorne would have never allowed that. He would have ordered the band to play "Charge!" He was fiercely loyal to his band members.

"He tried to protect his program that could have been perceived as doing stuff overboard, as I did with the basketball program," said Skip Hanson.

Indeed, Skip and Bob, who played cards together, at times competed against each other for students to play for them. One of them was Russ Hewett, a tall basketball player who was co-captain on Foxcroft's freshmen team. Russ also played a mean bass guitar and trumpet.

"Russ came to me after his sophomore year and said he was going to concentrate on music and I gave him a hard time, more than I should have," Skip said. "To this day I apologize to him. A kid shouldn't be badgered into doing something."

Skip had more success recruiting Russ' younger brother, Roger, to play basketball. He became Kevin Nelson's back-up at center when he wasn't playing in the percussion section.

No harm. No foul. No problem. The basketball players loved Bob Thorne. They used to play pranks on him, and that usually involved his unforgettable car, which was hard to miss. It was a yellow-and-black Volkswagen Karmann Ghia, a veritable bubble bee with wheels.

"There was a group of us who would come out after practice at night and we would walk by his house and, if his car was facing one direction, we would literally pick it up and set it down facing the other direction," said Kevin Saunders. "We did this for months and months. I don't think he ever figured out how that happened. The crazy shit we did. Small-town stuff you couldn't get away with today."

Oh, Bob Thorne knew about it and laughed along with it.

"He probably figured this out and thought it was funny. He loved pranks, even on him," said Jeff Thorne, Bob's son, who took his driver's test in that car.

Bob Thorne was as much a classic as his car. He became a legend at Foxcroft Academy. He turned the Foxcroft Academy Band into national and international stars. Their first big trip was to Virginia Beach, which was a learning experience as Foxcroft was among thirty or so high school bands from across the country at the music festival.

"Our show at halftime during the FA football games was rudimentary in nature until we competed at Virginia Beach," Lamontagne said. "We learned that quite intricate formations and changeovers could be accomplished by going to specific spots on the field all based upon timing of the music."

Thorne also handpicked about eighteen Foxcroft Academy Band members for its dance band and took them to the Berklee School of Music in Boston. In the first year of competition against larger schools from around New England, New York, and New Jersey, the Foxcroft Dance Band placed third overall.

"Mr. Thorne worked with the Berklee School of Music to create divisions much like our sports teams had that broke up classes/divisions by the size of your school," Lamontagne said. "For the next three years, the FA Jazz band won its division at Berklee competing against schools from all over the Northeast."

The Foxcroft Academy Band later on marched and played on Main Street USA at Walt Disney World and, though thousands of miles away from Pasadena, the FA Band was always Rose Bowl Parade quality. The FA Band was for the Memorial Day Parade in Dover-Foxcroft what the USC Marching Band was for Fleetwood Mac in "Tusk." The show wasn't over until they played.

Other than Dover-Foxcroft, the FA Band was a big hit in Bangor where the marching troupe was repeatedly invited to play in holiday parades. They were welcomed like the 5th Dimension were welcomed to *The Ed Sullivan Show.*

"We also recognized that we did not have to play conventional John Phillip Sousa marches all of the time, which we took to the Thanksgiving Day Parade in Bangor for many years to follow. The band blew the crowds away by playing 'Up, Up and Away' while marching," Lamontagne said. "All of this happened because Mr. Thorne learned from what we were exposed to and worked with all of us to make our marching and concerts just that much better than they were in previous years."

The venerable Bangor Auditorium was another venue where the Foxcroft Academy Band was appreciated. Whenever the Foxcroft boys basketball team was fortunate to play in the Eastern Maine Tournament in the late '60s and early '70s, the FA Band would accompany the Ponies and perform before the game and at halftime in the Bangor Auditorium. The FA Band received more praise, publicity, and better critiques than the Foxcroft basketball team in the *Bangor Daily News* sports section.

"Being a member of the FA Band did carry a great sense of pride," said Julie Mountain, a trombone player who graduated in 1975. "Bob Thorne was a master at turning children into musicians. He was very well respected and a little feared. No member wanted to disappoint him."

It was mandatory that FA Band members attend and play at Pony football and boys basketball home games. At Oakes Field, the band executed formations on the field at halftime when they performed, even late in the season when the autumn wind gave way to Jack Frost.

"Football season was the worst," Julie Mountain said. "Keeping the horn's mouthpiece in your armpit so it wouldn't freeze to your lips! Basketball season was a welcome change as it was indoors."

Welcomed unless you played one of the larger instruments.

"We'd literally play every home game and we'd be in those woolen uniforms in that hot gym? I played the sousaphone for four years. Let me tell you. Carrying a sousaphone to the back row of the bleachers wasn't always fun," Kevin Stitham said. "Especially when the team wasn't winning enough."

That started to change for the better in the 1973–74 season. The Ponies, led by Kevin Nelson and Kevin Saunders, had a team that was stirring excitement in the school and community, and the FA Band had a snappy tune that would have Pony fans clapping along with it.

Bob Thorne had introduced to the band an instrumental soul song called "The Horse" performed by Cliff Nobles and Company. Born and raised in Alabama, Nobles was signed by Phil-L.A. of Soul Records. "The Horse" was released in 1968 as an all instrumental song on the B side of a record whose A side was "Love Is All Right." Still, the B side "The Horse" was more successful and reached No. 2 on the U.S. Billboard Hot 100.

The soul song, which featured the horn section later known as MFSB (for Mother Father Sister Brother), was a catchy piece and Thorne thought "The Horse" was fitting to play with Foxcroft Academy's nickname and mascot being the Ponies.

"The Horse" became an anthem for the FA boys basketball team. Their musical rallying cry. Their fight song.

"I remember playing that until my lips fell off," said Jeff Thorne, who played trumpet. "That was a great inspirational tune."

Not that the Ponies basketball team needed extra motivation. With Kevin Nelson, Kevin Saunders, and Eric Annis, Foxcroft and Skip Hanson had three players with two years of varsity experience. With 6-foot-2 senior forward Francis "Junior" Bradbury and junior guard Jeff Dunn both improving and Mark Joyce transferring from Mount View

High School, Foxcroft finally had an imposing lineup to compete with Orono and Schenck and dominate the Penquis League.

The Ponies were serving notice, and Orono High School star Tom Philbrick was on alert. He had been watching intently the Foxcroft team progress since Kevin Nelson's freshman year.

"Kevin was a very, very gifted and special player. You just knew it was going to change Foxcroft's journey," said Philbrick, the Red Riots' 6-foot-5, 190-pound big man. "They just had a great chemistry and Kevin Nelson was in the middle and we knew how tall he was. And they had Kevin Saunders, Junior Bradbury, Eric Annis, and Mark Joyce. I knew who they were. I was like that when I played. I knew everybody. I knew their moves. Their strengths and weaknesses."

Though Kevin Nelson was getting most of the attention for Foxcroft's breakthrough, Kevin Saunders was rapidly developing into a great player. He was fooling people with his skill and potential. He wasn't particularly tall, and he was incredibly thin.

"My first driver's license I was 6–2, 135 pounds," Kevin Saunders said. "I tried out for the football team and the first two weeks we were without pads. But the start of the third week we had to wear pads. I'm walking out to practice with my pads on and Lap Lary comes up to me, puts his arm around me, and just turns me around and walks me back to the locker room. He says to me, 'I appreciate you coming out for football, but you are going to get killed out here. You're nuts.' So he made me team manager."

Kevin Saunders turned his focus to basketball and tried everything to gain weight. He opened packs of Instant Breakfast powdered mix morning, noon, and night and added ground-up bananas to the protein-rich drink. He took a part-time job at Pat's Dairyland, Dover-Foxcroft's version of Dairy Queen, not so much for the spare money but for the abundance of deep-fried calorie-heavy food.

Saunders recalled, "The owner there said, 'Don't worry. I'll fatten you up. Every time she made a steak, she'd bring it out and make me eat it. I still didn't gain an ounce."

Yet, despite his efforts to bulk up, Saunders could still out-leap players and outsmart them.

"Kevin Saunders was the best player I played with in high school," said Kevin Nelson. "He put up some gaudy numbers. Rebounding. Scoring. He had the whole package."

"Kevin Saunders was the real deal and he's the one who brought a physical presence for Dover," said Tom Philbrick. "He and Junior Bradbury. Kevin just wanted the ball. He brought Dover to the point that you had to take them seriously. Kevin Nelson was a nice guy and he played well and he had a magical body to play basketball, but Kevin Saunders was the heart and soul of that team."

As fate would have it, Foxcroft opened the 1973–74 season against Philbrick and Orono, the defending Class B state champions, in its dark, shoe box of a gymnasium. Ask Foxcroft Academy fans and they would say the Orono gym back then had the feel of a walk-in closet with a 40-watt bulb.

Though Philbrick had mononucleosis and missed most of the Red Riots' football season, he was cleared to play in the season opener against Foxcroft Academy. He scored a team-high 18 points with Brian Butterfield adding 14 and Scott McKay 13. But the Ponies pushed the Red Riots to the brink of defeat as Kevin Nelson had a game-high 21 points and 18 rebounds and Kevin Saunders had 18 points and 22 rebounds in a 64–63 loss.

The Ponies, falling a point short, proved they were pushovers no more.

"Orono was the aspirational team. Along with Schenck," Nelson said. "Those were the teams that held the reins back then."

Foxcroft quickly rebounded from that deflating 1-point defeat in Orono. The Ponies routed rival Dexter 70–48 in their next game as the Kevins combined for 41 points then FA rattled off a long winning streak to make Skip Hanson the winningest coach in FA boys basketball history, though only in his fifth season at its helm.

Skip's fantastic coaching feat, regrettably, barely got mentioned in the local newspaper.

Two of those victories in that streak were lopsided wins over a Schenck team that lost all five of its starters to graduation after barely beating FA in the tourney semifinals the previous season. Kevin Nelson had 26 points and 31 rebounds in a 77–53 victory over the Wolverines in Dover-Foxcroft and he teamed with Kevin Saunders for 48 points in a 71–42 triumph in East Millinocket where FA hadn't won in five years. Skip Hanson remembers that game because he was concerned with how lackluster the team appeared during pregame warmups. Dennis Kiah and Dave Clement, the school's new twenty-two-year-old freshmen basketball coach, confirmed the head coach's concerns about the team's low energy during layup drills.

"We got everyone in the locker room before tipoff, and I blistered them and I went after Kevin Nelson as captain," said Skip Hanson. "He had his head down and I said, 'I expect more out of you and the team when we get back out there.' And he said, 'I'm so sorry, coach, I let you down.' Kevin set the example so much. He was all about team. He was the superstar and everybody in the state knew who he was, but you would never know it on or off the court. He never tried to force his opinions on anybody. He was always encouraging kids to hustle. He encouraged himself to hustle."

If Skip Hanson needed to deliver a message to his team, Kevin Nelson always took it to heart. Based on uninspired pregame warmups and Skip Hanson's intuition, the Ponies were poised to stink at Schenck.

"There wasn't any sense of urgency from us, and he could sense that immediately and he wasn't happy," Nelson said. "I'm sure I was in his line of fire at some point, even though we had a terrific relationship. He knew which buttons to push, both individually and as a team. And that was a button he pushed."

Understand that Schenck was one of the teams Foxcroft measured its progress and success against. The Ponies were finally in a position to avenge years of embarrassing, lopsided losses to the Wolverines.

"It took us a long time to beat Schenck," Skip Hanson said. "We kicked their butt one night, and I remember Ron Marks coming up to me and saying, 'Jesus, if I had known Nelson was going to be that good, I might have stayed.'"

Getting over Schenck had been a major goal as well for Kevin Saunders for two years, ever since he heard the radio account of Foxcroft's 31-point loss to the Wolverines in the Eastern Maine Class B

Tournament quarterfinals in 1972. Saunders and Eric Annis were substitutes late in that game.

"I heard the radio replay of that Schenck game and the announcer saying, 'Foxcroft is throwing in the towel. They are bringing in the two sophomores.' That pissed me off to no end," Kevin Saunders said. "That was a major motivating factor for both Eric and I going into our junior seasons. That's when we started lifting weights and paying more attention to being in shape and the things you do to want to play better."

Instead of throwing in the towel, Foxcroft was revving up for revenge for Saunders and Annis. They were ready to *snap* the towel.

"I remember them telling me that, and I remember them saying in essence we'll show them, we surely can," Skip Hanson said.

Both Kevin Saunders and Eric Annis had been challenged to play up against older competitors for years, beginning as kids when they played basketball in the blacktop driveway at Annis' house, which also happened to be a mortuary. Lary Funeral Home Inc. was purchased by Phil Annis, Eric's dad, in 1957. The embalming room was behind a closed garage door only a few feet from the outdoor basketball court, which was a popular spot for pick-up games.

It was slightly creepy, but it was the biggest and best outdoor court in the Summer Street/Spring Street neighborhood.

"My brother, being a year older than me, had no choice but to drag me with him or he wasn't going," Kevin Saunders said. "I was competing against guys a year older so you grew up in that environment and you played up to their level."

Eric Annis had a different reason for playing against the big boys: leverage. He had extra basketballs stored inside the mortuary to keep them warm and properly inflated on cold days.

"I was just one of the little kids and eventually the big kids included me because they probably felt they had to," Annis said. "I kind of came with the hoop, I guess."

Although Annis was a starter and key contributor for the Ponies during the 1973–74 season, there were some Foxcroft fans who thought other players deserved more playing time than him. With a winning streak growing week after week, expectations for the FA team took flight like the Concorde. During one home game, Annis was actually booed by the home crowd.

"It wasn't so much that they disliked Eric," Skip Hanson said. "It was a packed house and the score was tight and I must have taken out somebody who was playing well. The first play Eric had when he came back into the game, he went the length of the court and laid the ball up and in. The boos turned to cheers."

Annis recalled, "I had had a bit of a rough game and was in foul trouble fairly early. It was a fairly big hoop."

The Foxcroft Academy gymnasium on game nights with sellout crowds generated a lot of natural heat. But, when the Ponies practiced after school without an audience and into the evenings on cold winter nights, they had a hard time staying warm. The country was engulfed in an energy crisis at the time, and there were long lines of automobiles parked at gas stations trying to get fuel.

The Organization of the Petroleum Exporting Countries, or OPEC, was refusing to sell crude to the United States as Arab oil-producing countries launched an embargo in response to U.S. support of Israel during the 1973 Yom Kippur War. Inflation was soaring. There was too much hippie flower power and not enough vehicle horsepower.

In addition to price controls and gasoline rationing, a national speed limit was imposed and daylight savings time was adopted. U.S. President Richard Nixon was feeling the pressure, not just from his inability to get Congress to pass effective emergency legislation, but from the ongoing Watergate scandal.

It was indeed a tricky time.

To save energy, Foxcroft Academy turned down the temperature in its spacious gymnasium. There were afternoons and nights it was so cold in the gym that the Ponies practiced wearing sweatpants over their basketball shorts.

"When it's like 15 degrees outside and you're in a 55-degree gym it's chilly," Nelson said. "So Skip, a couple of times, had us go out to Charleston Air Force Base and practice because they didn't have government restrictions there. The gym was nice and warm out there."

In the meantime, the Foxcroft Academy basketball team was on a winning streak and that produced a different kind of energy. The Ponies were hotter at the time than the movie *The Towering Inferno*.

Expectations reached a fever pitch when the much-anticipated rematch with Orono happened. On Saturday night, January 26, 1974, Foxcroft got its chance to avenge its season-opening loss. The Red Riots were coming to Dover-Foxcroft to play the Ponies in a 7:30 p.m. tipoff. Orono, defending state champ, had a thirty-three-game winning streak, and Foxcroft had won eleven games in a row since its 1-point defeat at Orono.

Fans were flocking to the Foxcroft Academy gym to see the rematch as if it was Ali vs. Frazier. The sudden surge of excitement was stunning.

"A lot of our games were packed, but not like that one," Dennis Kiah said. "Some fans started coming in for the freshmen game at four o'clock."

John Champeon arrived early as his father's job on game nights was to check tickets at the door for admission into the gymnasium.

"I remember walking into the lobby and the lobby was mobbed," John said. "I thought, 'Holy shit, this isn't your usual Foxcroft-PCHS game.'"

The Foxcroft gymnasium was packed for the Orono game in the opening quarter—of the *junior* varsity game. It was beyond a standing-room-only crowd. It was a stampede of hysteria.

"I know I'm a worry wart," Peg Hanson said, "but they must have been playing against the fire code with all those people in the gym."

"Fans were lined up three to four deep under the basket as you entered the gym," Kevin Nelson said. "I still can't believe that school custodian Roland Zwicker allowed this to happen. The fire marshal must have been sleeping."

There was no official gymnasium capacity listed at the time, so fans were backing up in the lobby trying to squeeze through the main door to the gym. There was enough seating for 1,200 fans but, on this night, the crowd must have been close to 2,000, if not more.

"A typical JV game, you don't get a full house watching, but that game by halftime it was full," said Dick Hatt, a star on FA's junior varsity team. "We were behind 31–28 going to the fourth quarter of the JV game against Orono that night, and late in the game I stole the ball and scored on an uncontested layup. Then I blocked a shot and threw a full-court pass to Dave Milner and we took the lead. We ended up winning by 46–40. I remember the noise from the crowd was phenomenal."

Kevin Nelson could *feel* the noise in the locker room as he got ready for the varsity game. He was nervous.

"Because our locker room was located immediately below the gym floor, the raw excitement and energy of the action above me was palpable," Nelson said. "There was no way to relieve my ever-churning stomach. When game time finally arrived, the team walked upstairs, we opened the door and ran out onto the court to go through warm-up drills. At that point, for me, the combination of intensity and adrenaline flow were at a zenith."

When the varsity game started, older fans were standing with their backs against the walls of the gym on both baselines. Younger fans were sitting on the floor in front of them. The only space between them were the gray protective wall mats under both baskets. The referees kept that space clear for player safety reasons.

In addition, there were fans standing/corralled/squeezed on the floor into the 4-by-12 foot space at mid-court between the two wooden home and visitor bleacher sections across the court from the team benches. That space was created to store a curtain/partition that was pulled across the court during P.E. classes to separate groups of students. On this night, the space was used as makeshift suite to watch a basketball game.

Furthermore, there were people standing and sitting in plastic portable chairs on both sides of the wooden bleachers that seat FA students and the FA Band across the way. More fans were sitting in plastic chairs right next to both the Orono and FA benches. Others were literally standing in the doorways and on steps leading to the stage just to catch a glimpse of the game.

Basically, the Foxcroft Academy gymnasium was packed like Times Square on New Year's Eve. Fans were waiting for the ball to go up, not down.

In the middle of this madness and nuttiness the Foxcroft Academy Band was in top form.

"I started going to the Foxcroft gym in 1970, and it was all about the band and seeing and hearing them," said Tom Philbrick. "We weren't really worried about their basketball team back then. The band was really cranking this time."

If the FA Band was prepared for the moment, the FA basketball team was not. The visiting Red Riots scored 10 consecutive points in the opening period and limited FA to only six field goal attempts in the first eight minutes. The Ponies trailed by 15 points, 19–4, at the end of the first quarter when they walked back to their bench a bit shocked.

A dream game upset scenario against the Red Riots appeared to be turning into a nightmare for Foxcroft on the same night, coincidentally, *The Exorcist* won the Golden Globe for Best Picture.

Annis recalled, "Skip said to us during the timeout, 'You guys are better than this. We can either stand up and fight the rest of this game or give up.' Well we worked and worked and worked and came back."

"When you're down big in a game like that in a gymnasium that was not symbolic of good basketball in the past, I told them we can pack it in or we can go after it," Skip Hanson said. "If we go after it, we can come back. We have the talent. The players responded really well."

Foxcroft scored the first 8 points of the second quarter and, with Nelson and Saunders combining for 18 points, the Ponies outscored the Red Riots 22–10 in the period. However, during halftime, Red Riots statistician Mike Grubb went downstairs to the visiting locker room to notify Orono coach John Giffin that his team had 2 points taken off the scoreboard at intermission. When the scorebooks for the home and visiting teams don't match up, referees side with the home scorebook as being the official scorebook of record. It had the Red Riots with 2 fewer points than the scoreboard.

Giffin had to wonder if he was being "hometowned" and if there was a conspiracy afloat. It didn't take a mathematician to see that.

With Orono still ahead 27–26, both teams had major setbacks in the third quarter. Tom Philbrick picked up his fourth foul, and Nelson was poked in the eye attempting a tip-in, fell to the floor, and went to the bench for more than four minutes.

"I dropped to the floor like a bag of wet mice, but I managed to finish the game," Nelson said. "I thought I lost my eye. I never had any feeling of pain like that."

With 1:55 left in the game, Philbrick fouled out, yet Orono, led by his younger brother Bert and Brian Butterfield, was in position to win the game. But, with 33 seconds to go, a missed free throw by Scott McKay on the front end of a 1-and-1 foul shot situation denied the Red Riots a chance to potentially expand their lead to 3 points. Instead, at the other end, Saunders followed up his own missed free throw for a basket to give the Ponies a 56–55 lead. Eric Annis then stole an Orono pass and was fouled. He sank both crucial free throws for a 3-point lead. Nary a boo was heard from Foxcroft fans.

With two seconds left, Annis fouled Butterfield. He made his first free throw and intentionally missed his second. A mad scramble for the rebound ensued, but McKay's potential game-tying basket was disallowed as time had expired. As it turned out, the Red Riots could have used those 2 points deducted off the scoreboard at halftime.

A wild celebration on the floor commenced after the final buzzer. Fans stormed the court. The Ponies had exorcized their basketball demons by beating the Red Riots for only the second time in thirty-six previous meetings and for the first time since 1970.

"That was the moment we thought we finally can compete with them. We're not the doormat anymore," Kevin Saunders said. "We can play with these guys. It kind of elevated a number of careers."

It certainly was a game for the ages, given the rivalry and the fans' response to it. Bob Thorne was so thrilled by FA's victory over Orono that he joined the celebration in the team's locker room afterward.

It was arguably the greatest game ever played in the Foxcroft Academy gym in its sixty-plus-year history.

"I would say it was probably one of the biggest basketball games in any gym anywhere in the history of basketball in the state of the Maine," said Kevin Nelson's brother Shawn. "It would have to rank right up there in the Top 20 of all time."

Afterward, Kevin Nelson was jacked up. He enthusiastically celebrated the victory. His dad, Hollis, greeted him on the court, beaming with pride.

"My dad wasn't as emotional as my mom, but he clearly had unrestrained joy and elation," said Kevin Nelson, who today has a framed photo of that occasion hanging in his den. "That moment is pretty special to me."

In his postgame exuberance, Kevin Nelson, who scored a game-high 26 points, also approached Tom Philbrick amid the celebration on the court. They shook hands.

"Kevin was such a nice guy and after they beat us at Dover, he was just so excited that he came up to me and said, 'We've been waiting for this for a long time,'" Philbrick said. "And I remember telling Kevin, 'Enjoy it right now. It's going to be different in the Eastern Maine finals.'"

Philbrick then walked away.

"I don't recall that conversation, but I can see myself saying something like that," said Kevin Nelson. "I probably should have kept my trap shut."

"That lit me up," Philbrick said. "He just wanted me to know how important it was to him. I didn't understand that until later on in life. As a kid I just took it as a challenge."

Orono was Foxcroft's main nemesis in football and basketball. But now that the town had a high school basketball team capable of beating the Red Riots, Foxcroft Academy fans were looking for every opportunity for Orono to lose to climb past them in the Heal Point standings.

Indeed, after Orono's thirty-three-game winning streak was stopped in Dover-Foxcroft, the Red Riots had to turn around and make another long trip. This game was in Skowhegan, about an hour's drive southwest of Dover on Maine Route 150, a long and winding road.

Philbrick said, "Skowhegan was a Class A team, and we should have handled them. But when we got in there the damn gym was full. And we were like, 'What the heck?' Where did all these people come from?'"

He looked around and saw some familiar faces. They might as well have been zombies.

"It was all the fans from Dover-Foxcroft," Philbrick said. "You see them so much you start recognizing people. They came down there and Skowhegan got fired up and upset us."

Meanwhile, Foxcroft kept on a roll. The Ponies closed out the regular season without a defeat. Hanson's ulterior motive was trying to get his team in a tournament frame of mind. He did not want his team to rest on its laurels in wake of the monumental win over Orono.

When the Ponies, seeded No. 2, beat Herman in the quarterfinals and No. 3 seed Mount Desert Island in the semifinals of the Eastern Maine Class B Tournament, Foxcroft ran its winning streak to nineteen. According to *Piscataquis Observer* contributor and sportswriting legend Lou "Scoop" Stevens, that tied the school's longest winning streak ever in boys basketball set by the Ponies' 1939–40 team.

Foxcroft also advanced to the Eastern Maine Tournament championship game for the first time in twenty-four years. It took almost that long for televisions to change from black-and-white to color.

The nineteen-game winning streak set up another meeting with top-seeded and reigning state champ Orono, which won its semifinal game by 29 points and was eager and determined to avenge its loss in Dover-Foxcroft weeks earlier. The Red Riots, who had dismissed Foxcroft for decades as a worthy opponent in their rivalry, now found Foxcroft Academy to be its greatest threat to returning to the state championship game.

"It became really intense," said Jeff Dunn. "Dexter-Dover football was a good rivalry, but this rivalry with Orono in basketball was better because there was a lot more talent. It was top shelf. They turned over good teams for several years and we did for a shorter time."

The third meeting between Foxcroft and Orono that 1973–74 season would be settled on a neutral court between the tournament's top two seeds. The Eastern Maine Basketball Tournament was always held in Bangor, then the second-largest city in Maine, at the Bangor Auditorium. It was an odd-looking building, narrow and long, with a V-shaped roof that earned a reputation for leaking whenever it rained or snowed. The building's weird design was to better protect it against high winds and to save heating costs.

The seating capacity in the Bangor Auditorium was about seven thousand. When it opened in 1955, the only bigger venue of its kind in New England was the Boston Garden. On opening day, the *Bangor Daily News* had proclaimed the Bangor Auditorium to be "Mammoth, Marvelous, and Magnificent." Bangor Auditorium provided a myriad of entertainment options, hosting everything from the circus to ZZ Top to Boston Celtics preseason games. And it was home to the Eastern Maine Basketball Tournament (until 2013, when the building was demolished and replaced next door by the new 5,800-seat Cross Insurance Center).

Located next to a harness racing track, the Bangor Auditorium featured four seating sections on both sides of the court: pull-out wooden bleachers at court level, a second section of stadium wooden seats and then lower and upper balconies of seats—the so-called nosebleed seats—near the ceiling, which seemed closer to Mars or Madawaska than the playing surface. Cigarette smoke would linger up there in the early days.

There was no seating for spectators on the baselines, only for cheerleaders who hung school banners on the bare steel walls behind them. There was room for a pair of standing baskets and, high above that, a pair of scoreboards on each end erected in a V-shape extending from the walls so spectators could see the scoreboards on opposite sides of the court.

"As a player it was like going to mecca. It was an out-of-body experience to play there," said Tony Hamlin, the only basketball coach to have won a tournament game at the Bangor Auditorium in five different decades. "When you are young, you are overwhelmed by the whole thing."

Tom Largay grew up in Brewer across the Penobscot River from Bangor. It was a special place to watch a basketball game but, for him, it went to another level of awe the first time he got to compete in the Bangor Auditorium when he played at Foxcroft and stepped into the building for a pregame shoot around.

"We got on that court, and it was like the movie *Hoosiers* and Hickory High getting off the bus and practicing before the Indiana state championship game," Largay said. "You walked out of the locker room and there were a lot of people there and it was like, 'Whoa!' That floor seemed so big. I remember dribbling down that court and it seemed like it took me forever. The whole experience of looking up in the stands. It was overwhelming for me."

It was the booming sound, not the cavernous sight, that struck Joanna Brown. She won two state Class B girls basketball title games in the Bangor Auditorium with Western Maine Tournament champion York High School in 1992 and 1994.

"The sound comes down at you in one direction," said Brown, a 2023 Maine Basketball Hall of Fame inductee. "I still get goosebumps thinking about it."

There was a ticket office and lobby at the entrance at ground level leading to stairs that either dropped down to court level and the lower section of bleachers or led up to the middle and top sections where the concession stands were located behind and beneath the stadium and balcony seats. The smell of freshly popped popcorn and steamed hot dogs tucked in soft split-top steamed rolls would drift up to fans sitting above.

"It was nostalgic. It's hard to explain sensory to someone who has not been there and smelled the popcorn and the hot dogs and the noise is right down on top of you. It was such an event," said Hamlin, who as coach of the Penquis High School boys basketball team won the last tournament game played in the Bangor Auditorium—the Class C state title game—before it was demolished in 2013.

"You drink in the atmosphere," he said. "Maine is unlike any other state when it comes to high school basketball—except maybe Kentucky and Indiana. Most of these high school tournaments are played in high school gyms until you get to the highest level. They don't have a facility to play in like the Bangor Auditorium until they get to the state championship games and then they play in big arenas."

There was a time in the 1960s when the Eastern Maine Tournament quarterfinals of two different classes—Class S and Class M, for example—were played on the same day, a total of eight tournament games that started at 9 a.m. and ended after 9 p.m. at the Bangor Auditorium. Spectators could conceivably watch four games for the price of one and delight in the wealth of excitement each one produced.

"It was a magical place," Tom Philbrick said.

It was the premium prized destination for all Eastern Maine high school basketball teams every winter. Making the tournament in the Bangor Auditorium was a crowning achievement. Van Buren High School in Aroostook County—which borders New Brunswick, a Canadian province—would bring busloads of students and make a day-long round-trip to the Bangor Auditorium about 200 miles and a 3½-hour drive away to cheer for their team in the tournament.

For the 1974 Eastern Maine Boys Basketball Tournament, Allagash High School, with a student body population of thirty-one, qualified for the Class D tournament for the first time. The Bobcats had to travel 250 miles and four hours to play in a building most of the team had never before seen in their lifetimes. They stopped in Houlton a day before the tournament to break up the trip and hold a practice session.

The Foxcroft Academy Ponies and their fans had to drive about an hour to get to the Bangor Auditorium. They arrived with much positivism. In their minds, Kevin Nelson was the best big man to come out of Maine since Paul Bunyan—who has a 31-foot tall statue right next to the Bangor Auditorium, symbolizing Bangor's history as a nineteenth-century lumber port. (Today Paul Bunyan's view of the Penobscot River is blocked by the Hollywood Hotel and Casino on the other side of Main Street.)

As obstacles go, Orono was the biggest for Foxcroft. To reach their ultimate objective—the state championship game—the FA Ponies would need to get past the battle-tested Red Riots.

"The rivalry was new to us because we were used to getting blown out and then suddenly we're playing those guys competitively," Kevin Saunders said. "And they were used to playing in those big games. Tommy Philbrick had played there before. None of us had been there in the finals. We weren't sure how to react to some of that, as evidenced by Kevin in his junior year. He played maybe half of that Eastern Maine championship game because he was in foul trouble. Tommy used him a little bit."

Certainly, the Ponies' nervousness and inexperience showed in the title game. Kevin Saunders was shooting the front end of a 1-and-1 foul shot situation but, after an official handed him the ball at the foul line to attempt the first one—and possibly add 2 points to the Ponies' score—Jeff Dunn stepped away from the foul lane. He was immediately whistled for a foul lane violation. Saunders never attempted a free throw, the Ponies were confused and embarrassed, and Orono got possession of the ball and a big laugh at the turnover.

"I don't know what I was thinking," Dunn said.

Dunn also had another costly turnover when he saw Junior Bradbury wide open in the right-hand corner, yet his pass sailed six feet over Bradbury's head and went out of bounds. The pass was high enough to clear the outside railing at the harness track.

"I don't know if I cost us the game or not, but I didn't help us win it," Dunn said. "Two mistakes. Of that whole season, those two things stick with me more than anything else."

The Ponies also were saddled with foul trouble. The Kevins both had four fouls with 4:43 left in the game, yet they pushed the Ponies into the lead, 50–45, on a 3-point play by Nelson with 3:40 to play and a basket by Saunders with 2:37 to go that forced the Red Riots to call timeout. Foxcroft fans were ecstatic.

Red Riots coach John Giffin in the huddle gave his Orono players the "backs against the wall" speech. It was the moment of truth, and Tom Philbrick was ready to take matters into his own hands.

"I told Barney [Brian Butterfield] give me the ball and I gave him a slap on the butt," Philbrick said.

Butterfield was given the nickname Barney in his youth by his dad, Jack, who worked on the railroad docks with a Frenchman named Barney. The Red Riots' guard executed Philbrick's game plan perfectly. Then things got frantic and chaotic.

Tom Philbrick took over for Orono and seized the momentum back for the defending state champs. With Foxcroft leading by 5 points, 52–47, and 1:48 left in the game, Philbrick went up to score a basket as referee Del Merrill whistled Nelson for his fifth foul.

This is forever known in Foxcroft Academy lore as "The Phantom Foul."

To hear Pony fans, Nelson might as well have been standing on Cadillac Mountain in Bar Harbor when the fateful foul was called.

"He was nowhere near it," Dennis Kiah said.

"I don't even remember who I fouled or where it was on the court," Nelson said. "I just remember I pitched a fit afterwards saying no way."

Skip Hanson swears he heard Tom Philbrick tell Del Merrill that Kevin Nelson did not touch him, therefore there was no foul on the play.

"Kevin didn't foul me. He was behind me," Tom Philbrick said. "I told Deli he didn't foul me, and he just looked at me like I was crazy for saying it, but I did say that. It was true. He didn't touch me."

"I always held Tom Philbrick in great esteem for doing that because he wanted to win with Kevin Nelson on the floor," Skip Hanson said. "I thought we could beat them because we were on a run then."

Merrill, inducted into the Maine Sports Hall of Fame in 1997, was a flame thrower for the 5th Marine Division in World War II and stormed the beach at Iwo Jima. He was more than prepared to take the heat and wasn't going to back down or change his mind. Foxcroft fans were enraged.

FA lost Nelson, disqualified with his fifth foul, and Nelson uncharacteristically lost his cool.

"I went back to the bench, and we had metal folding chairs and I kicked one halfway across that aisle behind our bench," Kevin Nelson said. "But they didn't 'T' me up because I just fouled out and the FA crowd was just beside themselves. I pitched a hissy fit."

Nelson was as mad at himself as he was at the foul call. Skip Hanson had coached him to move his feet and reach straight up. In Del Merrill's eyes and mind, Nelson must have looked like Godzilla going for Philbrick's shot.

"That was one of those calls that's hard to understand, like the pass interference calls in the NFL," Jeff Dunn said. "Sometimes you just don't make those calls and you let the game take care of itself unless it's something that really impacts the outcome. My recollection is it was under the basket and I don't think it had any impact on that particular play at the time, but that foul call made a difference."

Philbrick completed the 3-point play with a foul shot to make the score FA 52, Orono 50, then he tied the game at 52 on the Red Riots' next possession. Orono fans were suddenly ecstatic, as the positive energy suddenly swayed their way.

Fouling out Kevin Nelson was the way to victory for Orono. Kevin Saunders, struggling early in the game from a tough shooting night, was gallantly trying to carry the load with Kevin Nelson in foul trouble. Philbrick, the Red Riots' center, took advantage of both. He scored 13 of Orono's final 15 points, and his clutch defensive rebound in the final minute with Nelson on the bench set up Doug—who was injured and did not play in the Red Riots' loss at Foxcroft in January—to score what proved to be the deciding basket with 23 seconds to play. Tom Philbrick called the game-winning play coming out of the huddle, telling his brother to move along the baseline so that he would be wide open to take a potential game-winning shot.

"Tom Philbrick was Larry Bird before Larry Bird," said Dave Paul, whose father Joe Paul, an iconic coach at Greenville High School, was Giffin's assistant coach. "Tommy wanted one thing and one thing only. He wanted to win the game for Orono High School."

As Tom predicted, he was double-teamed leaving Bert Philbrick unguarded. Bert's shot rimmed around the basket where Carville was waiting to tip it in on the other side. While Carville was celebrating his go-ahead basket, Foxcroft nearly tied the game.

"The place is delirious and he's backpedaling back up the court with his arms in the air and someone from Dover snuck behind him and there's a long pass to someone—it might have been Junior Bradbury— who looked open for a layup," Butterfield said. "And Scotty McKay comes out of nowhere and intercepts the pass. It was a great play by Doug offensively, but Scotty saved our bacon with a hustle play."

Foxcroft had one last shot—a desperation heave—with one second remaining. But Saunders barely missed a potential game-tying shot on a play that he swears Tom Philbrick committed a real foul.

"Whoever was setting the pick on Philbrick, Tommy just pancaked this guy," Kevin Saunders said. "Tommy ran through him and pancaked him like he was a middle linebacker and he came out and put a hand in my face. Obviously in that circumstance the officials aren't going to call that and Tommy knew that. Tommy was very savvy. He understood the game very well."

Though the Ponies scored only 2 points in the final 3:40 of the game, Foxcroft coaches, players, and fans had a hard time fathoming how they could lose in such a fashion—on a "phantom" foul that turned the game in favor of the Red Riots.

Foul or no foul? The only debate more loud and intense at the time was Miller Beer's "Tastes Great" or "Less Filling."

"That was a sad game," said Duane Warren. "The referees? If I remember correctly, they just took it away from Foxcroft. I would never admit like Tom Philbrick that I didn't foul anyone. Oh my goodness. I spent my whole career since I was in fourth grade with like three or four fouls. I still own the record for most phantom fouls! If I got within 2 inches or 2 feet they'd call a foul on me!"

Philbrick, with a noble and honest effort, finished the championship game with 34 points on 15-of-21 shooting and added 13 rebounds. In a classy move, he also visited the FA locker room after the game to offer his condolences.

"It's one of the greatest exhibitions of basketball I've ever watched," Butterfield said.

Foxcroft fans were crushed by the defeat. They were more than sad. They were simmering. One of them was a young boy named Todd Hanson, Skip's son.

"My first memories was when Foxcroft lost in the Eastern Maine finals in 1974. I was in first grade and I remember crying in the stands when we lost," said Todd, who grew up to be a successful high school coach and was ultimately inducted into the Maine Basketball Hall of Fame. "And I remember my dad being really mad at the officials."

Driving back from Bangor didn't make things any easier. The nation was gripped in a gasoline shortage. Gas stations were running out of fuel with cars parked in long lines to get gas. It was like a drive-in movie without the movie.

A trip to and from the Bangor Auditorium was quite an investment in time and effort for Foxcroft fans, both emotionally and financially. Between phantom fouls and gas lines they had a lot of pent-up frustration.

Back in Dover-Foxcroft, the Ponies were commiserating over the season-ending loss to Orono that denied them the opportunity to play

Camden-Rockport in the Class B state championship game. In three games that season, Orono and Foxcroft were separated by a total of only 1 point. FA lost two of those games, but believed it had the 1–2 punch to knockoff Orono.

"Anytime you had Kevin Nelson and Kevin Saunders on the same team you had a chance to beat anyone," said John Champeon. "Kevin Saunders? If he hadn't played with Kevin Nelson he'd been thought of the one of the best players FA ever had. They were quite a duo under the basket."

"There weren't many guys on the 1974 team that were going to play at the next level in college. It was pretty obvious Kevin and I were going to play at the next level," said Kevin Saunders, who went on to a brilliant playing career at Husson College in Bangor. "But for Eric Annis and Junior Bradbury, that was their Super Bowl."

Some longtime FA fans thought the 1973–74 team might have been the Ponies' best—and last—chance to win a state basketball championship.

"I remember thinking our Gold Ball chance had gone with the graduation of Saunders and Bradbury," said Jim Harvey, who graduated from Foxcroft Academy in 1966. "As it was, we had some speed and would probably need to rely on pressure defenses with a heavy dose of Nelson on offense in the future."

The 1973–74 Foxcroft Academy boys basketball team was honored at a postseason banquet. The Ponies were awarded with jackets for winning the Penquis League championship. Kevin Saunders took his jacket with him to Husson College, where he became basketball teammates and friends with Tom Philbrick of Orono.

"We had jackets that had our season's record 18–2 printed out, and Tommy always took great delight whenever I wore that jacket around campus at Husson by saying, 'Yup, I'm the 2,'" Kevin Saunders said.

In the end, Kevin Saunders looked back at what might have been at Foxcroft. There were a lot of what-ifs capped by the season-ending loss to the Red Riots.

"In my opinion, we let that one get away. We should have won that game against Orono," Saunders said. "As Tom Philbrick readily admitted to me a hundred times afterward, 'You guys would have won the state championship because you guys matched up better with Camden-Rockport.'"

Camden-Rockport, which may have been the best team in Maine that season regardless of classification, beat Orono 56–48 the following week in the Maine State Class B Championship game at the Bangor Auditorium. Led by Charlie Wootton, the unbeaten Windjammers had defeated top-seeded Medomak Valley in the Western Maine Class B Tournament championship game.

Unlike Kevin Saunders, Kevin Nelson had another chance to make a wrong a right. He had one more year at Foxcroft.

While Saunders, Bradbury, and Annis were reflecting and grieving from the bitter loss to Orono at a postgame party at Fay Richards' house, Nelson was recovering quickly and moving on.

"I wasn't a real deep thinker back then. I was thinking, 'This really sucks, but I've got another year.' How long did I stay in a state of despair? Not that long. My vision was like 2 feet in front of me," Nelson said. "When you lose three players like that you're not thinking about, 'Oh boy, we're loaded for the next year.' I wasn't. There wasn't any expectation of an undefeated season."

Well, Tillson Thomas, the retired FA principal who paid the way for Nelson to attend summer basketball camp after his freshman year, had high hopes. Tillson sent a handwritten letter to Nelson dated April 15, 1974, on behalf of himself and his wife, Ruth—who taught Nelson in eighth grade—congratulating him on being named to the All-Maine team by the *Bangor Daily News*. They had been attending many FA games and were not a doubting Thomas family.

"From watching the games I seriously believe your 1973–74 team was the best team to represent Foxcroft Academy that I can remember," Tillson wrote. "Next year we will be cheering you and your teammates to go all the way to the State Championship and for you to receive a repeat of your All-Maine selection."

Tom Philbrick also was named first team All-State by the *Bangor Daily News*. Kevin Saunders was Honorable Mention All-Maine.

Nelson, the only junior named first team All-State, made it a point to attend and watch the Class B state championship game between Orono and Camden-Rockport in the Bangor Auditorium at the end of the season. But he did have one last game to play that year. The FA athletic department organized a fundraising basketball doubleheader in the FA gym on March 14 to benefit the FA Band which, on June 15, 1974, was scheduled to fly from Bangor International Airport to Romania to play fifteen concerts in a twenty-one-day tour for the Ambassadors for Freedom program.

The benefit basketball doubleheader raised money for the Foxcroft Academy Band, but it also spoke volumes about the respect, admiration, and appreciation FA basketball and the community had for Bob Thorne and the music program.

The FA Band was always behind the FA boys basketball team, quite literally. Band members in the bleachers sat behind the Ponies' bench when they performed at home games. The FA basketball program showed it had the FA Band's back by performing in the fundraising doubleheader in the FA gym.

In the first game, a faculty team from Old Town High School, led by Lionel Bishop and Skip Hanson's brother-in-law and Aroostook State sparring partner Bob Lahey, played the FA faculty. Foxcroft won 78–77 in overtime as Dave Clement had 22 points, former PCHS star Paul Draper added 21 points, and Wayne Champeon and Skip Hanson contributed 12 and 10 points, respectively.

The main event was the FA varsity team—led by Kevin Nelson and Kevin Saunders—playing the University of Maine All-Stars. Coached by FA trustee and booster Henry Gerrish, the Ponies got 30 points from Saunders and 13 from Nelson, but they were no match for the UMO All-Stars. Tony Hamlin netted a game-high 35 points for the all-star team that included future FA Athletics Hall of Famers Dave "Hawk" Anderson and Dickie Annis—and Orono's Tom Philbrick. He played four years of varsity basketball at Orono, and his teams compiled a record of 76–9 in that span, 6–1 in head-to-head matchups against Foxcroft Academy and Kevin Nelson.

Yet, the last organized basketball game Philbrick played while attending Orono High School was in the FA gymnasium. And he beat Kevin Nelson for the last time.

"Kevin was the most talented big man I played against in high school," said Philbrick, now owner and operator of Boothbay Lobster Wharf and the Philbrick Lobster Company in Boothbay Harbor. "I was very physical. That's the only way I could play Kevin. To this day I think Kevin felt I played dirty. I couldn't let him play in the paint and I talked to him. I told him, 'Stay out of the paint, Kevin,' but he didn't. He battled. He had a wicked heart."

Philbrick said he visited Digger Phelps at Notre Dame, Maryland's Lefty Driesell scouted him, and NCAA Division I schools from Arizona and Oregon recruited him, but he wasn't academically strong enough to move directly into those programs or the University of Maine where his father, Gib, was a basketball coach. He chose to play for future Maine Basketball Hall of Fame coach Bruce MacGregor at Husson College in Bangor with FA's Kevin Saunders. In their four years there as teammates, Philbrick and Saunders combined for 2,846 points, a 100–15 record, and one broken nose (Saunders broke Philbrick's nose in a rebounding drill in practice).

With that ferocious duo, Husson was NAIA District V champion before losing in the NAIA national championship games their first two seasons. Philbrick was All-NAIA District in 1977.

"I never regret going to Husson and what Coach MacGregor did for me," Philbrick said. "The only regret is not playing at The Pit at the University of Maine. I grew up there. My dad coached there. I'd shoot in there. We played games in there."

Tom's older brother, Jack, also went to the University of Maine. Jack Philbrick has made his mark in Hollywood as an actor, production manager, and director working on television shows such as *Hill Street Blues*, *Picket Fences*, and *White Shadow*.

Tom Philbrick was hoping he might someday even play basketball with Kevin Nelson in The Pit. Philbrick graduated from Orono High School having won a state championship and two Eastern Maine Tournament titles while appearing in three Eastern Maine tourney championship games in four years. The Red Riots lost to Schenck 59–27 in the Eastern Maine title game in 1971, and the Wolverines went on to win consecutive state Class B championships in 1971–72.

Nelson, meanwhile, was still chasing his and Foxcroft's first and elusive Eastern Maine Tournament title.

"Schenck and Orono. Schenck and Orono. Those two teams hammered us my freshman and sophomore years. They just hammered us," Kevin Nelson said. "All of a sudden, the tables were turning. Good players graduate and that's the way it goes. Tommy Philbrick was graduating, so my Orono nemesis was gone."

The Ponies, it seemed, finally had the opening that they had been looking for. Dark clouds were parting. Could there be a championship on the horizon?

The Cast of Characters

WITH THREE STARTERS GRADUATING FROM THE EASTERN MAINE Class B Tournament runners-up, the 1974–75 Foxcroft Academy boys basketball team appeared to be a new team in the works when in fact it was an updated version of an old team. Basically a reboot of the same undefeated "A" squad team that Skip Hanson saw developing in the Dover Grammar School gym when Kevin Nelson was an eighth grader and a messiah in the making.

They were just bigger, taller, better players who had grown closer through the years. They were ready-made to play to win. They were a gift for Skip. No assembly required.

The journey and destination are important, but sometimes it's the company you keep that matters.

"Something magical happened in the fall of 1974," Kevin Nelson said. "Skip selected an eclectic group of highly skilled, highly competitive kids who developed a team chemistry that was very special. From that point on, our team became part of FA basketball history."

The varsity team that Skip Hanson (with input from Dennis Kiah and Dave Clement) picked for the 1974–75 season consisted of nine seniors and two juniors who had been playing basketball together on and off for five years. Six of them played on the FA freshmen team in 1972. Six of them made the varsity team in 1974, and five were on the JV team. Five of them were teammates on the Ponies football team when they started their senior year at FA.

Foxcroft fans were thinking, *Ain't we lucky we got 'em? Good times.*

"The '75 team was laden with seniors, on purpose," Skip Hanson said. "We knew that we had an excellent chance to be successful, so we kept more seniors due to their experiences and abilities to challenge each other in practices."

Which begs the question: Does practice really, therefore, make perfect? That harks back to an Anglo-American phrase adopted from Latin in the mid-1500s and, more than two centuries later, resurrected from the diary and autobiography of John Adams, who was a heck of a coach during the American Revolution.

The Ponies thought they might have a revolutionary team for the 1974–75 season. They were a tight-knit group that had been close from day one. Literally. Kevin Nelson and Tim King were born a day apart at Mayo Memorial Hospital in Dover-Foxcroft. They were placed side by side in bassinets in a nursery room where their parents and relatives could view the newborn babies through a window outside the maternity ward.

Who knew then that the baby building blocks for a championship team had been birthed? They would be followed by a cast of characters ranging in size, personalities, and various chips on their shoulders.

Kevin Nelson and Tim King have been lifelong friends. Kevin just grew to be a lot taller. They went their separate ways in their youth and took similar paths in the outskirts of Piscataquis County. Kevin would work in the woods with his dad and bale hay in the afternoons in Southeast Monson. Tim would work on the family farm—Kings Royal Acres—on the East Dover Road and attend to the cows.

They were as rural as rural can get, yet they both managed to play basketball growing up. While Kevin was honing his craft in the family's barn, Tim was outside at his family's farm shooting at a hoop attached to a plywood backboard that his dad, Johnny, hammered and spiked into a huge elm tree about 7½ feet off the ground because the tree wasn't thick enough at the top to support a backboard and goal. Tim and his brothers had to shoot over a low-lying power line between the tree and house to get the ball in the basket.

Though technically separated at birth, Tim King and Kevin Nelson reconnected because of the SAD 68 consolidation.

"The first time I saw him it was like, 'Wow.' I had a brother-in-law who was just short of 6-foot-5. And I'm thinking this guy—Kevin

Nelson—he is like Jack in the Beanstalk all in one. In grade school I nicknamed Kevin 'Jack,' and I've called him Jack ever since," Tim said.

That's the fact, Jack. Nelson listed his nickname as "Jack" in the 1975 Foxcroft yearbook, *The Review*. That same yearbook shows that Nelson was voted "Most Likely to Succeed" by the senior class, which also voted Nelson as its class president each of his four years at Foxcroft. He served a four-year term in high school.

Kevin was named to the National Honor Society, received a Rose award for academic excellence, and represented Foxcroft at Boys State at the University of Maine. The kid garnered more honors and accolades in the '70s than *The Waltons* at the Emmys.

Moreover, Kevin was an all-around charmer. Dennis Kiah remembers a time his wife Betty Ellen was teaching at Foxcroft and was pregnant with their second child, Jill. Betty Ellen was standing on a chair, stretching to reach for an object on a shelf above her when Kevin walked into the classroom.

"He said, 'No, Mrs. Kiah. You can't do that,'" Dennis Kiah said. "Kevin stood there and took the items off the shelf one by one for her."

Hence, Kevin Nelson's impact on Foxcroft Academy was more far-reaching than the basketball court.

"We can't say enough good things about Kevin," said Peg Hanson. "He was the consummate student-athlete plus such a wonderful person. He's just so polite."

"He was so good, and he was such a nice guy," said Todd Hanson. "I think back to when I was seven or eight years old that year, and I think all the players remember me being a pain in the neck, but they were all really good to me, in particular Kevin. He never got mad at me. He was just such a perfect role model."

Kevin was a natural-born leader as well. His teammates realized he had the characteristics and charisma of a captain who could lead by example. Like his dad.

"Kevin set the tone for the team," said Mark Joyce. "If your star player for the state is gregarious and inclusive with everybody that sets the tone and that was no small reason for the chemistry that we did have. He was a good ballplayer and a good guy to be around."

With Kevin Nelson guiding the way, the 1974–75 season was more like a reunion tour than a revenge campaign following the bitter loss to Orono in the 1974 Eastern Maine Class B Tournament championship game. Nelson, in his fourth year on varsity, was reunited with practically all his teammates from the "A" squad at Dover Grammar School.

"You still have that commonality. We spent our eighth-grade year together and we won a championship together," Nelson said. "I got split apart from them as freshman, but it speaks to the quality of friendships that we had throughout our entire high school years."

Even the team managers on the varsity—Joe Dean, Keith Chadbourne, and Jim Herrick—were all seniors. Joe had been a team basketball manager since his freshmen year at Foxcroft Academy. He, too, was witness to the team bonding that took place starting at Dover Grammar School beginning with soccer. Joe played on the Eagles' soccer team coached by Gary Larson that went 10–0 and claimed a Central Maine junior high school championship.

"Even though this isn't the same sport, the Dover Grammar soccer team went undefeated and we only had one goal scored against us all season. Because SAD 68 had not been formed and Monson was not part of this team all the players, including me, were part of this soccer team at Dover Grammar," said Joe, who now lives in England and follows Premier League Football.

"I feel this was the basis of the championship mentality of the basketball team. I feel Kevin Nelson brought the final piece of the jigsaw that sealed this chemistry. Mostly by his kind and gentle manner of treating everyone equal."

To hear his classmates and teammates you'd think Kevin Nelson was David Cassidy and they were the Partridge Family. From the first day of school in eighth grade when he stepped off the bus from Monson, they came to embrace and admire him. He was their teen idol.

"It was almost written in the stars in grade school," Tim King said. "When Kevin came, that was the big hope for everybody. Even without verbalizing it they were wishing it because we needed somebody with his stature. I was hopeful but reasonably confident that if everybody kept their nose clean and did what they needed to do to develop going to our senior year we could win a championship."

Skip Hanson and his assistant coaches, Dennis Kiah and Dave Clement, had the same belief. It was their goal to stay the course and keep the team in line. They bounced ideas off each other and challenged the players in various ways.

"That coaching staff was such a good coaching staff for us," said Jeff Dunn. "Three different personalities and they had the right personalities to motivate us. And they had the right scheme and game plan. Obviously, the right scheme is to center around Kevin, but he wasn't a one-man team. The entire team contributed pretty much over the entire year to our success."

Kevin Nelson was again named one of the team's co-captains for the 1974–75 season. Jeff Dunn was named the other co-captain. Dunn was a 5-foot tall guard as a freshman, but grew to be 5–7 as a sophomore on the JV team and was 5–11 by the time he made the varsity team.

Though disappointed by key turnovers in the Eastern Maine Class B Tournament title game loss to Orono nine months earlier, Dunn was not haunted by them.

"The motivation our senior year just came from how good the team was, and the composition of it," Dunn said. "We all had very high expectations of what the season should be. We all thought we should come up nothing short of being in the state championship game."

Dunn was a quick, smooth, and deceptive player offensively. He was second on the team in scoring (10.3 points per game), but his forte was defense. He could steal chocolate chips out of a cookie and not leave a crumb.

"I always was aggressive on defense," Dunn said. "Hustle. I figured my hands were quicker than some of those guys a lot of times. I was always trying to hawk the ball. . . . It took me a while to get my confidence to play with the big boys."

That came when Dunn moved into the starting lineup in the second half of his junior season. With that promotion came more playing time and an opportunity to display his on-court demeanor.

"Jeff was soft-spoken but highly respected by everyone," said Skip Hanson. "We knew that he would lead by example, which he certainly did. I cannot recall Jeff ever disputing a call, or hanging his head when a coach got after him a bit. He was a real pleasure to be around and a terrific leader by his actions."

Dunn, though normally a quiet leader, was thrilled to be a co-captain and thought he earned it with his seniority. Though he might have liked to crawl under a rock when he made those two crucial turnovers in the Eastern Maine finals against Orono, Dunn was made for the spotlight. He did not shy away from those mistakes and owned them. He wanted to prove he could learn and lead from them as a team captain.

"I felt like I deserved it, but it was nice to get the recognition for it," Dunn said. "It was nice to have Kevin and I at mid-court meeting with the officials and the other team's captains. That was a highlight."

Shaking hands with the referees and opposing team captains at mid-court before each game was a big deal for Dunn, but that wasn't for show. Dunn knew his real worth to the Ponies.

"If Jeff was going into a game with me, he had this level of confidence that I might not have had without him," Nelson said. "He knew what his role was and he embraced it. He was the consummate teammate. Everyone on the team knew their role and embraced it."

Dunn was proud of being a team captain, much more than being mocked for his modesty by being voted "Class Flirt" and "Class Gossiper" in the 1975 *Review* yearbook. He suspected a conspiracy behind that vote.

"I think that was all just a big setup," Dunn quipped.

Of greater significance to Dunn and the team was what he said and did on the court and not in the hallway. He was slick.

"He had the quickest hands of anybody I ever played with or against in high school, college, men's league anywhere. It was almost like he was sizing up his prey," Nelson said. "He was one of the guys who told me, 'Do not bring the ball from a rebound down to your waist because I'm going to take it.'"

Dunn's running mate in the backcourt was 5-foot-8 Dave Ingraham. He was the starting quarterback on the Foxcroft football team that, in the fall of 1974, helped the Ponies to their first Penquis League championship since 1967 with a record of 6-2-0. They lost their final game of the season to Orono as Brian Butterfield ran for 143 yards and scored all the Red Riots' points in a 16–14 victory at Oakes Field.

Ingraham was probably the best three-sport athlete on Foxcroft Academy's basketball team. He was the steadying force for Foxcroft, especially when the team was pressured full court. He was all business.

"Dave never zigged and zagged. Dave was always like straight line," said his younger brother Peter. "He never changed expression. His emotions never showed. He was just cool as ice."

Kevin Nelson agreed, calling Ingraham the prototypical point guard.

"That season, he was absolutely the right player at the right time at that most critical of positions," Nelson said. "Dave sacrificed a lot for the betterment of the team our senior year. He averaged about 3.5 points per game, but I'm certain that had he played for most any other team, he could have averaged 12 to 15 points a game."

"Dave was definitely the court leader," Dick Hatt said. "He was always calm and quiet. There weren't a lot of spoken words."

Team came first regardless of what sport Dave played. He was not animated, preferring to lead by his actions on the court.

"Dave represented the team in a way only he could," Peter Ingraham said. "That was a real source of pride with my brother. That was his proudest achievement. He guarded it fiercely. He never had a bad word to say about anyone."

Dave also was the team's musical connoisseur. He would go with Scott Mountford and hang out with Alan Taylor or Tom Morgan, disc jockeys at Dover-Foxcroft's AM radio station, WDME, which was located right next to Central Hall.

The true musician on the team, however, was 6-foot-4 Roger Hewitt, who when he wasn't playing basketball for the Ponies was playing in the percussion section of the Foxcroft Academy Band. He played snare drum, tom drum, base drum, cymbals, claves, temple blocks, and so on.

Though Roger played in the Foxcroft Academy Band when he wasn't playing basketball, he had extra incentive to play hard. He loved Coca Cola, and sometimes Skip Hanson would offer a Coke and a smile to the player who had the best practice. Roger was the real thing in practice when it came to competing for a Coke.

Roger also found inspiration from a handwritten note by Foxcroft Academy fan John Milton, who praised Roger for his hard work and sacrifice and for always being ready when Skip Hanson subbed him into a game. Roger still has the note, dated December 26, 1974. Milton wrote, "Know that when Kevin comes out and you get in, the applause you hear is for you as much as it is for Kevin. You are the embodiment of the spirit that has transformed eleven individuals into a team. Patience, and self-sacrifice and desire—those are your virtues."

Mainer John Milton then cited seventeenth-century English poet John Milton's Sonnet 16 "On His Blindness" and ended his note with "P.S. Remember that, and be content, as we truly appreciate your efforts. We believe in you."

On the court, Roger Hewitt was Kevin Nelson's back-up at center and someone who never backed down to the team's 6–8 star.

"Kevin didn't have any peers and, though Roger couldn't move very well, he really made it hard on Kevin in practice," Dunn said. "Roger would mix it up with Kevin. He pushed Kevin really hard in practice and, without someone like that, our practices would have been a lot different."

Hewitt and Nelson—the two tallest players on the team—would be matched against each other in drills and scrimmages in practice. Sometimes their frustration would spill over on the court.

"He would always hang off Kevin and beat on him, but not intentionally and poor Kevin used to get mad," Jeff Brown said. "That's the only time I saw Kevin get mad. But I could hang all over Kevin and it never bothered him."

"Roger would pound me in practice," Nelson said. "He didn't care. He'd lay his body on you and push you around and fight you for rebounds, but he was a good teammate. Roger would wear you. He had some physical limitations, but when he stepped on the court, he was just like everyone else. He had that competitive nature. When he stepped off the court, we were all friends. We knew how to turn it on and off."

One time, their battles on the court led to a three-stitch cut in Hewitt's right eyebrow. Their competitiveness collided.

"I managed to get the ball away from Kevin and, while running past me to the other end of the court, Kevin tried to steal the ball back. In doing so, his forehead inadvertently made contact with the side of my head," Hewitt explained. "He ended up with an egg-size knot between his eyes, and I got a cut on my eyebrow. A visit to Dr. Bradbury for stitches ended my practice for the day. All was well the next day and practice went on accordingly."

Though Hewitt was comfortable being Nelson's back-up, the player on the Foxcroft team who may have been the most accepting of his role was 6-foot-1 forward Mark Joyce. He transferred from Mount View High School in Waldo County to Foxcroft Academy before his junior year. He was starter on the varsity team early in that season, but his playing time became more limited as he slid further down the bench.

However, Joyce evolved into the team protagonist. He was the best at poking fun, even at himself. When Joyce launched air balls on consecutive free throws in a game against Schenck, he turned a negative into a positive. He created a weekly "Air Ball Chart" and kept tabs of any teammate whose shots failed to make it to the rim or bounced off the side or on top of the backboard. He found a silver lining in stray shots.

"I took a lot of crap for those air balls, but after that I started tracking everybody's air balls," Joyce said. "I had a chart in the locker room. I was the official air ball scorer. I think we started tracking glass balls, net balls, and your garden variety of just-fell-short air balls and some that went over the hoop from the baseline. I was the Air Ball Tracker. I wish I kept the chart. That would have been an artifact."

Joyce also helped establish the FALS—the Foxcroft Academy Lounge Society. He and teammates after practices and some games would take folding aluminum webbed lawn lounge chairs into the shower in the P.E. locker room and literally spread out and relax under the spray of water from the shower heads as if they were sunbathing on a sandy beach.

Membership had its privileges.

"As long as you were part of the team and you could get a chair in there, no one was ever denied," Jeff Brown said.

Joyce wrote a story about the FALS in the *Pony Express,* the school's newspaper. It featured a photo of Kevin Nelson and Tim King lounging under the shower spray. Joyce was the editor of the *Pony Express* and co-commissioner of the FALS along with Nelson.

"The requirement was you had to be one of the people actually in the shower and you had to actually enjoy the shower experience, and Mark, Tim and I were always typically the last people in there," Nelson said.

Typically Nelson was the last to leave. Though he was quick to the ball on the court, he was notorious for being slow off it. It was one of the reasons his brother Shawn refrained from giving him a ride home when Shawn played at Foxcroft.

"He's absolutely right. Shawn was far more impetuous than me, and he doesn't have time to stand around and stop. He needed to move," Kevin said. "We were cut from a different cloth that way. I won't dispute that allegation. Guilty as charged."

Another holdover from the 1974 Ponies varsity team was Kenny Burtchell, a rugged 5-foot-9 junior swingman who was the strong, silent type. Think Clint Eastwood as Dirty Harry. Like several players on the team, Burtchell got off on the wrong foot with Skip Hanson, who was upset that Burtchell, when a freshman, reported late for basketball try-outs following the end of football season.

"Coach Hanson met me at the door on the following Monday night I went to practice and he gave me shit for not showing up for the first practice," Burtchell said. "I don't know if I had an attitude in play that he didn't like, but I was thinking I was out for the year because I skipped that first practice."

Burtchell eventually played his way out of Hanson's doghouse and made the Foxcroft Academy varsity team as a sophomore. Though a kid of few words, Burtchell let his play do the talking for him. He was a dogged football player with a soft shooting touch. His quiet, stoic demeanor masked the fierce competitor in him. He had a rock-solid body and a deadly shooting eye from long range.

"He was a quiet assassin," Dunn said.

"He never had a real presence, but he scored key points when we needed them," Peter Snow said.

"He was really underrated," said Mark Joyce. "He had like that country bumpkin look to him."

"You didn't want to piss Kenny off because he wouldn't say anything, he'd just shoot the ball," Nelson said. "Can you imagine if there was a 3-point line in Maine high school basketball at that time and Kenny was playing? His statistics would have been padded."

Like Burtchell, Scott Mountford—at 5-foot-10, 180 pounds—was built for football but had the right attitude to play basketball for Skip Hanson. It took Mountford a while to fully appreciate his coaches. Kiah once kicked Mountford out of a football practice, and Mountford dropped an F-bomb on his way back toward the locker room.

Jon Weatherbee, Mountford's football teammate, ran after him and put his arm around Mountford's shoulders and tried to calm him down.

"Jon, I'm fine," Mountford said.

"No, you're not," Weatherbee replied. "I think Kiah is going to come over and kill you. I'm here to protect you."

Mountford came around and made amends with Kiah, and it took him a bit to warm to Skip Hanson.

"He was known as a hard ass," Mountford said. "He wasn't well liked because he was so strict. Of course, we didn't know that he was just trying to bring what potential we had out of us. We thought he was being an asshole when, in reality, he was obviously a good coach."

Scott Mountford fit into Skip Hanson's master plan. He wanted a hard-nosed competitor to make his teammates better.

"Scott was a force his senior year, particularly in practices," Skip Hanson said. "He was rough and tough every night and consequently gave those around him the ability to play in those environments."

Other than Mountford, the rest of the newcomers to the varsity roster from the Ponies' outstanding junior varsity team were Dick Hatt, Jeff Brown, Peter Snow, and Tim King. They were starters on the Foxcroft Academy JV team that, coached by Kiah, accumulated a record of 19–3 during the 1973–74 season. They won their final nine games by an average of 18 points a game while defensively limiting their opponents to an average of only 37 points a game during that nine-game winning streak.

For someone who came to Foxcroft supposedly not knowing how to coach basketball, Kiah was obviously a fast learner.

"The kids were awesome. There didn't seem to be any jealousy about who was going to get the ball or who wasn't going to get the ball," Kiah said. "Every one of them contributed."

One of the biggest contributors on the JV team had been Dick Hatt, and he almost didn't make the team. His father was in the Air Force so Dick had lived in Florida, England, and Michigan before moving back to Piscataquis County in seventh grade. Though Hatt evolved to be one of the top three scorers during the 1974–75 season, his rise to varsity player was problematic. He said he was bullied by upperclassmen as a freshman, missed school, and decided not to play baseball, his favorite sport. Then he was cut from the JV basketball team as a sophomore and did not play.

Then, as a junior, Hatt was cut again from the JV team when he thought he belonged on the varsity team.

Had not Barry Church of Monson left the team because of transportation problems, Hatt said, "I very likely would have never played basketball again."

Instead, it suddenly opened a roster spot for Hatt. He had a second chance to play on a talented JV team.

"I am pretty sure I would have stopped basketball completely since being cut is pretty embarrassing," Hatt said. "But Coach Kiah came up to me to see if I wanted back on the team and I accepted. Then I ended up starting like three to five games into the season. Go figure."

That's when Hatt got past his desire to look elsewhere for a place to play high school basketball. Hatt, a 6-foot-2 forward with flair to his game, had another coach in his corner, too.

Dave Clement said, "I noticed that Dick Hatt was really progressing and coming into his own and taking on more responsibility offensively. He became a true basketball player and, quite frankly, he was questionable when Skip kept him on varsity. But he proved his worth as did Kenny Burtchell. They were both integral parts."

After not making the Foxcroft Academy varsity team as a junior, Hatt had considered transferring to Penquis High School in Milo before his senior year and was grateful that he didn't. His father was good friends with Eben DeWitt, who moved back from Dover-Foxcroft to Milo after he became superintendent of schools for SAD 68.

"I was pretty close to transferring," Hatt said. "I felt, in my honest opinion at the time, and I still feel that it was political how they picked the varsity team that year. My dad was pretty upset, and he was upset as much as I was mad, and he's from Milo."

Fortunately, Hatt stayed at Foxcroft Academy and became a starter on the 1974–75 team. He also was quick-witted and liked to pull pranks. One time he conspired with the Hathaway brothers, John and Will, to move John Arnold's desk in homeroom without the English teacher's knowledge but Arnold, equally quick-witted, figured out the culprit. He had Hatt move Hatt's classroom desk and park it in the hallway leading to the cafeteria for all to see as they went to lunch.

Though Hatt was voted "Class Clown" and "Class Scatterbrain" in his senior yearbook, his play on the basketball court was nothing to laugh at. He was completely serious when it came to his team.

"We had chemistry from day one," Hatt said. "Our practices were always competitive because the guys on the second team—and they always knew what we were going to run for plays so they cheated a little bit—they pushed us."

Jeff Brown was another Foxcroft Academy player who didn't like to be pushed around. He grew up playing and learning basketball at Jeff Howard's blacktop basketball court on North Street, where he often saw push come to shove, so to speak. Scott Mountford, who lived down the street after moving from Millinocket in elementary school, joined him.

That was where they watched brothers Dave and Trey Anderson—who also grew up on North Street—and their friends battle in legendary games of 3-on-3. Dave, Trey, and their father, Jack, are all in the Foxcroft Academy Athletics Hall of Fame. The Andersons were idolized in the community, and North Street was their proving ground.

"One day on the Howards' court, Trey and I were on opposite teams guarding each other when the next thing you know the shit hit the fan and Trey and I were rolling on the ground," said Dave, nicknamed "Hawk." "We got right into it. I think it was just our nature to be competitive."

Like Hatt, Jeff Brown thought he deserved an opportunity to play on the varsity team during his junior season. The top Foxcroft Academy player in the JV game was customarily asked to suit up with the varsity for its game, and Brown remembers a high-scoring game he played at Bucksport where he felt he earned the right to sit on the varsity bench that night. He sat in the crowd instead.

"I was hotter than a firecracker," Brown said.

Brown, however, always was one to put the team first ahead of his personal feelings. He was dependable.

"When it came time and when you called Jeff's number, he gave it to you," Nelson said. "When you have that chemistry and that camaraderie, when you have that, those little subtleties, behavioral subtleties, can make such a huge difference. And we are talking about sixteen-, seventeen-, and eighteen-year-old kids making these decisions."

Brown found his niche as the team's top substitute when he made varsity.

"Skip did a great job of promoting his kids and making a job or role for them," Gary Larson said. "I remember they made a big push for Jeff Brown to be the sixth man coming off the bench. He did a real good job of trying to give everybody a role so that everybody would feel important."

On varsity his senior year, the 6-foot Brown leaped into the sixth man role for the Ponies and also took the lead as the team's deejay in the locker room and on the team bus to and from games. Brown would bring 8-track tapes from his part-time job at LaVerdiere's drugstore downtown and pop them into a boombox. The Ponies favored two Bachman Turner Overdrive tunes—"You Ain't Seen Nothing Yet" and "Taking Care of Business"—which became their go-to songs and walk-out music when they left the locker room to play in the gym.

BTO was their mojo. The Ponies had a knack of knowing how to get fired up for a game or even for practice.

"We all got along pretty well and we all pushed each other very much in practice. We knew we were the second team, but we damn well weren't going to let the first team roll over us," Brown said. "So we were hacking and slapping and doing what we could to make everything work."

Tim King was a part of that. He and Scott Mountford became the tandem of tenacity for the second team in practice. As football players,

King was a prep All-American and Mountford was the Homecoming King. As basketball players, they were the Rock 'Em Sock 'Em robots.

"Scott Mountford? He would literally run through a concrete wall," Nelson said. "There was no question he would do it and he'd be happy about it and Tim King wouldn't be too far behind."

"I was a bulldog. I wasn't a high scorer, but I was really good on defense and I would harass the shit out of people," Mountford said. "Tim and I started playing together when we were young. We knew each other's strengths and weaknesses. He was a better player than I was. He could shoot better than I could. I was the muscle on the team."

Together, as a duo, Kiah was inspired by the high energy of Mountford and King. He created a new coaching strategy that he suggested to Skip Hanson as a way to utilize the team's depth and reward the reserves. It was shock and awe. Or shake and bake.

"We put five new players in and they were going to run and jump and apply pressure on the opponent and create all kinds of mayhem and havoc," Kiah said. "We wanted to let them loose while we rested our starters so we got everybody on the team involved. We had eleven on the team, and all eleven felt like they contributed."

This second unit, led by the 5-foot-8 King and Mountford, was dubbed the "Kamikaze Kids."

"They were like jet pilots giving everything they could and they would just lay it all out on the floor," Kiah said.

For Kevin Nelson, who rarely came out of games unless he was in foul trouble or the Ponies had a comfortable lead, the Kamikaze Kids and their comrades brought a sense of confidence and commitment.

"If I was on the bench or even on the court at the time watching them and how they played, seriously, that was inspirational," Nelson said. "Once again here's Skip. He's got to make a tough decision at the start of the season. 'Who am I going to put on this team? Who do I want on the team that's going to contribute to what he wanted to see happen as far as team chemistry and all that stuff?' Well, guess what? You put those two guys on the team for that purpose. That paid off. That paid dividends. We could go into a hostile gym or whatever. Scotty and Timmy didn't give a flying hoot. They would just go out and pressure the crap out of teams in those few minutes they got on the court."

Peter Snow was a member of that second group. For the first time at Foxcroft he was finally on the same basketball team as his Dexter Road neighbor Jeff Dunn. They grew up playing 2-on-2 basketball together in the driveway against their older brothers.

"Jeff and I always got our ass kicked. It was usually by Terry and Jeff's brother Tim," Snow said. "I don't think we won a game until we got to high school."

Snow, at 6-foot-1, was a scorer, but what distinguished him was his curly red hair and sharp shooting. Unlike his teammates on varsity, Snow hadn't had a chance to play with Kevin Nelson since he was in seventh grade at Dover Grammar.

"Boy is he big. I wasn't tall or anything and I was chubby back then and I could shoot a little bit, but that was about it," Snow said. "He was the man."

Snow was the man in waiting on the Ponies bench. He was good at picking his spots to make his shots.

"Peter was an unimposing guy and quiet, but every game he played in he contributed," Dunn said.

Snow had another noteworthy contribution during the season. He gave Skip's son, Todd, a moniker. After watching Todd squat and sit like a young frog on the sidelines, Snow took to calling him "Toad" and his teammates jumped in.

"He was always hanging around practice and we gave him a nickname and he kind of liked it so we went with it," Snow said.

Todd grew up on basketball to the point he became obsessed with it. When the schedule for the 1974–75 Foxcroft team was featured on a Pepsi-sponsored poster in preseason, Todd took it to school with him.

"After every game I'd go back to school and my teacher and report the score," Todd said.

Basically, his parents discovered soon after Todd was born that he was destined for a life with basketball.

"We wondered, what have we created in Todd because he just got so involved in this basketball thing starting when he was two years old," Peg

Hanson said. "He was humming and singing the 'Star Spangled Banner' and he had made a basket out of a milk carton and taped it to the refrigerator. A few years later, he was doing commentary like he was doing radio play-by-play of Ponies games in the kitchen. 'The Ponies stop, set and shoot!' And then he would pretend he was Orono. I thought, 'Oh my God what have we created?'"

Todd was the great pretender.

"They said I would wake up in the morning and reenact the whole game starting with the national anthem," Todd said. "Then I would do the starting lineups and introduced them for both teams and play a simulated game."

Todd and his brother Chad would go to practices at Foxcroft Academy with their dad. They became gym rats and math students. Todd learned to count by watching the football and basketball scoreboards at Foxcroft and figuring out the difference with the digits for the "Home" team and the "Visitor."

"Oh my God, he knows how to subtract," Peg Hanson summarized. "This is worth it."

Todd also took notice of Kevin Nelson and started following his career from Dover Grammar School. And Nelson found a pet in "Toad."

"His patience and his kindness to me to this day is what stands out about Kevin Nelson," said Todd, who later in life became such a standout basketball player and coach himself that he was inducted into the Maine Basketball Hall of Fame in 2023. "If you count Kevin's senior year, it was such a good five-year run of him being such a great role model at such a formative age for me."

Kevin had a positive influence on people of all ages on and off the court. With him in the starring role, the Ponies put together an intriguing roster for the 1974–75 season at Foxcroft Academy. They were looking for some stiff competition.

They didn't expect it to come from their teachers.

"There was great chemistry among them with everyone knowing and accepting their roles," Kiah said. "There was great competition in practice. And being able to play against a very talented faculty group once in a while was helpful as well."

Skip Hanson, even as Foxcroft's coach, still loved to play basketball and thrived on competition. Soon after he was hired at Foxcroft Academy, he decided to ask coaches and teachers to join him for pick-up games on Sunday nights in the FA gym. He sought out volunteers.

The first in line was a short and thin mathematics instructor, Wayne Champeon. But he was much more than a math teacher. Champ was a legend in the state.

"He was Maine's Bob Cousy," Tim King said.

In high school, Champ led Greenville High School to a state championship as a lightning quick 5-foot-7 poker-faced guard.

At the University of Maine, Champ was a two-sport star for the Black Bears. He was the first player to be named All-Yankee Conference in football and basketball. They are still telling stories of how Champ dribbled a punt return back for a touchdown.

Champ, in his prime, once competed against the Harlem Globetrotters and stole the ball not once but twice from Globetrotters' ball-handling whiz Curly Neal. The Globetrotters had to ask Champ to take it down a notch and act more like the Washington Generals.

"I didn't mean to embarrass him," Champ said. "The game was still going and Curly's hand was in my shorts and coming out the other side. He started waving to the crowd. I guess he evened the score with me."

Still, with all those accolades and achievements, when *Sports Illustrated* named its "50 Greatest Sports Figures" from Maine in 1999, Champ was not included. Joan Benoit Samuelson, who won the Olympic marathon in 1984, was first. The last basketball player on the list, at No. 49, was Mike Thurston who made a miraculous half-court shot for Caribou at the buzzer to beat Westbrook in the Maine Class L state championship game in 1969 that was televised statewide from the Bangor Auditorium. While Thurston's career may be best remembered by one long shot. Champ's amazing career, at 5–7, was a longshot to begin with.

John Champeon, Wayne's oldest son, bumped into Maine sports broadcasting icon George Hale one day at lunch. The sportscaster surmised that Champ's size was his only detriment.

"If your father had been six feet tall, he would have played in the NBA," Hale told John.

After college, Wayne Champeon started coaching basketball at Edward Little High School in Auburn and it didn't go as planned. His team didn't win a single game in his first season as head coach and they were 0–9 in his second season when a 9–0 Stephens High School team from Rumford came to play the Eddies in the infamous Lewiston Memorial Armory.

That particular Edward Little-Stephens game also delivered a stunning result: Champ's winless Eddies upset the undefeated Rumford team coached by Gib Philbrick, father of Jack, Tom, and Bert Philbrick from Orono.

"That was my first coaching win. The first person to greet me in the locker room was Mr. Philbrick," Champ said. "He came in and picked me right up off the floor and said, 'Champ, I'm glad it's over for you.' If I ever hear anyone say a bad word about him I'm not going to fight them, but I'm going to kick them in the nuts."

When Champ came to Foxcroft to coach the next year, he led the Ponies to their first Eastern Maine Tournament berth in eight years. Champ couldn't build on that and ultimately decided he was better suited to teach math than coach basketball.

Occasionally, Champ would play with "Jack's Five," Maine's first "Dream Team," a renown semi-pro team in the area founded by Jack Cashman with Jack Scott, a high school basketball sensation from Ellsworth, as its player/coach. The team included Skip Chappelle, Don and Dick Sturgeon, Larry Shiner, Leroy Patterson, Ted Leadbetter, Ned Robertson, and 6–10 Bob McCully. They all either played at the University of Maine or had Maine ties and, in the 1960s, they would tour the state and play exhibition games in places such as the Foxcroft Academy gym.

So when Skip Hanson offered Champ a chance to play pick-up basketball on Sunday nights in the FA gym—and in other gyms all throughout the area—word got out.

"I think it gave Champ a new life. We had some big crowds for those games and I always told the team I don't think they came to see us," Skip Hanson said. "They came to see Champ."

However, even without the crowds, the competition was heated when they scrimmaged among themselves in the FA gym. Tempers flared. Elbows flew. F-Bombs were dropped.

"Those games were intense," said Joe Champeon, who, along with his brother John, would go to the FA gym to watch their dad play.

One time Champ found himself guarding Skip Hanson under the basket. He apparently was under duress.

"I don't know what I did, but he didn't like it," Champ said. "I went up for a rebound with him there and I didn't come down back. He grabbed me."

There were other episodes of grabbing and one memorable act of kicking. Dennis Kiah became so mad at losing a pick-up game among fellow faculty one Sunday night that he drop-kicked the ball and it broke a window above the basket on the far end of the FA gym.

"I used to have an attitude," Kiah quipped.

If anything was broken, bent, or damaged—intentionally or accidentally—at Foxcroft Academy during that period, one had to face the wrath of one Roland M. Zwicker, the ultra-meticulous superintendent of buildings and the man most responsible for establishing the rules, regulations, and guidelines that have kept the FA campus pristine and beautiful for decades. Roland had an apartment in the basement floor of the Academy, so nothing got past him. If a blade of grass was out of place on the grounds, Roland would notice. He was scrupulous when it came to upkeep.

One time, Donna Albee Lindsay, FA Class of 1965—who played basketball for the Ponies and was a majorette with the FA Band—parked her beat-up black Volkswagen Beetle outside Foxcroft Academy and hurried inside. However, when she returned, her car had been literally picked up and moved onto the FA Lawn—Roland Zwicker's Lawn—by members of the Ponies football team as a prank. Donna was heavily interrogated by Roland as if she was a Russian spy until he was finally convinced that she didn't actually drive it onto the lawn.

Roland never cursed, but, as long as he was superintendent of buildings at Foxcroft, there were three things you never did: cross the immaculate FA front lawn, cross the shiny basketball court with shoes with black soles, or cross him.

"I worked for Roland one summer at Foxcroft and we were going to mow the grass. He said, 'No sense in mowing if you don't know how to trim,'" Champ said.

When Roland heard about Kiah's errant field goal attempt with a basketball and the broken window, he reported it to Foxcroft principal Tillson Thomas. He proceeded to call Skip Hanson into his office the very next morning.

"He asks me, 'What's going on Sunday night?' I don't want that to happen again, Skip. You make sure that doesn't happen again," Skip said. "And I'm thinking, 'Yeah, like I'm going to harness Dennis Kiah.'"

Kiah also was a culprit when the Foxcroft Academy faculty played a game against faculty at Hampden Academy. Kiah took out his frustration about his sub-par play by kicking the scorer's table, which forced the school's new foul indicator pole to crash onto the court.

"Champ was so embarrassed that he ran around the gym and hid under the bleachers," Hanson said.

Another time, in the Foxcroft Academy gym, Champ wasn't quick enough to disappear and duck out of sight. He threw a long, high, looping pass from one end to the other on the FA court but, in mid-flight, it struck one of the gym light fixtures hanging from the ceiling.

"I can still see that thing swinging, and I still remember in my mind. 'Oh Jesus. It's coming down.' And it came down and Roland was there."

Champ was reprimanded and Kiah was essentially put on double secret probation at Foxcroft Academy. Yet Kiah's unpredictability and fiery demeanor became an asset for the athletics program, particularly for the 1974–75 basketball team.

"At that point in his life, he was like Bobby Knight," John Champeon said.

Kiah's players learned if they didn't play well in a game, there would be consequences in practice, namely a lot more running and far less dribbling. As JV coach, Kiah had high expectations.

Tim King, when he was on the JV team as a junior, had to help his father on the family farm in East Dover one day and that meant he would be late for basketball practice and he didn't have a ride to get there. So King ran all the way from his house to the FA gym—a distance of about four miles—and when he arrived at practice 20 minutes late, a watch-watching Kiah was waiting.

"Kiah took one look at him and said, 'Well since you ran that far why don't you just keep on running' and Tim ran around the court for the rest of the practice," John Champeon said. "One thing about it, if you survived Kiah's practices he had a lot of respect for you."

"My lateness to practice and subsequent punishment to me was acceptable. Didn't bother me much. I was a team leader and I'm sure the point was valid, if not effective. Must have worked as John Champeon was never late," King joked. "I for one appreciated Coach Kiah's enthusiasm and dedication and only smile now when thinking about the aforementioned events. He definitely was the perfect ying to Coach Hanson's yang prepping the JV team members for the varsity level."

Coaches punishing players by making them run extra in practice was not uncommon at Foxcroft Academy, or any other school. There was one memorable football practice at FA in 1969 when Skip Hanson and Wayne Champeon were on Bob Stolt's Ponies coaching staff and the players were having a particularly poor practice. When quarterback Jere White made a snarly remark at athletic trainer Lap Lary, the coaching staff snapped. Feeling Lap was being disrespected, Stolt made the entire football team the rest of practice after every sloppy play run to the far end of the practice field—about 80 yards—and grab a leaf off any tree on the edge of the practice field and bring it back and put it in a pile by the huddle. Neatly.

"It seemed like 200 yards," Paul McKusick said.

Rick Pembroke counted and said he and the other players made the trip down and back 101 times. There were enough picked leaves stacked on the practice field to start a bonfire.

"It looked like the forestry students had cleaned out the other end of the field," Jere White said.

The exhausted players thereafter changed their team nickname from "Ponies" to "Leaf Pickers."

Kiah had his own unique way of motivating players. Following a 65–50 loss to Nokomis in Newport during the 1973–74 season, the JV team came to practice suspecting they would be punished in some way or form.

"We didn't even touch the basketball. Or a real basketball," Peter Snow said.

Kiah had lids put across the basket and had the team play with a weighted ball or a medicine ball normally used in training to build core strength. They passed it, shot it, and rebounded it. Kiah's message apparently was the JV team needed to get stronger—as much mentally as physically. His tactics evidently worked. The Ponies JV won their next twelve games—including a 36–23 win over Nokomis, a JV team that scored more than 100 points in a game on several occasions that season.

"We ran a four-corners offense against them and we're only looking for layups or in-the-paint baskets for us, and I told them that Nokomis was so bent on scoring 100 that they would panic and fire up shots all over the place," Kiah said. "Suddenly we were down 6–0 and I was talking to myself about what an idiot I was to come up with this plan and that we might lose 100-0. We proceeded to stay the course and went ahead 7–6 and eventually beat them. It was a big win for our kids."

Kiah, who learned to coach basketball by the book, relied on his motivational skills to prepare players, regardless if they were playing JV or varsity and regardless of the sport they were playing.

"Dennis was very emotional and he could channel it through the team," Dave Clement said. "He'd fire people up. He'd fire coaches up. That was one of his favorite sayings, in fact: 'fire up.'"

One time Kiah took fire up too far.

The Ponies were returning from a JV football game at Stearns on a Monday afternoon after Kiah chewed them out for their performance in the loss. The bus driver said, "You may be a good coach, but you're an awful poor sport."

When the team arrived back at Foxcroft Academy, Kiah addressed the players again and told them they had to put the game behind them and focus on playing better. He walked with Clement into the P.E. office in the boys locker room, passing Johnny King, a school custodian. Kiah then spotted a track starters pistol on Skip Hanson's desk.

Kiah, who was obviously having a bad day, thought he'd make a joke, lighten up, and poke some fun at himself following the defeat.

"Thinking that no one would ever leave a loaded gun around, I picked it up and said to Dave, 'I'm never going to lose another game' and put it up to the side of my head and pulled the trigger."

Let's just say a "Bang" sign didn't come out. But the sound of the blank blast knocked Kiah for a loop.

"The look on Dave's face told me I had just killed myself. Johnny heard me and the noise and came running into the office saying, 'What's he done this time?'" Kiah said. "What actually saved me was the pistol was blocked off at the end so nothing came out of it."

Years later, at Kiah's fortieth birthday party, Clement and Kenny Grant surprised Kiah with a special gift—a starters pistol with one bullet missing from the chamber.

"We've got a zillion Kiah stories and they are all well-documented and all well-deserved and they're not exaggerated, most of them," Clement said. "He was a character."

"Those type of things brought you together and brought the team together as well. The team could see Dennis was Dennis. He wasn't acting. They were fiery speeches, and everything he said, he meant it and he would go to war with you. And Skip again being the smart mentor, he exploited that and used it all to the benefit of the team and himself."

The FA faculty team was more than a formidable opponent in practice scrimmages against the Foxcroft varsity. There was Kiah, Champ, Skip Hanson, Skip's Aroostook State College teammate Gary Larson, former PCHS star Paul Draper, and Clement—who was a three-sport star and scored 1,260 points in his basketball career at Thomas College where he was inducted into its Athletics Hall of Fame in 2002. Hanson couldn't find a tougher foe to play his team after school.

Playing against hard-nosed faculty also put his team on its best behavior. They were like choir boys.

"All of us on the team had a little apprehension where the stuff would go if it went a little too far," Hatt said.

The varsity team didn't want to upset the teachers or coaches in those scrimmages for fear there would be punishment or retribution. The faculty team had the upper hand.

"They were brutal," Joyce said. "They didn't like to lose."

"The scrimmages were very spirited and indeed they schooled the 1975 team, which elevated our game," Tim King said. "It was a valuable contribution to our success."

Keeping up with Champ was particularly challenging with his no-look passes, dribbling, and competitiveness.

"How the hell is this guy this quick at forty years old or whatever? He was dribbling circles around us," Kevin Saunders said. "Truly men playing against boys. We couldn't get close enough to tackle him."

Joe Champeon said, "When I was in high school—and I'm twenty-five years younger than him—my dad was still the best player in the building."

"I think far and away they were the toughest team we faced," Dunn said. "They ran circles around us."

"Every time we scrimmaged them, it became very clear, very quickly that they were men and we were boys," Kevin Nelson said. "The physical nature of their play served to toughen us up. How could it not?"

Whether the players realized it or not at the time, Skip Hanson was using the Foxcroft Academy faculty team to teach his varsity team a lesson. The Ponies coach had a purpose for everything he proposed.

"Skip had me guarding Kevin Nelson to get Kevin in shape," Clement said. "Skip was thinking of every avenue you could think of."

Hanson always was challenging his players, testing them. And what better way to test them than to have them play their classroom teachers on the basketball court? In some ways during the 1974–75 season, the Foxcroft Academy faculty basketball team was the FA varsity team's toughest opponent all year.

"We had some pretty good players," Champ said with a grin. "They had to work."

The Ponies were finding motivation from all corners of Foxcroft Academy. One of their most inspirational stories came from team manager Keith Chadbourne. Born with cerebral palsy, Keith wound up following the footsteps of his older brother, Mark, who was a team manager for athletics director Lap Lary. Keith wanted to help out in any way he could.

Despite numerous operations on his right leg, Keith quickly earned a reputation for his hard work, dedication, tenacity, and his responsiveness to the team's needs. He was given the nickname "Mad Dog" by Tom Largay when Keith was a freshman manager for the Ponies' football team.

"His nickname was a means of inclusion," Largay said. "We wanted him to feel like he was part of the team."

Hanson recruited Keith as an equipment manager for basketball, but put him in charge of all team managers for the 1974–75 season. Mad Dog was asked to do many tasks, including shooting the ball at the hoop in practice to help the players work on their rebounding techniques.

Except the left-handed shooting Mad Dog was too accurate for their good.

"At one practice I was asked to shoot and hit the rim so the players could practice rebounding," Mad Dog said, "but I kept making the long shots to the point where they had to cover the basket with the lid."

Chadbourne, who was voted "Most School Spirited" by senior classmates in the 1975 *Review*, fit right in with a group of coaches, players, and managers at Foxcroft who would do anything to win and everything to support each other.

"We were easy going. Comfortable," Hatt said. "We didn't have any egos. We were calm. We were happy. We were having fun."

"That team was just so cohesive and it was right down to the team managers—Mad Dog, Herring, Joe Dean—everybody got along really well," Dunn said. "I don't recall ever any skirmishes or arguments or anything on that team. None at all. Everybody was along for the ride. We were all along for the ride and we wanted it to continue to the end."

Kevin Nelson likened the 1974–75 Foxcroft team to the NBA's Portland Trail Blazers who ultimately won a world championship in 1977. He saw how the Trail Blazers had clearly defined roles, and he personally identified himself with Bill Walton. Not because Walton was Portland's big man and star player but because Walton was playing through foot pain during his years at UCLA and particularly in his early years in the NBA in Portland.

"I loved the way he played the center position," Nelson said. "This was during my freshman, sophomore and junior seasons at FA. Back then, on those rare occasions when his games were nationally televised, his incredible skills—footwork, interior defense, shot blocking, rebounding, passing and court awareness—were mesmerizing to me. His outlet passes off the defensive glass were textbook. In my small universe at the time, I wanted to play just like him, but I didn't become aware of his chronic foot problems until his NBA career started with the Trail Blazers."

The Trail Blazers, in Nelson's mind, exemplified what the Ponies were trying to capture—an elusive championship with a team that had players who were aware of their strengths and how they could help the team succeed.

Nelson said, "I romantically looked at Bob Gross being Kenny Burtchell and Lionel Hollins being Jeff Dunn and Dave Twardzik being Dave Ingraham, and Maurice Lucas being Dickie Hatt and me being Bill Walton."

For the 1974–75 Ponies, it was role playing at its finest. And, like Walton, it was time for Nelson and the Foxcroft Academy boys basketball team to put its best foot forward.

Plywood Sign of the Times

THE ANNUAL RITE OF HIGH SCHOOL BASKETBALL IN PISCATAQUIS County tipped off the 1974–75 season with the Penquis League round robin, an exhilarating evening of hoops that was more a basketball tornado than a preseason tournament.

Hosted by Foxcroft Academy, all eight teams in the league—and their many fans—packed the FA gym to watch two teams at a time play fast and furious 12-minute games filled with up-and-down action and wild cheering, lots of turnovers and testosterone, and with enough time in between games to buy popcorn and hotdogs. With teams jumping on and off the court like a Ferris wheel ride, the round robin was a basketball carnival minus cotton candy.

It was a huge event that provided a small sample size for each team's prospects for the upcoming season. The Ponies, in their two 12-minute games, beat Schenck 19–15 and Penquis 16–6 in what was a preview for the upcoming season. Foxcroft appeared to have everything on their roster and in their arsenal except . . . a seamstress?

Kevin Nelson's No. 20 jersey needed some alterations.

"My new uniform, for some reason, it was short in the torso. I couldn't tuck it in," Nelson said. "Well, Skip gave my mother one of Joe Sand's knit coaching polo shirts and she sheared off the bottom half and sewed it on the bottom of my uniform so I could at least tuck it in."

With that adjustment, Nelson and the Ponies were a perfect fit. Foxcroft was prepared to leave every team in its wake from the opening tip, even Orono, winner of "The Phantom Foul" game. Mad Dog was still mad about that.

"After our junior year and that loss to Orono with a questionable fifth foul on Kevin, there would be payback in some form or another," said team manager Keith Chadbourne.

The Ponies didn't have to wait long for restitution and the form came in a fight. Foxcroft opened the 1974–75 regular season at home against Orono on a Saturday night, 270 days after they played in the Eastern Maine Class B Tournament championship game. The Red Riots had lost Tom Philbrick and Scott McKay to graduation. Another big man, 6–4 Anders Poforzelski, decided not to go out for the team.

Still, Orono fielded another formidable team led by Richie Pullen and F.T. Burpee award winner Brian Butterfield, whose father, Jack, was head football coach at Foxcroft Academy in 1953 and 1954.

Yet, by this point in Skip Hanson's FA coaching career, the Ponies' coaching staff had made beating Orono a case study.

"We were on top of it because Clement and I and Kiah used to do a lot of scouting of Orono and I think we had them pretty well pegged to be really competitive with them," Skip Hanson said. "We knew a lot of what they were going to do, so our team knew a lot of what we were going to do to try to stop what they were doing."

Another capacity crowd filed into the FA gym with an added attraction. George Hale and Steve Martin were calling the game for WABI Radio while positioned at a table on the stage next to the FA Band and behind the FA bench. Todd Hanson, Skip's son, watched the game from beneath the table, where he looked like a toad.

George Hale in person at Foxcroft Academy was deemed to be a celebrity sighting. He was a god in high school basketball circles.

"There's no question he was the king of sports in the mid-1970s, doing high school games, University of Maine broadcasts, as well as the sports segment on WABI-TV every night," said Rich Kimball, host of "Downtown with Rich Kimball" on WZON AM 620 in Bangor. Kimball started work at WABI Radio in 1975 and was mentored by George Hale.

"When George showed up for a game, it gave it a big-time feel, and his booming voice, even before he went on air, announced to all who were there that this game is special," Kimball said. "For my money, few people did more to make the high school basketball tournament the event that it became in the '70s and '80s than George."

For years, Ponies players, their parents, and their fans had watched George Hale on TV—with awe, as he was like the Walter Cronkite of round ball in Maine, and with anger, as he was perceived as anti-FA. Foxcroft fans felt Hale slighted their basketball team.

"We all believe very strongly that he was very much an Orono fan," Jeff Dunn said. "I don't think he was objective about our team at all. But that's my personal bias."

The WDME radio play-by-play voice of the Ponies, John Spruce, had moved from the stage to his new broadcasting digs in a press box high above courtside on the opposite side of the court. The new press box had been built by FA booster Henry Gerrish, a member of FA's Board of Trustees, who also later had a new office built for Skip Hanson behind the trophy case in the FA gym lobby after Skip was named assistant principal at Foxcroft.

"I remember Henry saying if people want to see the assistant principal they can't go down to the boys locker room," Skip said.

The student body cheering section at Foxcroft, situated in the bleachers on the stage directly behind the Orono bench and right next to the FA Band, was amped. It was dubbed "The Zoo" in the early 1970s. It rooted for the Ponies and razzed opposing teams to no end. When the visiting team's starting lineup was introduced, Pony fans in The Zoo would stand up, turn their backs to the court and read newspapers to ignore and mock the opposing team.

They did other annoying things—like pointing and chanting, 'You! You! You!' whenever an opposing player committed a foul—that principals and athletic directors would now frown upon in the name of good sportsmanship.

The Zoo also mocked the officiating crew. One of their favorite targets was referee Howard Seavey. The FA student cheering section created a special song for him, to the tune of the Mickey Mouse Club theme song.

S-E-A-V-E-Y . . . S-U-C-K-S!

Not so much. Seavey was inducted into the Maine Basketball Hall of Fame in 2024 as a "Legend of the Game." Seavey now R-O-C-K-S.

As it turned out, this latest renewal of the Foxcroft-Orono rivalry to open the 1974–75 season needed boxing judges more than basketball referees. The intensity was extreme, and the evening produced a brouhaha that would provide differing viewpoints and scorecards.

It was another close, hotly contested FA-Orono basketball game when, after a jump ball in the third quarter, Foxcroft's Dick Hatt and Orono's Pio Galbis were both diving on the floor for a loose ball before it rolled out of bounds. Bodies and wills collided in the process and a fight broke out.

Jeff Brown blames himself.

"I always felt bad in way because I think I started it," said Brown, who a couple of weeks earlier had been a tight end on the Ponies' football team. "I wasn't really trying to get to the loose ball. I was blocking for Dick."

"That's beautiful," Brian Butterfield quipped. "That is a football mentality."

The block led to a brawl between Hatt and Galbis, who may have been thrust into it by the force of Brown's block.

"Everything was real quick," Hatt said. "I don't know if I pushed Galbis away, but somebody shoved me in the back when I was on the floor. It could have been anybody who pushed me in the back, but that's what set me off. I thought it was Bert Philbrick and that's when I got up and took a swing. That's what instigated it."

Bert Philbrick was in the middle of it, though it's unclear if the 6-foot-2 Red Riots junior forward was trying to ignite the fight or break it up. One of his arms was cocked back, either to load up for a punch or pull back a player from the pack. In the meantime, fans spilled onto the court. Steve Hatt, Dick's brother, bounded from The Zoo in the bleachers then jumped off the stage onto the court.

"I was on the bench as they came over the top," said Orono's Dave Paul. "We had coins on the floor beneath us, thrown by Foxcroft students. We said, 'If you're going to throw money, throw dollar bills.'"

Everyone tried to get their money's worth before the fight broke up. There was pushing, shoving, yelling, and finger pointing, all the ingredients for a typical WWE wrestling match.

"It was quite a melee for a high school basketball game, but that's just how heated that rivalry was," John Champeon said. "There was a lot of emotions."

It was a spontaneous display of aggressiveness, anger, and frustration, but, thankfully, it didn't last long.

"The officials took care of it," said Wayne Champeon, who was standing by the door as a ticket taker turned peacemaker.

In fact, referee Jim DeFrederico took care of it. He lunged onto the floor and immediately tried to wrestle and pull Hatt and Galvis apart. As Wayne Champeon can attest, you don't mess with DeFred.

Though from Millinocket, DeFrederico was playing baseball in Greenville one summer for the town's semi-pro team. A pitcher, DeFred was good enough to be inducted into the Maine Baseball Hall of Fame in 1988, and he was a feared competitor. Wayne Champeon, in the 1940s, was a young bat boy for that Greenville town team, and several of DeFred's teammates coerced Wayne to run across the field one day and call DeFrederico a "spaghetti bender."

Not knowing any better, Wayne followed their orders and marched over to the Greenville pitcher to deliver the slur.

"DeFred looked at me and said, 'You know something young fella. Bigger men than you have been killed for what you just said,'" Champ recalled. "He knew some guys put me up to it. I was the messenger."

In the FA-Orono skirmish, DeFrederico was the mediator. The "spaghetti bender" was trying his best to straighten out the ruckus on the court.

No coach or player was ejected from the game nor was any fan thrown out of the gym. Play resumed. But the longtime competitive series between the two high school basketball programs had suddenly boiled into a rivalry with an on-court brawl.

Indeed, as Elton John said, "Saturday Night's Alright for Fighting."

"It was a tap dance. It wasn't very serious," said Butterfield, trying to put the fight into context. "The great thing is that rivalry by then had been established where emotions ran high and the fans' reaction in games at Orono and Dover was fantastic. It was like playing in the Final Four."

With The Zoo chanting the lyrics to Steam's "Na na na na, na na na na, hey hey, goodbye" song, Foxcroft pulled away for an 81–63 victory, as Jeff Brown, in his first varsity game, came off the bench to contribute 12 points and 10 rebounds, and David Ingraham helped hold Orono sharpshooter Richie Pullen to one field goal attempt in the second half.

Oh, and Kevin Nelson scored 39 points (9-for-9 from the free-throw line in the fourth quarter) with 22 rebounds in his season's debut in front of a crowd that included Peter Gavett, University of Maine freshmen coach and chief recruiter for the Black Bears. Gavett, a four-time All-American prep basketball player at Orono High School, sat next to Kevin's parents, Rose and Hollis.

Once the score went final, there was another score to settle. After the game, Rose Nelson made a beeline for George Hale and gave him a piece of her mind. She was convinced he was pro-Orono and anti-FA.

"You always say they're better and we keep beating them here," she snapped.

George Hale took it in stride. He smiled.

"George used to joke that, 'Half the people think I'm favoring one team, and half think I'm favoring the other, so I must be doing something right,'" Rich Kimball said.

The fist-clenching intensity of the game contrasted with Kevin Nelson's postgame ritual. Normally the last person to shower, dress, and leave the FA locker room after each home game, he would walk up the back stairs into a by-then empty gymnasium and soak in the quiet ambiance.

"My head was still buzzing from the sounds and sights of that Orono game," Nelson said. "I opened the door to the gym and immediately started experiencing a sense of solitude and peacefulness that was completely opposite from the extraordinary energy and excitement that existed in that same space a mere two hours earlier. The next sounds I heard came from John King, our janitor, who was pushing back the bleachers. John was Tim King's dad, and he always had a smile and something nice to say to me before I left the gym. I really appreciated his kindness and I always felt that he played a role—along with many other students, teachers, and staff—in our success that season. When John turned the lights out in the gym, I remember the stillness and darkness that followed. At that point, I couldn't help thinking about the profoundly stark contrasts I had experienced that evening. The drive back to Southeast Monson that night was dark and quiet although the accomplishments of the evening still hadn't fully sunk in, probably because my head was still spinning."

The Foxcroft victory and the fight were the lead story in the *Piscataquis Observer* five days later. A photo of the fracas stretched across the front page above the fold.

The fight even received special mention in 1975 Orono High School yearbook, the *Crimson Crier*, with the caption "TKO in the 3rd at Dover."

The Orono-Foxcroft rivalry was approaching Yankees-Red Sox.

"Those three years those were unbelievable matchups, unbelievable intensity. The crowds. The passion. The fights. Just tight games. Key plays. It meant so much to both towns," said Butterfield, who went onto a career as a third base coach for both the Yankees and Red Sox. "I do remember the passion, the noise, and excitement of Dover and Orono."

The Ponies started the season on a positive note after their "Duke It Out in Dover" victory over Orono. But, two days after the thrilling season-opening win, Kevin Nelson and his mother averted a potential major catastrophe.

Rose was then working at an insurance company in Dover-Foxcroft and she offered to drive her son home from basketball practice. However, the weather turned nasty and driving conditions suddenly became treacherous.

Freezing rain. In the dark. Danger lurking. Welcome to Maine winters.

Rose was driving with Kevin on the Guilford Road toward Monson when she decided it might be best to pull over and check in with her husband. She had a white knuckle grip on the steering wheel.

"We were going like maybe 10 mph and we were sliding down the grade onto the side of the road, which was gravel," Kevin said.

Once the car slid off the pavement, Kevin got out. He was crossing the road to go ahead to his friend John Danforth's house. Kevin intended to call his dad to ask what he and his mother should do. Keep driving, or stay parked on the side of road and wait for him to arrive?

"All of a sudden I looked back and saw this truck just bearing down on my mother and it crashed into the back of her car," Kevin said. "I just sprinted as fast as I could to get down there. She was hurt."

Rose suffered whiplash and was taken to Mayo Memorial Hospital. Kevin then realized had he stayed in the car and not set off on foot to John Danforth's house, he might have been in the hospital with his mother.

"That could have changed the trajectory of my season. If I had been in the car and I had been injured that could have changed my season as well," Kevin said. "Somebody was looking out for us."

Rose had to spend the next day in the hospital, which meant she would miss the Tuesday night game at Central High School in East Corinth. WDME play-by-play announcer John Spruce sent out a get-well message to her over the air during the game.

"It was like the farmer's report," Kevin said. "It was the only game she missed the entire season."

The broadcast of Foxcroft games on WDME became a must-tune-into event. As Foxcroft Academy home games were selling out, the next best option to follow the team was to listen to the local radio station.

One of WDME's most loyal listeners was Thurley Knowles, a relative of Hollis Nelson who also lived on Steward Road in Southeast Monson. "She was the most ardent supporter," Kevin said. "She couldn't go to the games, but she listened to them on radio."

The game against Central in East Corinth was a one-sided 97–52 victory. After the Ponies opened a 31–10 lead in the opening quarter, it afforded Skip Hanson to give more playing time to his reserve players, led by Tim King. King scored 13 points in the second quarter, when four of the five FA starters sat, and he finished with a career-high 17 points—2 fewer than Nelson who didn't play in the second and fourth quarters.

No one was more happy for King than "Jack."

"He knew what his role was and he embraced it," Nelson said. "He was the consummate teammate."

The Ponies won their first five games before the holiday break, including a 79–60 win over Schenck in East Millinocket, where Nelson helped FA overcome a 12–11 first-period deficit to finish with 34 points—24 in the second half—and nine blocked shots while Dunn added 18 points, 12 in the pivotal second quarter. Then Foxcroft hosted a six-team, two-day tripleheader holiday classic in the FA gym. The Ponies beat Hermon and previously undefeated Hampden Academy, a Class A team with an A-list author. In 1971, Hampden Academy hired a new English teacher by the name of Stephen King, who, in his spare time, was writing his first novel *Carrie,* which was published in 1974 and turned into a horror movie.

Unfortunately, the Ponies' holiday tournament wins over Hampden and Hermon were like ghosts. Those FA victories never appeared in the team's final record. They were considered exhibition games.

During the holiday break, Skip Hanson received a special visit from Kevin Saunders from Husson College. Saunders joined the Ponies in a practice to stay in shape. His presence contributed to a spirited practice capped by "suicides," the nickname given a fitness drill of repetitive sprints from baseline to baseline where players are asked to run and bend down and touch the foul lines, the mid-court line, and end lines to complete each trip.

"I was running suicides the whole length of the court and it was pissing guys off. Scotty Mountford was determined he was not going to let this asshole—who was a freshman in college—beat him in suicides. And he tried his damndest to chase me down," Saunders said. "It didn't work."

Though playing at Husson College in Bangor, Saunders still maintained close ties with Foxcroft Academy. His younger sister, Susan, played in the FA Band and he even recruited the band to perform at a Husson game.

"When they came to Husson College and played, I don't think I had had a better warm-up session going through drills before the game," Saunders said. "And all my teammates were making comments like, 'You played in front of this band for four years?' They were a talented group and played some upbeat music, and my guys absolutely loved it. They asked our coach if we could bring them back again."

Husson also would have liked a visit from Kevin Nelson. But, by his senior year at Foxcroft, the 6-foot-8 center was the center of attention from college recruiters in NCAA Division I.

"Kevin had made enormous strides. He finally had the confidence that he should have had since his sophomore year," Saunders said. "He realized he was head and shoulders above most everybody else and he had learned to take advantage of that. It didn't surprise me at all."

Recruiting letters started coming to Kevin Nelson from big-time college basketball coaches, beginning with Notre Dame coach Digger Phelps, who first wrote to the FA star on December 28, 1973, and reached out again before the 1974–75 season. Legendary Indiana coach Bobby Knight mailed a letter to Nelson on September 2, 1974.

"Be assured we will be following your progress with a great deal of interest, and, it is my hope you in turn will show an interest in Indiana," wrote Knight, a Hall of Fame coach.

Other big-name college coaches such as Villanova's Rollie Massimino, Seton Hall's Bill Rafferty, and the University of Detroit's—and later ESPN's—Dick Vitale wrote. Boston Celtics legend Bob Cousy wrote Nelson on behalf of New Hampshire coach Gerald Friel. And another Celtics great, K. C. Jones, on Washington Bullets team stationary dated March 13, 1975, eventually wrote for Maine coach Skip Chappelle. Chappelle once roomed with Celtics and NBA Hall of Famer John Havlicek during training camp in 1962.

The scrutiny was overwhelming for Nelson. It's rare for a high school basketball recruit in a tiny rural town to receive so much attention and notoriety. A few come to mind. College recruiters famously flocked to French Lick, Indiana, to watch Larry Bird. The Los Angeles Lakers' Austin Reeves was raised on a 300-acre farm in Newark, Arkansas, and won a pair of state Class 2A titles. Otto Porter Jr., who played eleven years in the NBA, was recruited out of Morley, Missouri, a town of less than seven hundred people in a high school graduating class of thirty-two.

Then there was Bryant "Big Country" Reeves, who grew up in Gans, Oklahoma, with a population of 218. He went on to play at Oklahoma State University and become a first-round draft pick in the NBA.

"Being a big fish in a really small pond, I was getting recruited," Nelson said. "It was very weird. It was just very weird. I wasn't ready for a lot of stuff."

More than 100 recruiting letters were addressed to Nelson at Foxcroft and his home address in Southeast Monson. He was receiving more mail than the North Pole.

"I was just a kid from Monson that was getting attention for something and I didn't know how to handle a lot of it," Nelson said. "Obviously it blows up your ego, but at the same time you're thinking, 'I've got a job to do which is go to class, keep my grades up and play ball and try to win games.'"

He remembers, "That was so friggin' intense to me. It started my junior year and that senior year I didn't react to it very well. My life consisted of going to practice, playing games, and doing homework. That's all my life consisted of. That winter I would have coaches calling on the phone and, back in the day, there were no cell phones. They'd call your home. My mother and father would answer and I didn't have time to talk. I was doing my homework. They would leave messages. I didn't know how to handle a lot of that, but I think I grew into it and Skip was enormously helpful to me to help navigate my way through this."

Boston College became a constant presence at Ponies' games. The Eagles, coached by Bob Zuffelato, were in the midst of a 21–9 season that would earn them an appearance in the Sweet 16 of the NCAA tournament. They were building a program that would eventually lead them into the creation of the powerful Big East Conference in 1979.

"There was one guy from Boston College who just would not leave Skip alone," Dennis Kiah said. "I remember Skip telling me one night I'm going to ride with you tonight. I don't want him following me home. Skip said, 'I don't want him at the house anymore. I'm tired of him. I don't want to talk to him anymore.' So we drove all over town. I didn't even know where I was going."

Instead, Peg Hanson had to talk to Drayton Miller, the energetic and persistent Boston College assistant coach, an excellent recruiter assigned to scout Kevin Nelson. She inherited the role of entertaining the nice yet nettlesome recruiter.

"We drove by the house a couple of times and saw his car and we kept going. He was inside," Skip Hanson said. "When I got home Peg said, sarcastically, 'Thanks a lot.'"

Not only was Miller trying to spend time at home with the Hansons, he was trying to spend quality time with Nelson and his teammates.

"He asked me if he could ride the team bus to away games," Skip Hanson said. "I said, 'I'd get my ass in such a sling with other coaches. I don't want to jeopardize anything for Kevin. Why don't you follow the bus?'"

Miller, it was presumed, did manage to get new sneakers into Nelson's hands. Prior to the season, Skip Hanson had ordered new high-top sneakers to give his players better protection against ankle sprains.

"We wore high maroon canvas Converse sneakers. We ordered them from Converse because Skip believed in a sharp uniform and everybody on the team having the same thing," Nelson said. "I think one of the reasons is North Carolina that year started wearing powder blue Converse."

"The kids at first weren't happy. 'Geez, we've got to wear these?'" Skip said. "I said, 'C'mon, let's try them. Then it became our trademark and everybody started talking about it."

However, before Christmas, Nelson's favorite pair of practice sneakers, which were Adidas, gave out in practice from wear and tear. Santa Claus delivered a new pair.

"Kevin's shoes were different. They were huge, but we all had leather Converse, but there was something different about his shoes," Mark Joyce said.

"Drayton would show up at our practices all the time and he knew I needed a new pair of sneakers," Nelson said. "Guess what shows up at Foxcroft Academy in a package not long after that but a brand-new pair of Converse leather sneakers? The same type of sneakers that Boston College was wearing."

Except the sneakers, size 15, were too big for Nelson.

"I mentioned this to him and a set of size 14s showed up and I kept them. That's what I played in for the second half of the season," Nelson said. "Was that an NCAA violation? Maybe it was. Maybe it wasn't. I probably could have handled it better, but I'm trying to go to high school then and play basketball. Nowadays that's what gets the juices going with these kids."

Nelson already had visited Boston College on a recruiting trip the same weekend Texas and Heisman Trophy winner Earl Campbell played the Eagles on Chestnut Hill. Ironically, one of Nelson's hosts was 6-foot-10 Boston College center Paul Berwanger, the youngest son of Jay Berwanger, who was the first recipient of college football's Heisman Trophy in 1935.

In addition to Boston College, Nelson had a strong interest in playing college basketball at the University of Maine, the University of New Hampshire, and the University of Vermont. The first time Kevin flew on an airplane was to Burlington when he was a high school senior.

In the meantime, Nelson tried his best to keep his team unbeaten and avoid any trap games. In a January 7 game at Dexter, the Tigers controlled the pace of the game and outscored the Ponies 11–9 in the first quarter and were tied with FA at 33-33 after three periods. Foxcroft outscored Dexter 25-7 in the final quarter and ultimately won 58–40 as Nelson scored 19 of his game-high 29 points in the second half.

"They were trying to goad us. They knew they couldn't win, so they were like yanking on our jerseys and trying to trip us," Mark Joyce said. "I remember I almost got in a fight in that game. They were trying to goad us into something stupid and they slowed the game down."

Then the Ponies played their next game against Mattanawcook Academy in its new gymnasium in Lincoln. The Lynx, too, held the ball, ran the clock, and were limited to 10 points in the first half.

In all honesty, the Ponies weren't as concerned about the ability of the Lynx—FA built a 36–10 lead at halftime—as they were about the *smell* of Lincoln. There was a paper and tissue mill in the middle of town at that time and it emitted a distinctive sulfurous odor that earned the town the nickname "Stinkin' Lincoln." The smell wasn't so bad playing basketball inside. But Foxcroft football teams for years dreaded going to Lincoln, particularly on windy days having to play on the football field above Mattanawcook Pond while wearing protective mouthguards that forced players to have to breathe more through their noses.

There were occasions where visiting football players literally gagged from the smell in the air in Lincoln.

Fortunately, Foxcroft's basketball team came out of Lincoln smelling like roses and kept rolling toward another game date with Orono. On January 25, 1975, Nelson, who the previous week passed the 1,000 rebound mark in his high school career, validated Miller and every head and assistant college basketball coach who was trying to recruit him with a record-breaking performance in a big game before a capacity crowd. It came right down the road from the University of Maine.

That night the Ponies brought a twelve-game winning streak to the Orono High School gymnasium. Two days before the game, a *Bangor Daily News* sports brief announced that the game was already a complete sellout.

There had been discussions about moving the game to the 3,100-seat University of Maine's Memorial Gymnasium—The Pit. But Red Riots coach and athletics director John Giffin didn't want to lose his team's home court advantage in the Orono gym, which featured a stage on one end of the court and fans not willing to give up an inch.

"I remember talking with Giffin about that a few weeks after the tournament and told him I thought that playing in The Pit would have given Orono the upper hand, as it would have kept Kevin, Dick Hatt, and one or two others running more," Skip Hanson said. "Kevin certainly had the advantage on a smaller court."

The game was never played in The Pit, but it was a packed house in Orono High School. A snowstorm late in the week didn't stop people from still getting into the Red Riots' gym. Some secretly slipped in through a side door to the visitor's locker room. Another group of FA fans reportedly paid $20 to a scalper for tickets for four people. That was the going rate. A single admission ticket was selling for twice to three times its face value outside.

That was what Bill Patterson and his friend and classmate Arnold Stevens paid to a scalper.

"I had to go to that game. Just had to. Arnold and I got down there. We went on faith. We didn't have tickets. We will get in somehow," Patterson said. "That was big-time money for us. So we got in and, boy, was it worth it."

During the JV contest, George Hale happened to bump into Skip Hanson. Hale spent a lot of time in Orono as he was the play-by-play radio broadcaster for University of Maine football and men's basketball games. He wanted another look at the Ponies. He considered them to be Kevin and the Kevinettes.

Hanson was flustered by Hale's take and dared him to change his mind.

"He was all over me before the game about being a one-man team. He kept riding me, saying, 'You're nothing but a one-man team,'" said Hanson, growing defensive. "So I said, 'We've got other good players on this team that complement Kevin. We'll see, George. I'll see you after the game."

In the first quarter, Nelson *was* a one-man team. He scored all of Foxcroft's 14 points in the opening period. Then he scored 12 of Foxcroft's 16 points in the second quarter.

"He took that game over in terrible conditions. Their court was dark and dirty and their fans right on your hip," said Hatt, who was the first Ponies' player other than Nelson to record a field goal with 20 seconds left in the first half.

Hatt, Dunn, and Ken Burtchell combined for three field goals in the third quarter and Nelson matched them. Foxcroft took a 43–38 lead to the final quarter and Nelson, for once against Orono, was not saddled with foul trouble.

"Most games went pretty smooth for us unless Kevin got in foul trouble, then everybody started to panic," Peter Snow said. "It was all in the game plan. It wasn't him showboating. He just had one of those games."

Orono, behind Galbis and a full-court press, made another push for the lead, cutting FA's advantage to 44–41 early in the fourth quarter. Red Riots fans were aroused by the rally. Skip Hanson called timeout. He knelt on the floor facing his starters sitting on the bench in the first row of the bleachers.

There was a sign on the wall behind them: "This year like last year the best is right here!" The Ponies were in Orono. They knew what they were up against.

"They had a good team, and they had some big kids and some tough kids, and John Giffin was a good coach. We all knew it's going to go down to the wire," Hanson said. "What I was doing during the timeout was just telling the kids to be cautious about some things. You don't need to heave up a 25 footer or throw it over a guy's head or something like that."

At that instant, Nelson abruptly interrupted his coach. It was his Jimmy Chitwood *Hoosiers* moment. He reassured his coach and his team that he wasn't going to let them lose.

"He told Skip to relax. It's not a problem and Kevin was obviously in the zone," said John Champeon, who was promoted from the JV team to varsity for the game. "Kevin said, 'Don't worry, coach, we've got this.' And it wasn't like Kevin to speak up."

With a shot to take over the game, Kevin, in so many words, said, "I'll make it."

"I won't say it was unlike me, but I remember being intensely emotional about getting that win down there," Nelson said. "A loss would have kept their winning streak going, but a win would have removed our last obstacle to going undefeated for the regular season. No one wanted to say it, but in our mind's eye we were thinking if we get this second victory over Orono this season we might be able to run the table."

Out of the timeout, Nelson proceeded to score the next three baskets for Foxcroft Academy and had 15 points in the final quarter. The Ponies sealed a 60–52 win when Dave Ingraham sank two free throws, the only points not scored by Nelson in the final eight minutes.

"Jeff Dunn and the other kids played like hell, but once Kevin got the hot hand, they were getting the ball into him," Skip Hanson said. "A lot of times in different games Kevin would pass it back out, but he was so confident in what he was doing he just took the ball to the hoop."

Nelson finished the game with a Foxcroft Academy single-game record 47 points on 21 of 27 shooting. He also added 21 rebounds and had five blocked shots.

"He put the game on his shoulders. He just went to a level I've never seen before," Dunn said. "You always knew what you were going to get out of him—like 25 points and 25 rebounds on average. But that game the rest us . . . we didn't stand around and watch, but we *almost* stood around and watched."

Oddly, Orono and Giffin, a defensive-minded coach, played Nelson straight up. The Red Riots rarely tried to double team the Foxcroft center.

Years later, Orono Athletics Director Mike Archer said, "They should have gone box-and-one and put the four on Nelson."

"There were other really good players on Foxcroft, but when you have such a great player it shows the unselfishness of the team. They're thinking, 'We've got to get the ball to this guy," Brian Butterfield said. "They would get the ball to him at mid-court or the top of the key and sometimes Kevin did a lot of his work dribbling to the basket. That was a great exhibition that night."

"That was the type of team we had," Skip Hanson added. "As long as someone was hot, they didn't care. They just wanted to win."

After the game, George Hale, taking Skip Hanson up on his pre-game invitation, sought out the Foxcroft Academy coach. Nelson had scored as many points in the game as Orono's entire starting lineup. Hale's "One-Man-Team" reprise had been validated in theory, but Skip wasn't ready for a "I Told You So Lecture."

"I saw George coming to me after the game. I just went the other way," Skip joked.

Years later, George Hale, who was still doing sports and political commentary on radio at the age of ninety-two, acknowledged Nelson's place in Maine schoolboy basketball.

"Kevin was the best high school player ever from Maine," Hale said. "I can name a lot of great kids, but he was one of the best."

George Hale also had praise for Skip Hanson and the rest of the team.

"I do recall George's respect for that team, as he made a point of talking about how 'that Kevin Nelson team did things the right way,'" Rich Kimball said.

With his momentous record-breaking performance at Orono, Nelson was now primed to lead the Ponies to even greater heights. The prospect of a perfect regular season was moving from a possibility closer to probability.

"That win was the game we thought, 'We're going to run the table,'" Dick Hatt said. "We're going to go undefeated."

Nelson, however, didn't allow himself to think far ahead in wake of the win at Orono. His mentality remained nose-to-the-grindstone.

"The next game we played made me the most nervous," Nelson said.

That was in Newport against Nokomis. Nelson was held to 19 points, but Jeff Brown came off the bench to score 12 and FA prevailed 57–45.

Hatt was hurt during that game when Nelson mistimed his jump and caught Hatt with an elbow that opened a gash over Hatt's left eye that needed six stitches to close. It was the first game Hatt's grandmother attended, and it was a bloody mess. Not only was her grandson injured but Nokomis fans hurled insults at him after the game in the parking lot.

"They said, 'That's what you get for coming here,'" Hatt said. "Whatever."

The injury forced Hatt to play without his glasses for the next game. Fittingly, it was an eye-opening performance. Hatt had a game-high 20 points, 12 rebounds, and seven assists featuring a couple of dazzling, crowd-pleasing behind-the-back and no-look passes that caught the attention of everyone in the Foxcroft Academy gym, including Boston College recruiter Drayton Miller. After the game in Skip Hanson's office downstairs in the Ponies' locker room, Miller loudly proclaimed the star of the game and spelled out his name.

"H-A-T-T," Miller shouted.

Hatt had a different perspective of that performance. Because he was nearsighted, he had been wearing glasses playing basketball, but they kept slipping off his nose. He started attaching strips of white athletic tape vertically to the arms of his glasses so they would stick to the sides of his head.

Anyone could plainly see those glasses were a sight for sore eyes. However, the 20-point game against Schenck convinced Hatt he didn't need his glasses to see the hoop or pass to teammates.

"That's what I told Skip after the game. I'm not wearing these frigging things anymore."

Contrary to George Hale's "one-man team" observation, Foxcroft's winning ways were becoming more of a team effort. After Nelson had 26 points and 23 rebounds in three quarters of action against them earlier in the season, the PCHS Pirates decided to hold the ball on offense and play keep away when the Ponies played in Guilford a week later. The Pirates scored only 4 points in the opening quarter and limited FA to 10. Foxcroft won 52–29—its lowest offensive output of the season—as Nelson scored 19 points and Ken Burtchell added 14.

Several of Foxcroft's other opponents employed the same stalling tactics. With no shot clock and seemingly no chance of winning, opposing teams would hold the ball or pass and dribble it near mid-court. The strategy PCHS employed was, if Kevin Nelson et al. can't touch the ball, they can't score.

"It was interesting to see the different tactics that the teams played, but that one was the most dramatic. They literally would pass the ball around for two, three, four minutes," Dunn said. "They held the ball for, like, minutes and minutes at a time just passing it around trying to keep it out of our hands so we couldn't score. It didn't work."

Hanson relied on his whole roster in such instances of inhibition.

"He put Scott and Timmy in there as guards and two or three others and told them to chase the ball," Peter Snow said.

Mountford and King were the co-pilots of the Ponies' counter strategy.

"That was almost unfair," Dave Clement said. "We were playing a bunch of guys off the bench who would probably be starters on most of the schools in our league and they would just run our opponents ragged and wear people out and give our starters a blow. That was kind of a one-two punch."

In its final home game of the season, Hanson decided to do something special to acknowledge the nine seniors on the team. The Ponies had become darlings in the community and such a hot ticket that there were team posters and calendars popping up all over town and bumper stickers and seat cushions were being sold at home games. The seat cushions had a designated spot for autographs on the back side so fans could have their favorite players sign it.

The Ponies had morphed into a brand. They were like Basketball Kens in a Barbie World.

So, before the opening tipoff against Dexter in the final home game for the seniors on the FA team, it was arranged by Skip Hanson that John Spruce, the voice of Ponies basketball, would introduce each senior over the public address system as they ran onto the court. A spotlight shone on them from above. It was dramatic theater in the Foxcroft Academy gym. The gym floor was turned into a red carpet of sorts to greet each member of the famous local team.

Dexter coach Ed Guiski was not amused. He saw the scene as overkill.

"He was pissed," Skip Hanson said. "He came up to me after that and said that was bullshit. It was probably too much. If I were Ed, I'd probably be pissed."

At Foxcroft, Dexter threatened to spoil Senior Night. Led by Galen Chapman's 12 first-half points, the Tigers were ahead 33–32 after two periods, the only time during the regular season that the Ponies trailed at halftime. Ingraham was shifted onto Chapman in the second half and held him to two field goals, and Dexter scored only 16 points in the second half.

Foxcroft prevailed 57–49—the 8-point margin of victory being the closest any team other than Orono had come to beating Foxcroft Academy during the regular season. Nelson, in the final home game of his career in a Ponies' uniform in the FA gym, scored 15 of his 27 points in the second half.

Guiski had to be impressed. He had worked with Nelson at the Pine Tree Basketball Camp at Thomas College the previous summer and coached a team that included the FA center toward the end of the week. The Dexter coach gave the Foxcroft player a bit of advice when he prepared a written evaluation of Nelson's performance and skills at the end of camp.

"In Ed's younger days as a high school and collegiate player, he was an aggressive player and a ferocious rebounder. So, naturally, as my coach, he advised me to be a 'wide' big man as opposed to just being a 'tall' big man," Nelson said. "This proved to be incredibly helpful advice, although I found it particularly interesting that he would want to give me suggestions on how to become a better player in light of the fact that FA and Dexter High School were arch enemies located just 13 miles apart and that we would be playing each other twice during the upcoming 74–75 season. Nevertheless, it was pretty clear that Ed's commitment to coaching and passion for the game were off the charts. Following high school, I had the good fortune of getting to know, like, and admire Ed both as a person and a coach."

As the 1974–75 regular season was winding down, colleges recruiting Nelson were hoping he was ready to make a decision. Skip Chappelle, who grew up in Old Town, had driven the backroads to visit Kevin and his family in Southeast Monson.

"It's the typical great Maine road trip," the Black Bears coach said. "We stayed after Kevin."

Chappelle loved recruiting all over Piscataquis County. He became teammates and friends with Wayne Champeon from Greenville at the University of Maine when *Sports Illustrated*, in a preseason preview issue, called them the "best backcourt in the Yankee Conference." When he coached at Maine, Skip was always on the hunt for big men, but a friend, Al Hackett, convinced him to go to Milo to watch Wally Russell, a 5-foot-6 guard, play.

"Wally limped onto the court and I guess he had had a sprained ankle, but he played and he lit it up," Chappelle said. "I told Al, 'OK. We'll track him.' Wally came to Maine and was one of the better players we had."

Chappelle was ready for Nelson, a prototype center, to come to Maine. He thought he had the inside track to signing Nelson to a letter of intent when Skip Hanson arranged a phone call for the UMO coach to talk to his star player.

"Kevin got on the phone with him, but didn't commit. Kevin at the time was talking to a coach at a D2 school around Boston that he really liked," Hanson said. "So after the call, Chappelle calls me up and says, 'Geez, I thought he was going to commit.' And I said, 'So did I. But I think he's still leaning that way, so be patient with him.'"

In the meantime, the Ponies were growing impatient to play in the Eastern Maine Class B Tournament. They were losing their grip on securing the top seed for the tourney. Mount Desert Island of Bar Harbor, with an 11–6 record, had closed to within a fraction of a point of overtaking FA in the Heal Point rankings. The Heal Point System rewards teams who play higher up in classification and win, and the MDI Trojans were accumulating more points than the Ponies, who had a weaker schedule playing in the Penquis League, which included two wins over a Class C team, Central High.

In its regular season finale, Foxcroft had its hands full against Penquis in Milo. A pair of Penquis students—one sitting on the shoulders of the other who was covered by a sheet—were parading around the court prior to game holding a sign that read: "PENQUIS' ANSWER TO KEVIN NELSON."

Nelson chuckled at the sight, yet he wasn't in the best of moods. He was sick and forced himself to play. He had only 14 points, a season low, but Jeff Dunn netted a career-high 22 points and Burtchell pumped in 14 as the Ponies pulled away for a 67–54 victory.

"I was running on fumes the whole game," Nelson said. "And we had the tournament coming up."

Hanson again reminded the Ponies that they needed to get into tournament mode.

"I knew Kevin wasn't feeling well. And I knew the last three or four games of the regular season the players knew they were going to the tournament as a top seed. So I thought it was appropriate to let them think about how they had lost focus," Hanson said.

Drayton Miller was waiting for Nelson afterward in Milo for a chance to converse about the Penquis game and chat with him about his college plans. Dennis Kiah didn't have his get-away car in the parking lot to get around Miller.

"He's in the locker room and I'm in the shower," Nelson said. "I asked Skip if he would let me go home with my mom and dad because I was so sick. I just didn't want to talk to him, and I just walked out of the locker room."

Miller ultimately lost out in signing Nelson, but he did help recruit a strong freshman class for the 1975–76 season led by Tom Mergers, a 6–9 center who averaged 34.5 points and 17 rebounds a game for Prosser Academy in Chicago.

For Nelson and Foxcroft Academy, their focus turned toward the tournament. Though they were taking an undefeated record to the Class B tournament, they wound up being the No. 2 seed behind MDI and its 12–6 record. The Trojans' final Heal Point tournament index score was 126.12. Foxcroft's was 125.91.

That disparity in record exposed a flaw in the Heal Point System. The Ponies had hoped to earn the No. 1 seed in the Eastern Maine Tournament for the first time since 1950.

"We weren't steamrolling anybody, but we played well enough to win and found a way to do it," Nelson said.

The Ponies, in spite of their 18–0 record, still needed a pick-me-up to get prepared for the tournament. They found one in an unexpected manner in the form of a plywood sign.

The success of the team had simply captivated the community, which had fallen in love with the team. Not an Ali MacGraw/Ryan O'Neal kind of "Love Story," but Ponies fans and boosters had become infatuated with the team. For starters, there was a full-page advertisement with forty-two business sponsors in the February 13 edition of the *Piscataquis Observer* noting "Ponies Strive for Championship."

However, FA's biggest booster may have been Neil Johnston. He was consumed with the team and its march toward a title.

Johnston was a multitalented, multifaceted custodian at Morton Elementary School and SeDoMoCha Middle School. He serenaded teachers and students with song. He lived on the Milo Road and owned a workshop there.

In short, Neil Johnston was a peculiar personality and quite a handyman. His best friend, Ted Harvey, was his partner in crime. They were both carpenters and often co-conspirators.

"Neil was always the instigator of something, and he and dad always had a blast raising Cain," said Tom Harvey, Ted's son.

There are many Neil Johnston stories, such as the time he tried painting a house but became intoxicated to the point he couldn't climb a ladder to finish the job.

Indeed, during a "Foxcroft Follies Talent Show" in November 1974, Neil portrayed a drunk in comedy skits on the FA stage between acts.

"He was one crazy son of a gun," Jere White said. "He would pull pranks and did all these practical jokes on all the teachers."

One time, Neil pulled one over on the new pastor at the Congregational Church, Rev. Kenneth Dale. Neil, a deacon at the Catholic church, was in charge of putting grape juice in the pastor's chalice for serving Sunday communion.

"Neil put whiskey in it," White said. "Ken takes a big pull on it and his eyes bulged out. That was his first communion in his new church, and he thought it was going to be grape juice and it was whiskey."

Neil was good at hijinks. He was good with his hands, too. He was always building something.

"Neil was just a friggin' character. He built a houseboat on Sebec Lake—the Little Toot," Jeff Weatherbee said. "He built it at his house on the Milo Road. We had a big procession going to launch it into Sebec Lake. I remember Neal saying, 'I hope this thing floats.'"

Neil had a camp at Sebec Lake on the Bowerbank side. He would often steer his boat to the Dover side to the camp of Bob and Ruth Weatherbee and dock it. So often, in fact, that Bob convinced Dover-Foxcroft Police Chief Herbie Green to give him an old metal street parking meter so Bob could put it to use by sticking it in the cove next to his camp.

"The next day Neil came over and saw the parking meter there and cracked up," Jeff Weatherbee said. "I think it's still got coins in it because we didn't have the key to open it."

The success of the undefeated Foxcroft Academy boys basketball team opened Neil to a whole new world of possibilities and pranks. He decided to honor the Ponies and humor their fans by creating a big sign, and he recruited Ted Harvey to help him.

"Neil and dad's partnership for the deed was done," Tom Harvey said. "As far as Neil's inspiration for doing it, I suspect it was simply recognizing that the entire town would be traveling to the Bangor Auditorium to witness the big game."

One certainly couldn't miss the plywood sign. Painted white it was estimated to be 12 feet wide by 6 feet high attached to two 4-foot tall posts.

The sign certainly generated a lot of smiles and memories. Its black letters read: THE LAST ONE OUT OF TOWN TURN OUT THE LIGHTS.

It was a familiar refrain in Maine for fans following their small-town basketball team at tournament time, but Neil Johnston made a big deal— and big sign—out of it. Never had those words been so prominently displayed.

"Neil had a great sense of humor," Kevin Stitham said. "That wouldn't have been a big project for him. If you can build a house, you can make a billboard."

"Neil was a firm supporter of Foxcroft's athletics; he and Ted just had a good time wherever they went," said businessman and FA super booster Jim Robinson, FA Class of 1959. "You could never tell what he was going to do next. Never."

What Neil created was a rallying cry. The sign was stuck in a snowbank on the outskirts of Dover-Foxcroft near Bear Hill Road on the side of the highway leading to Bangor where the Ponies and their fans were headed for the start of the 1975 Eastern Maine Class B Tournament at the Bangor Auditorium.

You couldn't miss the sign or its message: Poniesmania had arrived!

"What a phenomenon," Kevin Nelson said.

The team saw the sign for the first time as it headed to Bangor in a yellow school bus on a Thursday afternoon to play its quarterfinal game against No. 7 seeded Limestone. The Ponies rose from their seats, looked out the windows on the right side of the bus and erupted in cheers.

"We all got a great roar out of it," Peter Snow said.

"Neil was just a sweetheart. He was a big supporter of the team and all the kids," Jeff Brown said. "We loved that. I've said that so many times throughout my life."

The Ponies were followed soon to Bangor by their fans and the FA Band.

"My first reaction was the whole town is behind us and they were all going to be at the Bangor Auditorium," Dave Clement said. "That was awesome."

The Ponies got an unexpected test from Limestone in the quarterfinals. Had they been the No. 1 seed, they would have played eighth seeded Herman, who they easily beat in the Foxcroft Holiday Classic. Limestone was highly motivated as it was making its first tournament appearance in twenty-three years and one of its wins was over third-seeded Van Buren.

Foxcroft built an early lead but had to hold on as Nelson, for the first time all season, fouled out of a game with 22 points with 2:29 to play with Foxcroft Academy ahead 61–47. Skip Hanson decided to replace Nelson with Scott Mountford instead of Jeff Brown or Roger Hewitt and instructed the Ponies to go into four-corners offense to thwart an Eagles comeback. Mountford wound up getting an assist on a clutch basket by Burtchell and was on the receiving end of a high post pass from Hatt for a backdoor layup that sealed a hard-fought 65–55 win.

Hatt had 20 points and 10 rebounds and saved the day. Skip Hanson came up behind Hatt in the locker room and patted him on the back and said so.

The tournament semifinal game against Van Buren, with a school enrollment of 613, was the best the Ponies had looked in weeks. It represented their twentieth consecutive win, Foxcroft's longest winning streak in thirty-five years, topping their nineteen-game winning streak the previous season and the nineteen-game winning streak of the 1939–40 FA team.

With Dunn scoring half of his 16 points in the first quarter, Foxcroft Academy jumped to a 20–8 lead, then Nelson scored 13 of Foxcroft's 17 points in the second quarter en route to a convincing 74–41 victory over the Crusaders. The Ponies had their mojo back and headed to the McDonald's on Broadway on their way home to celebrate.

"We all decided to line up and sing the Big Mac song: 'Two all-beef patties, special sauce, lettuce, cheese, pickles, onion on a sesame seed bun.' You deserve a break today, so get up and get away to McDonalds," team manager Joe Dean said. "The manager there then told the servers to give us all free drinks. Jeff Brown ordered two milkshakes and two Coca-Colas. Most of the team thought Jeff was being greedy, but I had been to McDonalds with Jeff before and he always ordered that many drinks."

While the Ponies were dining at McDonald's, fourth-seeded Orono was upsetting top-seeded MDI in the other Class B semifinal game 57–45. Thus, to win the tournament and go to state, Foxcroft would have to get past the Red Riots again. Orono would be without 6-foot-3 senior forward Mike Leveille, a star baseball player who quit the basketball team before the tournament, though Brian Butterfield and Richie Pullen went to his house and tried to talk him out of it.

Nevertheless, Foxcroft was more than ready to avenge the previous year's Eastern Maine championship game loss to Orono. The Ponies figured their time had come. For the first time in decades, Foxcroft Academy had beaten the Red Riots twice in the regular season in basketball and a third time would vindicate perhaps the most painful loss in FA basketball history one year after blowing a late lead and losing on "The Phantom Foul."

Playing its third game in three days and passing the The Last Out of Town Turn Out the Lights sign once again, the Ponies were plenty pumped to play Orono. Skip Hanson gave them even more motivation.

Hanson, before the 1975 Eastern Maine title game in the Bangor Auditorium, huddled his team together in the locker room and played a cassette tape of the radio broadcast of the final minutes of the 1974 Eastern Maine title game loss to Orono.

Kevin Nelson sat in silence and listened. Then he started banging his head either against a concrete wall or a metal locker.

"That got everybody pretty spun up," Mark Joyce said.

"He was so devastated by that loss and it was still raw," Tim King said. "When he heard that tape it brought back bad memories of the game and he was going to ensure that whatever it took to make that right this time."

The sight and sound of Nelson pounding his head into an inanimate object got everyone's attention.

"I don't remember Kevin getting *that* motivated, but it certainly motivated all of us. Kevin probably more than anybody, apparently," Dunn said.

"Kevin is sitting there banging his head against a beam in the locker room. That tape really fired him up," Dennis Kiah said. "I walked over to him thinking, 'Oh my God, he's going to get a concussion and won't be able to play!'"

Hanson, however, was wondering if playing that tape may have been too over the top as a motivational tool. Wes Jordan, the head athletics trainer for the University of Maine, observed the locker room scene and questioned the pregame strategy as he walked back out to the court with Skip.

"I just wanted them to have memories of how we lost that year, and Wes says, 'What the hell are you doing, Skip? Christ, I walked in there and everyone is tighter than a drum,'" Hanson said. "I said I never thought of it that way. Hopefully it helped. I just wanted them to recall the last 2 to 3 minutes of that game and what went on, and I think it helped."

It didn't hurt, or at least he didn't hurt Nelson. He doesn't even remember it.

"If anybody is banging their head against anything, he's the guy. I will never, ever dispute Kiah's assessment," Nelson said. "I might have been in the zone at that point and time, as we all were, but it's entirely possible that could have happened. I won't deny that."

The Red Riots weren't fazed. They played like two-time defending Eastern Maine tourney champs in the opening quarter and missed only three shots in taking a 19–18 lead. Butterfield beat the buzzer with a layup to close the period. However, in the second quarter, Nelson regained his senses and sense of purpose. He scored 13 of Foxcroft

Academy's 17 points in the period as the Ponies took a 35–29 lead to halftime despite twelve turnovers.

Hanson implored his team to do better in the locker room and turned again to Nelson to rally the team around him. Nelson had 19 points and 9 rebounds in the first half, one more rebound than the entire Orono team.

"We didn't play too well in the first half, and I could always get after Kevin, because I knew Kevin would accept it as a challenge. He never said anything back and it would impress the team," Hanson said. "I think Kevin came out for the second half and got the ball at the top of the key and he went by five defenders, and he put that ball up and in. I think he scored three or more baskets right after that and he dominated."

As did Foxcroft. After years of aggravating lopsided and close losses to Orono and constant frustration and failures against the Red Riots, the Ponies proceeded to win going away after the Red Riots pulled within 3 points, 39–36. Foxcroft ended the third period on an 11–4 run then Nelson scored the first 4 points of the fourth quarter and Burtchell scored 8 of the next 10 for the Ponies. Burtchell, who made nine of his twelve shots in the game, methodically built the Ponies' advantage to 20 points, 67–47. Scoring 30 of the game's final 41 points, Foxcroft won by 24, 73–49.

"Things just flowed our way in that game," Burtchell said. "I don't know how the chemistry came together so good, but that was a good time to come together."

"The Orono games were the ones you looked forward to because you wondered who would step up," Dunn said. "You knew Kevin was going to do his thing, but guys like Kenny Burtchell stepped up a bunch of times and really made a difference in games and probably didn't get nearly enough credit."

Nelson finished the game with 31 points, and Burtchell had a season-high 22 points. Burtchell joined Nelson and Jeff Dunn on the *Bangor Daily News* Class B all-tournament team, and Hatt was named Honorable Mention.

"It's amazing how much you have games in your life in high school that you remember," said Butterfield, who was named to the *BDN*'s Class

B all-tournament team. "I wake up thinking about the games we lost more than the games we won."

It was Foxcroft's most lopsided win over Orono in at least fifteen years. For fans of the Ponies who had grown to resent the Red Riots over the years, this was a blessing. The fans of Orono were miffed.

"The Red Riots of Orono were at the time a perennial power, and their proximity to Bangor gave them a familiarity bias of which they were quite aware. The idea of some school 20 miles further out from their center of the universe prevailing for a championship was unthinkable. And they tended to act like it," said Dave Cheever, WEMT-TV sportscaster. "I attended that championship game and was quietly thrilled that Foxcroft pulled what some idiots thought was an upset."

The Ponies' victory in the Eastern Maine Tournament championship game marked the first time since 1967 that neither Orono nor Schenck would represent Eastern Maine in the Class L or Class B state championship game.

Foxcroft fans in the line of cars that followed the Ponies home that night were as happy as they could be. Not only did they turn the lights back on in Dover-Foxcroft, there was the sound of church bells ringing as the team's bus drove through town back to the FA gym for a homecoming reception to greet the new Eastern Maine Class B Tournament champions. It was if the Ponies had finally been freed from the curse of Orono.

It was during this celebration in the FA gym that word was received that undefeated Medomak Valley would be the Ponies' opponent in the State Class B championship game the next Friday in the Augusta Civic Center. The Ponies didn't have much time to savor their sensational win in the Bangor Auditorium.

"It was almost like after we beat Orono that we cast aside that demon from the year before," Nelson said. "Then we found sort this new world of, 'Now we've got one more game? Really?' So we had to get our focus."

State Championship Win for the Ages

WHILE THE PONIES KNEW VERY LITTLE ABOUT THEIR OPPONENT IN THE Maine State Class B championship game, Al Baran and his Medomak Valley Panthers teammates knew everything they needed to know about Foxcroft.

They scrimmaged against Kevin Nelson, Jeff Dunn, and Jeff Brown when they attended the same Pine Tree Basketball Camp at Thomas College in the summer of 1974.

They even drove two hours up and back from Waldoboro to Dover-Foxcroft in the winter of 1975 to personally scout the Ponies from the stands during a game in the Foxcroft Academy gym.

Both times, the Medomak players came away with the same observation: Foxcroft had a worthy team, but the Panthers were decisively better.

"It was incredible. It was a Cinderella season for us. They still call us The Big Team From Medomak," said the 6-foot-6, 210-pound Baran, the Panthers' star player. "We had a major run that season and took everyone down and went through the Western Maine Tournament like nobody has ever gone through it before."

The unbeaten Panthers scored 93 points and routed defending state champion Camden-Rockport by 40 points in their Western Maine Class B Tournament quarterfinal win then scored 100 points in their 20-point semifinal win over Lake Region. In the Western Maine final, the Panthers put up 91 points against Mexico led by Baran's 36 points.

To the Ponies, Medomak Valley was like a mythical giant.

"When we learned about Medomak being the Western Maine champ, we weren't surprised," said Kevin Nelson. "My first reaction was, this is going to be difficult game. They went to that camp at Thomas

College we were at and I remember they had a lineup of Al, who was 6-foot-6, Russell Luce who was 6–4, Chuck Begley was 6–4, and Dean Erickson and Wayne LaHaye. I remember them being very formidable. They were averaging well over 90 points a game, and they were undefeated and they were crushing people."

Medomak Valley, like Foxcroft, benefited from a school consolidation. That was in 1968. However, Baran grew up in Danbury, Connecticut, and was attending Norwalk High School, a school of some three thousand students, when his family decided to move to Maine and buy a farm. They were looking at real estate as they stopped to eat in Moody's Diner off Route 1 in Waldoboro when a waitress noticed how tall Baran was and asked if he played basketball. Baran said yes.

"Then we noticed someone running to a phone booth," Baran said. "Within 20 minutes, Medomak Valley coach Art Dyer was standing there at our table."

Dyer actually invited Baran into his home in the aptly named town of Friendship for a short time until Baran's parents found a place in the town of Washington where they could grow vegetables, chop wood, and live off the land.

Al Baran, then a junior in 1973, was the missing link for the Panthers basketball team. He became Medomak Valley's version of Kevin Nelson.

"These guys wanted to win so bad. These guys had been trying to win a Western Maine title for years," Baran said. "I fit in well with them."

Baran instantly became the Panthers' starting center. Medomak Valley went 15–3 but lost to rival Camden-Rockport in the 1974 Western Maine Tournament Class B finals. Camden-Rockport was to Medomak what Orono was to Foxcroft.

"It was what it was. They had a better team," Baran said of Camden-Rockport. "I wasn't bitter, but we were trained to dislike them. But it wasn't a cult. That's who we were."

With Baran, the Panthers became a confident lot. Most of the team attended the Pine Tree Camp at Thomas College in the summer of 1974. So did Nelson, Dunn, and Brown for Foxcroft.

Baran by then figured Medomak Valley was going to be good enough to win the Western Maine Class B championship in his senior year, and he figured they would be facing Foxcroft and Kevin Nelson in the state title game. So Baran tried to arrange an impromptu scrimmage against the FA players at Thomas College on an outdoor court as a measuring stick. He wanted to know how they sized up in talent.

That summer scrimmage at Thomas College convinced Baran that the Panthers would be the team to beat come state championship time.

"We knew Dover had a good team and all week long we were saying we wanted to play those guys. Let's have a scrimmage. We wanted to win the state right then. We didn't want to wait until next February," Baran said. "So we finally got them down on one of the outside courts. Kevin and I were there, but I don't remember if their full team was there, but we beat them pretty handily. We were thinking, 'We've got this. We won the state already.' But we tended to get too cocky as things went on. We knew they were probably the only team in our way to win the state."

For good measure, Baran and several other Medomak players on a whim one winter night decided to drive two hours to Dover-Foxcroft, sit in the stands and size up the Ponies one more time. Baran jumped into a 1968 Pontiac GTO driven by teammate Drew Butler.

"We walked into the Foxcroft gym with our hats tucked down so no one would recognize us like we're here to kick ass and win state and then we're leaving. We were too arrogant," Baran said. "We sat up high and we walked in with our Medomak hats and shirts and it was like we were here to conquer. We got there fast, we watched the game, then we got home fast. Dover beat somebody. We drove up to scout them and, I hate to say, but we came out of there with the opinion we could beat Dover. We didn't think there was anybody who could beat us. That's a bad attitude to get, when you are seventeen or eighteen years old."

To Foxcroft, Medomak Valley was more a mystery, a nameless and faceless opponent next in line. The Ponies had focused on beating and getting past Orono, and they allowed themselves for a short spell to bask in the glow of that accomplishment. Over the weekend before its week of preparation for Medomak, the Foxcroft players were reveling in their new-found fame.

"I think we became celebrities that year in that town," said Dick Hatt. "They would have never known me if I hadn't been on that team."

"The town was really into it. I was this new kid in town and every-body knew who I was," Mark Joyce said. "It was a little bit intimidating. I thought I didn't deserve the notoriety or I hadn't earned it because I haven't learned the names of any of these people. I'd walk into a place for the first time, and I'd hear, 'Hey, Mark! How you doing?' I'm doing pretty good. How the hell do you know my name?'"

Beating Orono and qualifying for the state championship game had its benefits. Players, coaches, and managers were invited to have free haircuts at "Be Curlee See Shirley," the beautician shop owned by Shirley Mae Warren, Duane Warren's mom.

The *Bangor Daily News* sent a photographer to Foxcroft Academy to capture players and managers in poses in the hallway and school library. The newspaper also ran a full-page ad saluting the Class B Eastern Maine champs.

Kevin Nelson and Jeff Dunn drove to Bangor to be interviewed by Dave Cheever, the sports director of WEMT-TV Channel 7, the ABC affiliate in Bangor. That was a big production.

"To us, it was like being interviewed by Howard Cosell," Kevin said.

"Well, I am 5-foot-6 and Kevin is not. I remember speaking with him and wondering if the juxtaposition was ridiculous. This was at a time when being on television—any television—was a big deal, especially for high school athletes," Cheever said. "Our signal at Channel 7 blanketed the state and went as far west as Lake Champlain to the west and Prince Edward Island to the east. Never mind that on any given broadcast hour we were seen by more moose than people, we filled a niche and the tournament was a big deal. Having the Ponies' captains for an interview was a good get for me and for them. They had airtime that their fans and family could see, and I was able to bridge some of the gap of not calling the games live."

Cheever's day job in 1975 was teaching at Bangor High School. He had limited contact with the Foxcroft basketball team in his media job, but Kevin Nelson and Jeff Dunn and the Ponies' plight impressed him to no end.

"Bangor was a perennial power in that half of the state based on its enrollment alone. I had more students daily in my English classes than were enrolled at Foxcroft," Cheever said. "One thing remains, however, and that is the affection I had for Skip Hanson and his team. Win or lose, they did it the right way. It so happened that they won."

The Foxcroft Academy team was treated like royalty in their community and their school hallways. With their sudden fame, some players were invited to elementary school classes in Dover-Foxcroft to speak to kids.

"The momentum grew over those four years in high school. You could see them getting better every year and everybody started thinking, 'Oh, they're going to do it. They're going to do it.' It was so exciting. Every school was involved," Peg Hanson said. "They knew we had a chance at winning the Gold Ball. The whole community was engaged."

On Monday of Medomak week, Skip Hanson and assistant coaches Dennis Kiah and Dave Clement drove to Cony High School in Augusta to get a scouting report on the Panthers. The Foxcroft Academy coaches didn't have much to go on other than team rosters and newspaper box scores as there were no game tapes to view back then. The FA coaches targeted Mike Haley, a football coach at Cony who had refereed several Medomak Valley basketball games. Haley, a friend of UMO coach Skip Chappelle, agreed to give Hanson and his coaching staff some pointers about the Panthers as long as they kept it secret.

"We stayed with him for three hours and went over Medomak's strength and weaknesses," Hanson said. "He was a big help."

Meanwhile, back at Foxcroft, Wayne Champeon was running practice for the Ponies. It was a routine to shoot free throws at the end of practice and, once one player made 10 consecutive foul shots, practice was officially over and the players could go downstairs to the locker room and shower. Dave Ingraham, the team's best and most clutch free-throw shooter, was shooting foul shots and he got on a roll. Swish. Swish. Swish.

"Champ says no one can leave until someone makes 10 in a row. My brother is at the foul line shooting and he makes 10. Then he makes 20 in a row. Then he makes something like 30 in a row and everybody is getting restless and wants to go home," Peter Ingraham said. "It's the end of practice and Wayne says, 'Wait. We are going to stay here and wait until Dave misses one.' I think Dave made like forty or forty-five foul shots in a row and everybody had to stay and wait until he finished. It incapsulates the whole Dave foul shooting thing."

Before getting the scouting report from their coaches, about the only particulars the Foxcroft Academy players knew about Medomak Valley was its record and the size of its front line. There wasn't a newspaper within reach to read games stories about the Panthers or see their box scores. There was no YouTube or MaxPreps.

"When Foxcroft played Medomak, it was close to a sure thing that no more than two of the twelve players on either roster had ever set foot in the opponent's community," Cheever said. "The coaches could scout all they wanted, but the freshness of the competition was due in large part to the fact that these kids had never played against each other and would have had difficulty finding the opponent's school on a map."

Mark Joyce was the only Foxcroft Academy player who had set foot in Waldoboro. He had competed against the Panthers when he was playing for Mount View High School in Waldo County before moving to Dover-Foxcroft.

"And they just smoked us," Joyce said. "We were a good team, but we didn't have any height."

Foxcroft, with Kevin Nelson, had considerable height. But Medomak Valley had more.

"The first thing I thought was, 'Holy shit, these guys are big,'" said Tim King. "They must have been eating Aroostook County potatoes, because they were tall. That intimidated me with my stature. I was hoping I wouldn't play."

The Panthers started an imposing front line of 6–6, 6–4, and 6–4. They all took to wearing gold wristbands that were intended to identify their teammates yet also serve as a display of rebounding superiority.

"So you knew when you were up there for a rebound, don't take it away from a guy wearing a gold wristband. He'd take your whole arm off to get that ball," Baran said. "You would try to ensure that your own teammate didn't take the rebound from you. If you saw the wristband, you would back off."

On paper, Medomak Valley looked mighty intimidating. During the regular season, the Panthers averaged 80 points a game with an average winning margin of 24 points. They played Dexter twice, scoring more than 80 points both times and beat the Tigers by an average of 27 points.

By comparison, the Ponies also beat Dexter twice, yet struggled in their two wins against the Tigers. Expecting a tough game with Medomak, Foxcroft had a vigorous week of practice to prep for the Panthers.

"It was brutal. Not because of the coaches, but because we were so competitive," said Jeff Brown, who was nursing an ankle injury suffered in the Orono game. "I told Kevin he was a mean SOB that week because, in one practice, I took a shot and he blocked it. I caught it. I took another shot and he blocked it. I caught it. I took another. He blocked it. After the fourth block I said to hell with this and threw it to someone else and everyone split a gut laughing. He blocked me four times straight. I tell my kids that story and they laugh."

One player who stood out in practice during the week was Peter Snow. He was upset that he didn't even play in the Eastern Maine Tournament championship game. He and sophomore Steve Mountford were the only two Foxcroft players who didn't get on the court against Orono in the Eastern Maine title game in Bangor. Hanson explained to Snow afterward that he wanted the seniors to be on the floor at game's end.

That served as extra motivation during practice for the Medomak game.

"I was still pissed off," Snow said.

During the season, Foxcroft at times had difficulty handling a full-court press. Though they never lost a game, several were closer than expected as the Ponies committed too many turnovers for their coach's liking.

Breaking Medomak Valley's full-court press was a point of emphasis leading up to the state title game. The Panthers preyed on turnovers forced.

"We drilled and practiced scenarios in practice," Nelson said. "How are we going to break this press? How are we going to attack it?"

Medomak's turbo-paced style was predicated on its full-court press. The Panthers, coached by Art Dyer, would create turnovers and turn them into fastbreak points.

"It drove Coach Dyer crazy. He was a defensive coach his whole career and we showed up and all we wanted to do was run and gun that ball," Baran said. "We pretty much rolled over everyone."

While Medomak preferred a more up-tempo game, Foxcroft's style was more deliberate and patient. They were trying to work the ball into Nelson and play an inside out game.

"That didn't work on us too well," Baran said. "It was harder to slow the ball down on us, because we'd just hammer you into running no matter what."

Hanson laid out the game plan for Medomak. He would have the Ponies alternate between a 2–3 zone and a 1-3-1 zone defense, challenging the Panthers' shooters to hit from outside.

"No man-to-man defense, as we did not want Kevin away from the hoops," Hanson said.

The game plan also called for Foxcroft to play pretty much mistake-free basketball on both ends of the court. There wasn't room for errors and erratic passing or ball-handling miscues.

"Al was a force, LaHaye was a good player, and a couple of others," Hanson said, "We knew they were good and we're going to have to play a top game just to be competitive."

The week of practice was coming to an end, and Hanson had some surprises in store for his team. First, the team was going to be treated to a steak lunch on Friday at what was considered the finest restaurant in Dover-Foxcroft, the historic Blethen House, with its white linen tablecloths. The Foxcroft Academy team came to the Blethen House dressed for their final away game of the season. Judging by their wardrobe at the time they could have been called "The Polyester Ponies." Low-cost, iron-free polyester clothing was the fad, the so-called Leisure Suit Era. Skip Hanson wore a checkered leisure suit to the Eastern Maine Class B championship game win against Orono with matching pants and jacket.

"I don't remember what I wore, because my wife had laid my clothes out for me every day," Kiah joked. "As long as we hadn't lost a game in them, I wore it."

The rest of the team wasn't quite as superstitious. Though they were super competitive on the court when they practiced or played, there was no competition for whom might be the best dressed off the court.

"I do remember we were always checking out the young ladies, though," Dick Hatt quipped.

For the state championship game trip, Tim King was dressed in polyester plaid pants with a solid-colored sport coat, a dress shirt, and a white tie. His parents took a photo of him standing next to a snowbank in the driveway on the family farm before he left for the Blethen House.

Kevin Nelson's choice of clothes came from a mail-order big-and-tall place in Brockton, Massachusetts. Because his inseam was 39 inches and sleeve length was 38 inches, he couldn't find clothes that fit him at Koritzsky's in Dover-Foxcroft. Kevin also had a pair of blue and white pattern leather platform shoes.

"I think I was 6-foot-10 with those on," he joked. "No wonder I had chronic back problems."

In its heyday, the Blethen House—which was demolished in 1998 to build a Rite Aid—served only the best, and the FA basketball team certainly qualified as elite. After their send-off lunch, the Ponies were going to board a bus to Augusta, but not any bus. Hanson had arranged for them to travel in a chartered Greyhound bus.

"We felt like we were Schenck," Nelson said. "They always showed up to games with a Greyhound for crying out loud when the papermills were operating up there. They had the best of everything. They had warm-up pants!"

"That Greyhound bus was pretty exciting. That was pretty fancy for back in those days," Burtchell said. "I think it added to the team's morale and the energy of the whole thing. It was like a boost to be treated so well."

Skip Hanson, who was Foxcroft Academy's athletics director, discovered he had enough surplus money in the sports budget to charter the bus. But, when he approached FA principal Bob Perkins with the proposal, Perkins was at first reluctant to approve it. He thought it would send the wrong message to the community.

"Look, it's up to you, Bob," Skip said.

Perkins relented, and he never regretted the decision to go Greyhound.

"He said, 'That was the best idea you ever had, Skip. The kids loved it. The parents loved it,'" Hanson said.

Though fearing that Foxcroft may have finally met their match, the Ponies boarded that bus in Dover-Foxcroft with the full support of the community and with complete faith in the team's star player. In Kevin they trust.

"We thought that the only one who had the confidence was Kevin Nelson. Everybody thought this team they were going to play was going to beat them. Except for Kevin," said longtime FA booster Jim Robinson. "He seemed to be the only one to think that wasn't going to be a problem."

Well, it certainly was going to be a tall order. Nelson looked at the Medomak front line he would be facing which, across the board, was the tallest he had ever gone up against at Foxcroft.

"Jeff Dunn and I were sitting in my car and getting ready to get on the bus, and we saw their size and I think we had a little deer-in-the-headlights look," Nelson said.

As the Ponies' chartered bus left town south on Route 7, they saw that Neil Johnston had amended his sign from the previous week by replacing Turn Out the Lights with Put Out the Cat. The updated sign was erected at the bottom of the South Street hill, next to the A. E. Robinson building, as the team bus started its two-hour trip to Augusta. Hanson also had arranged for the team to check into a Holiday Inn, where they would stay after the game, win or lose.

Following a brief pit stop to look inside the then-empty Augusta Civic Center, the team arrived at the Holiday Inn that Friday afternoon. They were paired and given keys to rooms with two double beds. They spent most of that free time watching TV, and they didn't like what they saw and heard and had read most of the week in newspapers. They weren't given much of a chance of upsetting the powerhouse Medomak Valley team.

"Everyone pumped them up because they were down in Southern Maine and we're not supposed to compete well with those teams," Brown said. "We all felt we could beat them. We had the drive to do it. We had the talent. We had nine seniors. We had seven guys who could start for any team. I believed it then. I believe it now. I will always believe it."

The Ponies, however, didn't have many believers outside the Penquis League and Piscataquis County. They were annoyed that Eastern Maine media personalities, such as WEMT's Dave Cheever and WABI's George Hale, were predicting that Medomak Valley would beat Foxcroft in the state championship game.

"First, Medomak was a really strong and deep team," Cheever said. "They did not have anyone 6–8 with a shooting touch and brains, and Skip Hanson did. Despite saying that, I thought that Medomak was likely too strong for the mighty Ponies."

Those predictions were probably warranted. Medomak Valley was licking its chops. The Panthers and their fans had been waiting for a long time to win a state championship. They, too, had never brought home a Gold Ball. Medomak, in its seven years as a consolidated school, had made the Western Maine Class B Tournament six times and was seeded No. 1 three times.

The Panthers felt it was their time and their turn. They had the team to finish the job and beat the much-ballyhooed Nelson and the Ponies.

"When Kevin was a sophomore and a junior, we were in Western Maine and the Heal Point rankings would come out every week and we'd always kept an eye on Eastern Maine to see who we might play," said Scott Graffam, a senior on the 1974 Medomak Valley team who was inducted into the Maine Basketball Hall of Fame in 2023. "We were always keeping track of him. Kevin Nelson's name was always in the Bangor paper, and if they won a game we were always reading about Kevin Nelson. He was in the news and he was a big guy and his battles with Orono were epic. Those games were always big newsmakers."

Predictably the main storyline for the Foxcroft/Medomak showdown was the matchup of two undefeated teams led by their two big men. It was the Maine basketball equivalent of the Irresistible Force vs. Immovable Object.

"Kevin had incredible strength and a wingspan and he could shoot and he could do it all," said Baran, who was at least 10 pounds heavier. "One headline in the local paper read, 'Baran, Nelson: Mountains

Meeting in Augusta.' When you read that when you're eighteen years old it's like, 'Whoa.' It went on to describe that I was probably stronger, but he was more a finesse player and all that, although he was goddamn strong. He was no weakling, that's for sure."

Nelson said, "Alan got off the floor really quickly. He was an inside player who had a good 10-to-15-foot game. Inside offensively and he was a strong rebounder. He himself could block shots and he did. I gained an immense amount of respect for him."

The main event was set, and the team's superheroes had been identified.

"That was sort of the setup for the state championship game: The Clash of the Big Men," said Ernie Clark, a 1976 FA graduate who played on the Ponies' JV team that season. "He [Baran] gave us a different look on the low post, but Kevin could play from the high post in. He had that advantage."

The site of the state title game was the nearly new Augusta Civic Center. It had been built for economic development off the I-95 Belgrade exit on a 59-acre plot of forest and farmland that previously contained a chicken house. Called "The Sports Hub of Maine" by *Kennebec Journal* sports editor Ken Marriner, the Augusta Civic Center, with a listed seating capacity of 6,100, hosted its first basketball game on December 26, 1972—the Cony Rams vs. Waterville Purple Panthers—even though only 3,000 seats were ready and toilets were still being installed.

Only 1,500 fans showed up for that game, a 60–40 Cony victory.

The Boston Celtics—with John Havlicek, Dave Cowens and Jo Jo White—played an NBA exhibition game in the Augusta Civic Center against the Buffalo Braves and heralded rookie guard Ernie DiGregorio on September 21, 1973. General admission was $3.50.

The first Maine high school state championship boys basketball games in the Augusta Civic Center were played on March 3, 1973, when Jonesport-Beals beat Wiscasset 100–77 in the Class D title game and Sumner beat Yarmouth 100–63 in the Class C state championship game. The most anticipated game of the day, however, was between two undefeated teams—Orono and Camden-Rockport. Both teams entered with 21–0 records, and Camden-Rockport had a home court advantage among the standing-room-only crowd of 6,500. Droves of Orono fans who traveled by car and bus to the Class B state title game could not get inside the packed building.

"I told Barney it's a good thing we are wearing our red uniforms because we are playing away tonight," Orono's Tom Philbrick said.

Camden-Rockport sent the game into overtime when Charlie Wootton hit a long shot at the buzzer, setting off a thunderous cheer. The noise was so deafening that Brian Butterfield, who played with an abscess in his ear, raised his hand to cup it as it hurt him so much.

"My mom and dad were at the game, and dad had been at so many great sporting events in his lifetime," Butterfield said. "When Charlie Wootton made that shot, my dad told me after the game that was the loudest crowd noise he had ever heard. The sound staggered me. It felt like it was an onset of vertigo. For a second there it felt like I was punched by a heavyweight fighter."

Orono prevailed 60–55 in overtime as 6–7 Stevie Gavett, Peter's brother, finished with 23 points and Tom Philbrick, then a sophomore, added 22 to give their coach, John Giffin, who had attended Camden-Rockport, his first state championship.

The Augusta Civic Center also hosted multiple sporting events including roller derby. Its biggest entertainment event was on March 24, 1977, when Elvis Presley made his one and only Maine appearance, still noted by a plaque in the lobby. Hence, Elvis left the building long after the Foxcroft Academy Ponies arrived in it.

Baran's only concern about the Augusta Civic Center was that he and his teammates were not allowed to have a practice or shoot around in the arena during the week to acclimate themselves to the new surroundings. The facility had two free-standing baskets and an overhead scoreboard. The Panthers were about a half-hour drive from Augusta to practice, but Foxcroft's drive would have been nearly two hours, maybe longer. There is a 10-mile stretch on southbound I-95 that has a warning sign MOOSE CROSSING.

"I remember being told that because we were so much closer—30 to 35 minutes—that it would have been an unfair advantage," Baran said. "I think Dover would have come down in a heartbeat, but State High

School Principals officials said no because Medomak Valley was closer. That didn't make any sense."

As it turned out, both teams had equal time to shoot around in the Civic Center before the game as they arrived at about the same time in the parking lot. The Panthers were stunned by the sight of the Ponies pulling up in a Greyhound bus.

"We came there on a school bus because we weren't that far away, and they're coming in on a chartered bus and that was like 'Holy shit!' to us. We are never going to charter a bus for the last game of our careers. Wow," Baran said. "I looked at that and that's not something you're going to forget. We came on our usual school bus with the same bus driver who drove us to every game."

Foxcroft also had several booster busses filled with students and adults traveling to Augusta. Arline Dean, who graduated from Dexter High School in 1939 but married a FA graduate, Ronald (Class of 1937), was supposed to go to the game with her daughter, Barbara, FA Class of 1966. But Arline decided to stay home after a fire broke out in the attic of their home on the Sebec Lake Road. Her daughter, Grace Dean Langley, FA Class of 1972, took her place at the last minute.

Tragically, that bus was delayed getting to Augusta. Glen Bugbee, the bus driver, was taking his wife, Ruth, to the game. One minute he was looking at her through the rear view mirror above him, seeing how thrilled she was about going to the game as she sat behind him. The next minute, he looked and she was slumped in her seat. Glen heroically tried to attend to her while safely steering the bus to the side of the road. She did not make it. The passengers had to get off the bus until a replacement driver arrived.

"We continued on to the game in a very quiet bus, but once we got inside the Augusta Civic Center, there was a very different atmosphere," Grace said. "I ran into Annalee Korsman, who noticed I had a maternity shirt on. She asked, 'Are you pregnant again? Ewww.' She was funny like that."

Most Pony fans drove on their own to the game in Maine's state capital, Augusta. They had plenty of incentive with Foxcroft playing in the state basketball championship game for the first time. That novelty was addictive.

"It was about the only game that I didn't play in that my parents went to," Ernie Clark said. "We all piled into the car and went to Augusta and sat in the top row of the Civic Center."

Al Baran also was impressed by the Foxcroft Academy Band when it filed into the arena. The FA Band was positioned across the court from the Ponies' bench. Twice during pregame, they played "The Horse"—the team's anthem—and both times thousands of Foxcroft fans around the band in the lower and upper sections stood up and clapped in rhythm with the song.

"The FA Band owned the arena that night," said Eric "Punch" Anderson, FA Class of 1962.

It was a powerful show and sound of support. The FA Band fired up the FA team as it warmed up.

"One hundred percent," Dick Hatt said. "'The Horse'? I still listen to this day. Every time they played that song it was just pumping through my body."

"That would jack us up," Mark Joyce said. "We weren't just a one-act show. We had one of the best high school bands probably in the country playing at our games and they were just awesome. They would get people pumped up. It had to get in Medomak's heads. They're thinking, 'If the band is that good, the basketball team must be good.' That had to psyche them out."

"It was a 100 percent totally community-supported event," Tim King said. "And it wasn't just the final game. The whole season it was that way."

If the FA Band wasn't intimidating, Nelson surely was after the opening tip. Scott Graffam, who was sitting near the baseline, claims the 6–8 Foxcroft center blocked a shot by each of the Medomak starters in the opening period. It's his story and he's sticking to it.

"It changed the whole game," said Graffam, a 2023 Maine Basketball Hall of Fame inductee who played at Medomak Valley from 1972 to 1974. "At one point, Chuck Begley had a kind of breakaway and he was going to lay it in and cut the lead to one point and he was looking over his shoulder for Nelson and missed it."

Medomak Valley's starting lineup consisted of four seniors and one sophomore—Dean Erickson, who went on to play basketball at Brown University and, in 2018, was inducted into the Maine Basketball Hall of Fame.

Foxcroft's starting lineup consisted of four seniors and one junior—Ken Burtchell.

The Ponies never trailed in the first quarter and led by as many as 5 points as Burtchell scored 6 points and Nelson had 5 points and seven rebounds. His driving basket down the lane gave FA a 13–10 lead at the end of the opening period.

The Panthers were struggling to get their running game going. When Medomak Valley went into a full-court press, Nelson would come back and use his height to take the inbounds pass then either dribble across the mid-court line or pass to a teammate when the Panthers' pressure subsided.

On offense, Medomak Valley had a tough time adjusting to the free-standing baskets and the deeper background and optics behind them. The Panthers weren't as worried about the Ponies' depth as they were about the arena's depth perception.

Medomak Valley played its Western Maine Class B Tournament games at Edward Little High School in Lewiston. "No one on our team had ever shot at one of those free-standing baskets before," Baran said. "Our shots were going in and out, in and out, in and out."

Russell Luce, who had scored 34 points on 17-of-17 shooting in the Panthers' Western Maine semifinal win over Lake Region, couldn't find his mark. Nor could Dean Erickson.

"That game is not something I relive often," said Erickson, now a chartered financial analyst (CFA) at Bionic Capital LLC in Melbourne, Florida.

Still Medomak, which trailed by as many as 5 points in the first quarter, managed to take the lead in the second period with a 12–4 run that pushed the Panthers ahead by 5 points, 24–19. Hanson called a timeout and following the timeout, Peter Snow, who did not play a single second in the Eastern Maine Class B Tournament championship game, checked into the game. He immediately scored a basket in the state title game that thwarted Medomak's momentum. Nelson closed the first half with a layup that beat the buzzer and narrowed the Panthers' lead to 26–25.

The decision to put Snow in the game instead of Brown, who had been the Ponies' sixth man the majority of the season, did not go over well with Brown, who thought he was healthy enough to play.

"It was one of those deals. Jeff Brown was sometimes our sixth and seventh man and Peter had really looked good in practice," Hanson said. "Peter was a junior and Jeff was a senior. And I thought, 'I've got to put Peter in now the way he has been playing.' Jeff never forgave me for that."

The game at intermission was getting tighter and the crowd was still getting bigger. Event organizers were scrambling to find more seating to accommodate fans.

"Our crowd beat their crowd. There was like 7,500 people in that Augusta Civic Center," Baran said. "At halftime they were still putting out folding chairs, right on to the edge of the court. I'll never forget that. We walked out from the locker room to start the second half and they were still unloading cartloads of folding chairs. People wanted to sit down next to the court. It was amazing. I've never played in front of a crowd like that."

In the second half, Foxcroft regained the advantage on two free throws by Nelson, then the two teams battled back and forth, swapping the lead on six consecutive possessions. It was a frenetic pace. The pulse of the game was thumping. The pressure was building. Fans were cheering and screaming on both sides. Heart rates were rising as each minute and second ticked off.

It was a virtual ping-pong match of emotions and energy.

Baran put the Panthers back in front 39–38 with a layup, but Nelson's driving layup to retake the lead for Foxcroft was waved off when he was charged with an offensive foul, his third of the game, with five seconds remaining in the third quarter. Any foul on Nelson raised the anxiety level on the FA bench and added to the jitters in the FA crowd.

The Panthers appeared to be in excellent shape early in the final quarter. They increased their lead to 5 points, 43–38—their largest lead of the game—with 7 answered points before Butchell answered with a crucial basket. Then Baran drew a shooting foul on Dick Hatt—his fourth foul of the game—and made two free throws with 6:30 left in the game for a 45–42 Medomak lead. Snow again came off the bench as Hatt sat down with his fourth foul with Foxcroft trailing.

"We felt, given Peter's abilities—he was a smart player, he would give the ball up if somebody had a better shot—Jeff was a better defensive player," Hanson said.

"You've got to give credit to Skip for that decision," Mark Joyce said. "That must have been a tough call, and I know Brownie hated it and he may not be over it yet."

"I don't remember much of it, because I was sitting on the bench stewing," the ultra-competitive Brown said.

The Nelson-Baran matchup that was publicized in days leading up to the state championship game was beginning to materialize and live up to top billing. Nelson scored back-to-back buckets to give Foxcroft the lead 46–45 with 5:40 to play, then Burtchell fouled Baran who completed a 3-point play with a foul shot for a 48–46 Medomak lead 10 seconds later.

Burtchell countered with a corner jumper to tie the contest, then Luce regained the lead for the Panthers with a layup. Following an Ingraham free throw, Peter Snow made his presence felt. After a Nelson rebound, Snow scored inside to give the Ponies, with 4:27 remaining the game, a 51–50 lead, the fourteenth—and what turned out to be final—lead change in the game. Foxcroft was anxious to slow down the pace of the contest and control the ball with the lead.

Following a Medomak timeout, the Ponies defense held, and Snow scored again on another layup off a pass from Nelson as the Panthers' Dave Strout struggled to guard Snow. Foxcroft's lead swelled to 3 points, 53–50, with under four minutes to play, and Snow grabbed a rebound on the other end of the floor that gave Foxcroft a possession to extend its lead to 5 points. The momentum was again back in Foxcroft's favor with Snow's efforts. Snow made one of two foul shots to push the Ponies in front 54–52 with 2:07 left in the game.

"He was the torpedo at water level," Baran said.

The underdog Ponies were beginning to feel like top dogs. There was a little sense of panic in the Panthers, who seemingly had seized control of the game five minutes earlier with a 5-point lead.

"I always had a feeling they had a feeling they were going to steam-roll through everybody that year," Nelson said. "When it came down to the last few minutes of the game and we were actually ahead, they probably found themselves in some real dark territory."

Medomak, to its credit, kept coming. The Panthers had the ball with a chance to tie the game. Baran and company were bearing down.

"I don't care how much Baran scored, he just couldn't keep up with Kevin," Jeff Brown said. "He couldn't run the floor with Kevin. He was a big guy and pretty good player, but we could break the press with Kevin. He could out dribble anybody his size and close to his size."

However, with 1:11 to play, Nelson picked up his fourth foul. Panthers fans were elated. Foxcroft fans fretted. LaHaye made one of two free throws to cut Foxcroft's lead to 54–53. Hansen called timeout and Pony fans dialed 9-1-1.

The message to Nelson in the team huddle was simple. Do not lunge. Do not leave your feet and try to block a shot.

DON'T JUMP, KEVIN! DON'T JUMP!

"You could clear a rebound over someone, but it didn't matter. There was a presumption of guilt," Nelson said. "Anybody who was tall in high school basketball, if you created any sort of contact that was it. The referees were likely to blow the whistle on you."

And Baran, who had only three fouls, had an advantage. He had scored 11 of his team-high 17 points in the second half, which included three made free throws.

"That's the only time I really felt pressure. Toward the end of the game we started getting a little bit of an idea that we may not win this thing," Baran said. "It just became obvious that we were in a war and things might not turn our way."

The intense pressure was building with each possession, and fans for both teams were on the edge of their seats. Cheers erupted and hearts sank with each point scored and every whistle blown. Hanson was walking the sidelines and working the officials. He accidentally stomped on Kiah's foot arguing one call. Hanson called four timeouts in the fourth quarter.

"We knew that would have to be a good part of our game plan, particularly at the end if we were tied or had the lead just to calm things down. Sometimes it makes the other defense a bit lazy," Hanson said. "We used four timeouts in the last six minutes or so."

"It was tense. Tense. Tense. Tense. Tense. It just was tense," Nelson said. "There was no great divide or lead in the game. The thing I remember most was the crowd. There was a lot of pressure on sixteen-, seventeen-, and eighteen-year-old kids, and we took it seriously. There was a lot of pressure. Wow. That game could have easily gone the other way."

It almost went to Medomak in the final minute. Hatt, Foxcroft's second-tallest starter, fouled out, and the Panthers, trailing by a point, 54–53, had a chance to tie the game or possibly take the lead when LaHaye went back to the foul line to shoot the front end of a one-and-one with 54 seconds remaining.

LaHaye, who had 16 points in the game, missed the first free throw, but Baran grabbed the critical rebound under the basket. Nelson was defending him. Baran was in the paint in position to score and possibly induce a fifth foul on Nelson that would certainly shift the game's momentum and send the Medomak star to the foul line again.

Baran could have faked a shot and caused Nelson to jump into the air and into a vulnerable position to draw his fifth foul. Baran did what came naturally to him.

"Ball fakes were not part of my game," Baran said. "I played upstairs. I could outjump Kevin. I could outrun him. I was a very good shooter and could shoot from further than he could. But it wasn't any of that. It was just that I just didn't do ball fakes. I never had to. There was nobody I played against that I needed ball fakes."

But Baran had never played against a player like Nelson that season. He snatched the rebound and immediately went back up for the shot. Nelson naturally went to block it. The memory of "The Phanton Foul" against Orono was on his mind.

"He took a jump shot in the lane, and I just said, 'I've got to go after this.' I knew I couldn't go anywhere near his hand. I went up and I cleanly blocked it and no one called a foul," Nelson said. "I'm thinking, 'Wow, maybe the refs are going to let us play and let us decide the game and its outcome.' Luckily it just worked out that way that it happened. I was able to tip it. I easily could have missed it, and he could have made the shot. That's the way it goes sometimes."

Ingraham grabbed the rebound and was fouled by Dean Erickson. Ingraham went to the line where the team's best free throw shooter—who four days earlier kept his teammates after practice by making forty-something consecutive foul shots—made his teammates proud by sinking two in a row for a 56–53 lead, the final points of the game. He was Mr. Dependable.

Dave Ingraham, with his parents, John and Ann, and brother Peter in the crowd and his sister Susan playing in the FA Band, sealed the win after Nelson eliminated Medomak's best chance of beating Foxcroft with his blocked shot on the other end of the court.

"That was our last hope," Baran said. "If I make that, then we probably win."

"Had he pumped fake, I would have gone for it. No question. He would have had me," Nelson said. "In the excitement of the moment I would have gone up and he would have probably drawn a foul on me and the game would have worked out a different way."

Trailing by 3 points with time running down, Baran had one more shot in the game, but Nelson blocked that one, too. The poor-shooting Panthers didn't record a field goal in the final three minutes of the game, in part because Foxcroft's stalling tactics in its version of Dean Smith's North Carolina four-corners offense was playing keep away.

The final photograph during game action was LaHaye launching a shot—worth 2 points, not 3, if he made it—over Burtchell with eight seconds showing on the overhead scoreboard and Foxcroft leading 56–53. LaHaye missed and Nelson grabbed the last rebound of the game.

Both teams played their hearts out until the final buzzer.

"That was a nail biter. It could have been anybody's game. . . . However, I felt we had karma on our side—a juju—that we had survived this monster team and we were ahead," Tim King said. "I felt it was going to happen. We had Jack."

As great a game as it was—an instant classic, if you will—it was not televised. Today, high school basketball fans in Maine can watch regular season games every day of the week through live streaming. But, in 1975, only the state's Class A championship game appeared on TV.

There were two radio accounts of the Foxcroft Academy-Medomak Valley Class B state championship game, one from WDME in Dover-Foxcroft with John Spruce doing the play-by-play and John Doe providing color commentary. When the final seconds ticked off, John Spruce gave an account of the pandemonium from his broadcasting perch.

"They're going crazy down there on the floor," he announced. "They are just mobbing there and WHOOP-EE!"

A radio recording of the 1975 Maine Class B state championship game is a rare find. WDME 1340 was an AM station from 1967 to 1991 before changing to FM. In 2001, WDME 103.1 was acquired by The Zone Corporation, a broadcast company owned by authors and philanthropists Stephen and Tabitha King. In its heyday, WDME was broadcasting out of an actual train passenger car converted into a radio station. It was located on outer West Main Street and managed by Bill Mack, a popular morning deejay and radio personality. In The Zone Corporation WDME morphed into WZLO.

John Spruce's WHOOP-EE was just the start of a wild evening of celebration. At game's end, the contrast in emotions was evident at court side from smiles to smirks. From disbelief to delirium.

"I felt euphoria," Skip Hanson said. "I felt so good for the kids, because they had worked so hard for four years and they were good kids to coach."

"We were crushed," Baran said. "There was no question about it. We were so pissed off we just wanted to get out of there. We didn't know what to do."

Foxcroft fans started chanting "We're No. 1!" That was the typical universal chant of champions in 1975, which was two years before Queen created "We Are the Champions."

The FA Band played on, belting out the school song—"Oh Foxcroft We All Assemble"—to celebrate. Foxcroft, the best! One FA Band member, Earl Moulen, pounded his base drum so hard and so often that the drumsticks broke through the drum.

The Ponies cheerleaders, all eight of them, danced with joy.

"I was dating John Warren at the time, and he was at the game, so I went running over to him and jumped into his arms," said FA cheerleader Lindy Strout. "He wasn't nearly excited as I was."

It was the culmination of a championship dream decades in the making. After so many years of falling short of expectations, Foxcroft Academy fans had a team that exceeded more than they could have hoped for. Some might say it was pure fantasy, which wouldn't be too far off. February 28 is now National Tooth Fairy Day.

The Ponies left their fans with a season they will forever adore. The No. 1 song on Billboard's Top 100 that day was the Eagles' "The Best of My Love."

The Foxcroft Academy Ponies were finally state basketball champions.

"It had been something that had been building that whole season," John Champeon said. "It was like a magic carpet ride."

John was among the many delirious FA fans who ran onto the court at the final buzzer. But he had a purpose. He wanted to grab the game ball to make sure it got in the right hands to place in the Foxcroft Academy trophy case in the gym back home.

"I remember thinking, 'Well, we can't let just some Joe Schmo grab that ball. We need to have that ball for the trophy case," Champeon said. "I was going to be the big hero and get us the ball, and I made a beeline for it. I was probably three feet away from catching it and someone else reached out for it and I ran full blown right into the guy's elbow and broke my nose. They had to find a handkerchief. I had tears running down my face, half because I was happy that we won and half because my nose hurt like hell."

Years later, John's broken nose story was recounted to his brother and father.

"He's got a pretty good-sized target there," Joe said.

"Where did he get it?" said their dad, who has the most recognizable nose in the Champeon family.

Kevin Nelson—who averaged 25.5 points per game in the regular season and 25.1 ppg in tournament games—followed the Ponies' players one by one up the step ladder to cut down the ceremonial nets. He was the last one to snip and waved the net in circles above his head. His crowning achievement of the 1974–75 season came on the night of his mother's forty-first birthday.

Skip Hanson invited the retiring Lap Lary to join him on the court to revel in the victory, and Todd Hanson also rushed to the coach's side. A memorable photo was taken of Todd being hugged by his father, who was sitting in front of Foxcroft Academy principal Bob Perkins, who was patting Skip Hanson on the shoulder as he sat waiting for the postgame awards ceremony.

"I don't remember much about the game besides winning, but I do remember distinctly running down on the court and dodging my way around people and finding my dad and sitting in his lap," Todd said. "We used that picture in our media guide at Brunswick High."

The photo was one of the few times Skip Hanson sat and relaxed all night. He had been pacing the sidelines and used all of his timeouts in the fourth quarter to keep his team composed.

Weeks later, Skip received a letter from Tony Hamlin praising him for his Dean Smith–like strategy of using timeouts and the four-corners offense to keep the game under control.

"For you to beat Medomak you had to be really good because Art Dyer's teams were tough defensively. They were patient. They were disciplined. He was a great coach," Tony Hamlin said. "So for FA to beat them in a state championship game, even though it was close, speaks volumes because they beat a hell of a good team."

One that Scott Graffam figured could beat Foxcroft.

Graffam, who later coached the Panthers, had analyzed the two state championship combatants before the game and had created in his mind his own blueprint for a Medomak victory.

"When the game first started, I said, 'If Al Baran scores 15 points and Kevin Nelson scores 25, Medomak will win the game.' But what happened is Medomak had a great offensive team and Kevin Nelson changed the whole game with his blocked shots," Graffam said. "Russell Luce made 17 field goals in the Western Maine semifinals—it might still be a Western Maine record—and scored 34 points. He was 0-for-8 against Foxcroft. Dean Erickson, who became one of the best players in the state, was only a sophomore at the time, but he was 0-for-6. So if those two players score 10 points apiece, Medomak would have scored 70 and they held Foxcroft to 56. So they did the job defensively, and Kevin got 25 and Baran got 17. If you had told me that before the game, I would have said there's not a chance that Medomak would lose."

Then how did the Ponies win?

"Foxcroft won because of Kevin Nelson," Graffam said. "If you look at the ten top players in that game, Kevin was first and the next four best players were on Medomak and Foxcroft had the next four. Those four for Foxcroft didn't score very well, but they rebounded well. The other thing Skip Hanson did was, Medomak was a pressing team and he had Kevin come down to the foul line and they would lob the ball into him and he held onto it and let everyone clear and they broke the press. So, Medomak never got any turnovers and they lived by that in the Western Maine Tournament."

Nelson, in addition, believes Medomak underestimated the heart of the Ponies and their will to win.

"There was a time during the week I took notice that they started 6–6, 6–4, 6–4 up front and I thought, 'Are they going to roll us?' I don't know if that acted as motivation or more fear to make us play well," said Nelson, who finished the game with 25 points, 26 rebounds, and 4 blocked shots. "I respect Art Dyer so much. But even though he was a hard driver of his players, I really think he might have thought that maybe we, Foxcroft, didn't have the team he thought we had and that he made a very grave error if he felt that way. The kids on our team knew how to play well and they knew how to play together and win."

They knew how to celebrate, too. Publicly and privately.

"The celebration can be divided into two parts," Jeff Dunn said. "The celebration on the floor afterwards was fantastic. Every fan of Foxcroft stayed for the end of the game, but nobody just went to their car afterward to beat the traffic. Everybody was out on the floor, just milling around and celebrating. That was a really special time for the team. It topped off the year of support we had. That court was jammed with people."

"I just remember relief and going into the locker room with this enormous amount of relief. There was just a lot of pressure. I hadn't felt that kind of pressure to that extent," Nelson said. "A lot of coaches who were recruiting came up to see me. Looking back on it years later, I'm glad they got to see a great game."

After the game, Kiah and Clement were gleefully thrown into the locker room showers and doused. Several Foxcroft players visited the Medomak locker room as, unlike now, there was no routine or ritual where opponents exchange handshakes in a postgame sportsmanship gesture on the court.

Baran was lamenting the loss and Medomak's missed opportunities, including his clutch rebound when he might have drawn a fifth foul on Nelson. Baran's rebound shot with fifty-some seconds remaining may have been destined to give the Panthers the lead until Nelson blocked it in a do-or-die play.

"That, to me, was the turning point of the game," Baran said. "For a long time, I blocked that out of mind. I owe Kevin credit on that one. He got me. There's no doubt. I'm not too proud to admit it. Without video who the hell will ever know, but there's enough to know that I had confidence if I make that shot we've got a hell of a chance of winning that game that had been torturing us the last hour and a half. But it didn't work."

While Medomak Valley fans were wallowing in the defeat, Foxcroft fans were cheering at the top of their lungs on their way home.

Infamous sign-maker Neil Johnston celebrated Foxcroft's victory at a nearby fast food restaurant. He was shouting "Icky Icky Gower, We've Got Pony Power" for all to hear.

"He was right on top of a table singing that," Jim Robinson said. "Everybody who was there was clapping and asking, 'Where did this guy come from?' Everybody thought he was under the influence, but he wasn't."

Ted Harvey, Neil Johnston's sign-making buddy, was reveling in his good fortune. Before the game, he had supper at a Chinese restaurant and his fortune cookie contained a message so encouraging that it indicated, in his mind, an FA win and he came within a point of predicting the final score.

The student booster busses returned to Dover-Foxcroft all smiles for many miles. They were all hoarse from chanting "We're No. 1!" and "We Are FA!"

"It was a natural thrill all the way home, yet as we got closer, our excitement could not be contained," said Dianne Albee, who had been a cheerleader for the Ponies earlier in the season.

"The first people to hear our excitement was the town of Dexter. Down went the bus windows and out came our fingers. Not the usual middle one, but the one signifying Foxcroft was No. 1."

By the time busses passed Burtchell's Market and started the descent down South Street into downtown Dover-Foxcroft, the windows were opened again. There were a group of people standing outside LaVerdiere's drugstore waiting to greet the student busses as they turned onto West Main Street.

"We spread our victory with unison cries of 'We're No. 1!'" Dianne said. "I swear, we floated off that bus when we got to Foxcroft Academy and not one person was without a big smile. Hugs and sore voices accompanied us as we found our rides home. And, boy, was my dad, Earl, so happy."

The bus that Grace Dean Langley was on also pulled into the FA parking lot. Her husband, Rick, had stayed back with her mother at the house and it's a good thing they did because the attic fire had rekindled.

Fate comes in many forms. That attic fire allowed Grace the opportunity to use her mother's ticket to go to the greatest basketball game in Foxcroft Academy history.

Meanwhile, Part Two of the Ponies' postgame celebration was underway at the Holiday Inn. The Foxcroft team had retreated in their Greyhound bus to their hotel about two miles away from the Augusta Civic Center. They left the facility after taking one last team photo with Kevin Nelson kneeling with the game ball and Mark Joyce holding the Gold Ball and players either signaling No. 1 or victory or simply beaming from ear to ear.

Back at the hotel, the jubilation continued. The Ponies' coaching staff and their wives went to visit Peg Hanson's cousin, who lived in Augusta. That was their post-state championship party location.

The basketball team remained at the Holiday Inn (now a Hampton Inn). The "World's Innkeeper" couldn't contain the players' excitement.

"I kicked myself for leaving and going over there and not staying to monitor them," Skip Hanson said.

"We were running around. We didn't know what to do," Mark Joyce said. "This wasn't our place. We didn't have a friend's house to go to. We were all pent up and no place to go."

The drinking age in the state of Maine at the time was eighteen, and most of the FA team were of legal age. Some players managed to get six packs of beer to their rooms, and they stacked the beer into the bathtubs in a couple of the rooms and covered the beer with ice from the ice machines in the hotel.

Some other players decided to prance through the hotel's bar. Kevin Nelson remembers seeing Roy Taylor, a starter on the 1968 Monson Academy state championship team, when he walked through the bar/restaurant.

"It was very jovial and friendly at the Holiday Inn," Tim King said. "I think that was the first time I had a screwdriver, and then I graduated to mai tais."

By the next morning, the coaches had been made aware of the players' assorted activities. Nothing was broken or stolen. No one was hurt. No harm. No foul. No arrests. The boys were just in a celebratory mode.

"The coaches were pretty unhappy with us after our behavior the night before and rightfully so," Dunn said. "We were young and at the time the state drinking age was eighteen, and most of us were eligible to drink. We took advantage of that."

They also paid for it.

"It was a quiet bus going home. We were all hungover," Peter Snow said.

The mood on the bus ride home changed once the team's chartered bus steered off Interstate 95 at the Newport exit, about 28 miles from Dover-Foxcroft. As the bus prepared to turn left onto Route 7, there were Foxcroft Academy fans already with signs on the side of the road, waving and cheering wildly. The team had no idea of the homecoming that awaited them ahead.

When the team bus drove through the tiny town of Corinna—about 21 miles from Dover-Foxcroft—it was greeted with a fire truck escort. But it wasn't the Dover Volunteer Fire Department. It was the Dexter Volunteer Fire Department.

Wait! What? Dexter never bends over backward for Dover and vice versa.

Because Dover and Dexter are longtime natural rivals, Skip Hanson never considered asking Dexter coach Ed Guiski for his help to give Foxcroft a scouting report on Medomak Valley prior to state championship game. Guiski and Panthers coach Art Dyer were friends.

"After it was all done and over with, I jokingly said to Ed that he did a pretty good job of telling Art about our offense, defense, and special plays," Hanson said. "With a big grin, Ed replied, 'Not good enough.'"

To celebrate the Ponies' state championship game victory, the Dover Volunteer Fire Department had asked the Dexter Volunteer Fire Department to intercept the Ponies' chartered bus, according to Rick Pembroke, who served more than fifty years as a volunteer firefighter including six as fire chief in Monson and fifteen as fire chief in Dover. The plan called for the Dexter FD to escort the team through Dexter to the Piscataquis County line, where the Dover FD would escort the team into town down South Street then left up Main Street. Skip Hanson later sent a thank-you letter to the Dexter FD.

The Ponies were absolutely stunned by the community's response to their state championship win throughout the area. Announcements on WDME radio, a blurb in the last paragraph of the *Bangor Daily News* game story, and word of mouth on the street alerted their fans of their estimated time of arrival back in Dover-Foxcroft. Groves of Ponies' fans were gathering.

"This is Nokomis and they're doing this? Then Corinna? And then Dexter? C'mon! We were brutal enemies in the sports realm," Tim King said. "This impressed a lot of us. It was surreal. It was definitely surreal. It was like riding a surfboard on a perfect wave and it culminates when you come out of the wave at the academy."

As the bus passed Peter Snow's house near the Board Eddy Road on the Dexter Road, neighbor Jane Grant had made a sign that read: 22–0 THANKS, CHAMPS!

Another sign down the road got the Ponies' attention, too. It read: HALE ATE HIS WORDS.

By the time the chartered bus rolled down South Street into the edge of downtown, it was apparent that the homecoming was going to be epic. Horns were honking. Sirens were blaring. People were waving, cheering, and smiling on both sides of the streets.

"That was tremendous," Peter Snow said. "There were people just about at every house on every street all the way up to the high school and the high school was just packed."

Though it was cold out and beginning to snow, the players opened the bus windows and waved to fans from both sides of the bus. They also stuck out their arms and pretended like they were flying.

"Like Big Bird flapping his wings," Mark Joyce said. "And it just got crazy from there. People were leaving their homes to come out and see us. I haven't experienced anything like that since."

It was a homecoming parade for the ages following a victory for the ages.

"We felt like kings just being able to ride it," Dunn said.

"The atmosphere around town was electric," said Mark "Bagga" Stevens, FA Class of 1972. "Most of the pundits thought we would lose. They thought 6–6, 230 pound Alan Baran would be too much for Kevin Nelson. They were wrong. Nelson dominated that game."

"There was elation after the game, but we wondered our fate after the hallowed Nelson era. Would we ever get a Gold Ball again?" said Jim Harvey, FA Class of 1966.

The homecoming state championship celebration peaked in front of a full house in the Foxcroft Academy gymnasium. Each coach and player was asked to speak. There was no shortage of gratitude and ovations.

By the time the state championship reception ended in the Foxcroft Academy gym, there were already three or four inches of fresh snow on the ground outside and it was still dumping.

Ironically, there was a full moon above those snowstorm clouds that night. Spiritually, a full moon symbolizes a time of release and completion, the culmination of positive energy after a period of work or effort.

The players, who were partied out from the night before, pretty much went their separate ways after the state championship reception at Foxcroft Academy. A small group did gather at Kenny Burtchell's place next to South Street Market.

"The flurry of activity that went on those forty-eight hours or whatever after the game was overwhelming," Kevin Nelson said.

Some fans may have stayed inside that Saturday night to watch the 17th Annual Grammy Awards on television. It was a feel-good day and night and there was a lot of love in the air. Barbra Streisand's "The Way We Were" was named Song of the Year and Olivia Newton-John's "I Honestly Love You" was named Record of the Year. Art Garfunkel accepted the award on her behalf from Paul Simon and John Lennon.

The Ponies coaching staff was in a spirited mood. They were celebrating at Wayne Champeon's house. However, their party was interrupted by a phone call from Southeast Monson. Rose Nelson was inviting Skip and everyone to her house to celebrate with her and Hollis.

"It was snowing. And those roads? But she just wanted Skip and the coaches there so off we went. We were probably crazy to do it, but you get caught up in the moment," Peg Hanson said. "You couldn't say no to Rose. It was a very nice celebration and Rose had enough food to feed the town of Monson."

The Champeon state championship party moved from Mayo Street to Steward Road, 20 miles away.

"We had enough trucks to get us up there through the snow and I'm glad we did. We had a good time," Skip Hanson said. "We didn't get home until probably 3:30 or 4 in the morning."

Hanson was in such a good mood that he had forgotten where he placed the keys to his truck. It took him two weeks to find them, partly because there seemingly was one party after another.

"We celebrated right up to baseball season," Kiah said. "Every weekend there seemed to be a party. That was unbelievable."

The whole season was unbelievable. The probability of a high school player such as Kevin Nelson going on to play NCAA Division I basketball is about 1 percent. It's even more minuscule for someone to do it from a town the size of Monson. Or *Southeast* Monson.

The accomplishment of a team winning a state basketball championship and going undefeated in the process is so rare and exclusive. For the players who do it, it's their crowning achievement in high school and, for the vast majority of them, the greatest athletic feat in their lifetimes. While college and professional athletes nowadays talk about and expound on their quest to win a championship ring, high school athletes treasure their forever team trophy. Winning a Gold Ball is the pinnacle of their playing careers.

For nearly half a century, that Gold Ball from 1975 has rested front and center in the trophy case in the Foxcroft Academy gym lobby. It's a perpetual gleaming, shining reminder of probably the greatest sports championship in the 200-plus-year history of the school, its one and only Gold Ball. Foxcroft's crowned jewel of joy.

While Dover-Foxcroft basked in the glow of the Gold Ball the Ponies brought back from their state basketball championship triumph in 1975, Monson was quieter and more private in the way it celebrated the triumph.

In fact, the Nelsons' neighbor, and Hollis' cousin, Thurley Knowles, had taken what looked like an empty furniture or appliance box—quite large—and flattened it to create with others a large sign to commemorate Foxcroft Academy's state title. She wanted to celebrate Foxcroft's state basketball championship in her own way with a nod toward Kevin Nelson and his family that spoke volumes about the way Monson viewed the feat.

The sign read: MONSON POWER KEVIN NELSON HELPS PONIES.

That sign had been stored away and was discovered thirty-nine years later in 2014 when Shawn found it in the Nelson family barn in Southeast Monson, while he was clearing out the place to sell the property. It immediately became a collector's item.

"It was one of those family things. She was so proud of what we had done. She was a Monson person and she was proud of the fact that somebody from Monson—whether it be me or anybody else—could be successful at Dover," Kevin Nelson said. "I'm not sure if it was her who made the sign or if she had someone else do it for her, but her finger-prints are all over it."

It was a rectangular sign encompassing a full-circle moment. Kevin Nelson's basketball path was supposed to be through Monson, where he was destined to win at least one state championship for the Slaters. But a school consolidation sent him in another direction, toward Dover-Foxcroft and the Ponies.

"In 1969, when Monson Academy closed its doors forever due to consolidation, I was too young to fully appreciate the profound sense of loss felt by many Monson Academy alumni and residents of the town," Kevin Nelson said. "I can't speak for all the folks in Monson, but I'm fairly certain that six short years after the closing of Monson Academy, Thurley was especially proud of the fact that someone from Monson played a key role in helping the FA Ponies go undefeated and win a state basketball championship."

That sign is now preserved and prominently displayed upstairs in the Monson Historical Society. It lies a few feet from the last Gold Ball the Slaters won for Monson Academy in 1968.

Thurley also sent a handwritten two-page congratulatory letter to Kevin a week after the state championship victory in 1975, which she said, "never would have happened without you." She had attended the state title game in Augusta and the homecoming celebration in Dover-Foxcroft the next day but wished she had been able to attend more Foxcroft Academy games while working at Hardwood Products in Guilford, where she worked the night shift for forty-three years.

In the letter, Thurley, who died in 2006 at the age of ninety-two, promised to cut out newspaper clippings from the games and store them in a folder. The letter included a handmade bookmark Thurley created with a photo of Kevin on one side and Skip Hanson on the other.

"P.S., Oh yes. We are keeping the folder in the Monson Historical records as years from now someone may say, or want to know, facts forgotten," Thurley wrote. "Who was the Monson power, who did they play and the score."

Kevin Nelson has kept that letter all these years. In his mind, all's well that ends well.

"For people in my family, there was element that had a certain provincial to it. There were Monson people who thought bad things, though," Nelson said. "What prevailed above all that emotion was happiness that we won this major prize. High school basketball in Maine, regardless whether you're in Fort Kent or you're in Kittery, it's the same deal. In the wintertime basketball is the central figure in a lot of these small towns. It is the primary source of entertainment and a major source of enormous civic pride. Particularly when the team is winning."

And turning out the lights.

The Epilogue and Everlasting Impact

THIS IS THE HAPPILY-EVER-AFTER PART.

When the parades end, the memories last, and the Gold Ball is put away for prosperity. When the once-in-a-lifetime undefeated team grows up while its legend grows as other teams who follow them fall short of the standard they set. When a dream-come-true season morphs into questions such as "remember when," "whatever happened to" and "where are they now?"

Kevin Nelson—after winning a state championship for Foxcroft Academy, having his uniform number retired in the FA gym and committing to play college basketball at the University of Maine—returned to the Monson Academy gymnasium.

Not so much as a conquering hero, but for a summer job working for the Dover-Foxcroft Parks and Recreation Department. Whereas Nelson's return to the Monson gym lacked the fanfare that he experienced when the 1968 state champion Slaters triumphantly came home, it still had a life-altering impact on a young kid. As Buddy Leavitt was to him, Kevin Nelson was a hero in the eyes of a youngster in that gym named Dean Smith.

"Monson being as small as it is, the Nelson family were friends," Dean Smith recalled. "I was introduced to Kevin initially when he was a summer recreation coach/counselor and he took time to introduce me and my friends to many different sports—including basketball. But probably the most significant aspect of my interactions with Kevin was related to his introduction of me to boxing."

Wait. What? *Boxing!* Did Jimmy Chitwood become Mickey Goldmill?

"We were in the Monson gym one day and I placed a mat on the floor to simulate a makeshift boxing ring," Kevin said. "Dean was mixing it up pretty good with a kid named Robbie Sawyer, who was about four or five years older and much larger than him. Dean never backed down. Thankfully, Robbie was a good kid and things didn't escalate although, looking back, it was probably not one of my more responsible decisions to let them go at it in the first place. I'm very grateful that no blood was spilled. . . . Whew!"

But there was a valuable lesson learned. Dean—the son of Jake and Glenda (Brown) Smith—thought he was annoying Kevin and that was the reason behind him being paired against a taller, stronger kid to box. Dean thought it might be a form of punishment. It ended up being an inspirational moment.

"Kevin decided to have me box a much older and bigger kid—likely to have me be put into my place," Dean said. "I had never boxed. I had no idea what I was doing, but as soon as I got hit—once a fire was ignited in me—I did not stop swinging. I would not give in and let a bigger, more experienced kid beat me. If Kevin would not have intervened, I am not sure that I would have stopped."

Essentially, Kevin's boxing challenge brought something out of Dean—an inner confidence or competitiveness—that was a revelation. Whatever Kevin's intentions might have been, they served as a critical moment in Dean's development.

"From that day on, I paid special attention to Kevin and his path and I wanted to follow it," Dean said. "He was a great role model from a time and a place where I needed one."

Like Kevin Nelson, Dean Smith wound up attending Foxcroft Academy and became an extraordinary student-athlete and star basketball player.

"Every day upon entering FA I saw the state championship ball and the net and pictures with Kevin holding it," Dean said. "He was an inspiration in leadership and the virtues of hard work."

Like Kevin Nelson, Dean Smith went on to play basketball at the University of Maine where he made an indelible mark. He was a three-time Academic All-American and, in 1990, was named the recipient of the

NCAA's Walter Byers Award as the nation's top scholar-athlete. He had the top grade point average among electrical engineering majors at UMO. The University named an award after him, which is given annually to the top female and male student-athletes at Maine.

Dean Smith is now Vice President for Engineering at Orono Spectral Solutions in Hermon. In 1987, both he and Kevin Nelson received Distinguished Athletic Citizenship Awards from Foxcroft Academy and, in 2016, they were both inducted into the Maine Basketball Hall of Fame.

Many years after their first meeting in the Monson Academy gym, Dean Smith surprised Kevin Nelson with a thank-you gift—a pair of boxing gloves.

The moral of this story? Though there is physical evidence of Foxcroft Academy's one-and-only state basketball championship and a trophy case and scrapbook of memories to last a lifetime, the impact of that accomplishment and the people behind it lasts forever. And while Kevin Nelson was never given a chance to try to win a state basketball championship in Monson, his imprint on the community is immeasurable. It pays it forward after all the accolades end. Greatness breeds greatness.

The praise and attention kept coming for the Foxcroft state champions in their March of madness in 1975. The team received a proclamation and congratulations from the Maine State Legislature for its achievement, and the hometown heroes received maroon-and-white vinyl jackets with an "FA" patch on the front and "Class B 1975 State Champions 22–0" embedded on a basketball logo on the back.

These kudos came at a postseason winter sports awards banquet with Maine coach Skip Chappelle as guest speaker. The 1975 state title team was honored in the Foxcroft Academy gym, where it was announced that Kevin Nelson's No. 20 uniform would be the first jersey number retired in FA's athletic history.

The final score of the tension-filled, pressure-packed state championship game appeared on the scoreboards in the Foxcroft Academy gym at that post-championship season banquet. When a buzzer sounded, it was the cue for FA principal Bob Perkins to turn to Skip Hanson and joke, "Skip, I think we finally won the game."

Sadly, Perkins lost a brief battle with cancer five months later at the age of forty-nine. More than 350 FA teachers, trustees, and students attended his memorial service. The *Piscataquis Observer* published a story along with the unforgettable and touching photo of Bob standing and draping his right arm around the shoulders of Skip who was sitting and holding his son, Todd, during the state championship postgame trophy presentation in the Augusta Civic Center.

About a week after the special inaugural Winter Sports Banquet at Foxcroft Academy, the Maine High School Basketball Coach of the Year award was announced at a banquet in Brunswick that Skip, because of a previous obligation, did not attend. Ron Marks, who preceded Skip as coach at Foxcroft, was given the honor of calling Skip to tell him that he had been selected and announced as Coach of the Year.

The Foxcroft Academy Trustees also rewarded Skip for his coaching contribution. They gifted him a new aluminum Old Town canoe with paddles and four lifejackets. It's still being used by the Hanson grandchildren at the Hanson family camp at Sebec Lake.

"It meant so much to Skip when they thanked him because they thought about his whole family," Peg Hanson said. "It meant everything to him. He achieved his goal. That's what his goal was, and he worked very hard to accomplish it. It was a big sense of pride with him to be able to do it, especially in his hometown and just give back to the town."

To put the Ponies' Gold Ball achievement in historical perspective, that state championship game was won on February 28, 1975 B.C. That's B.C. as in Before Cooper was born. The Duke University recruit Cooper Flagg, who grew up in Newport, is projected to be a top pick, if not No. 1 overall, in the NBA Draft in 2025. As the Maine State Player of the Year as a freshman, the 6-foot-9 Flagg led Nokomis High School to a state championship then transferred to Montverde Academy in Florida.

In 1975, Kevin Nelson was Maine's Cooper Flagg, the most sought-after schoolboy basketball player in state history.

"He was The One at the time," Skip Chappelle said.

Chappelle won the Kevin Nelson Sweepstakes and signed Kevin to play his college basketball at the University of Maine. Kevin wanted to stay close to home so his parents could attend his games. His father bought a used front-wheel drive Jeep Wagoneer, because he and Rose planned to attend their youngest son's games even if the roads to Orono or elsewhere were dicey in the wintertime. The Nelsons even joined the Gerrishes—Henry and Louise—in Boston when Kevin played there.

"A lot of good stuff came from my mom and dad. I really am a product of them. No question about it," Kevin said.

Kevin was home in Southeast Monson when word leaked out that he had signed a letter of intent to play basketball at the University of Maine. He became the first-ever in-state student-athlete at UMO to receive a full-ride basketball scholarship from the Black Bears.

"It was a coup for Skip Chappelle to recruit Kevin successfully," said WEMT's Dave Cheever. "Nelson had enough credentials that he could have gone to a number of schools. Orono was convenient, and I think it fit with his academic interests, too."

"I remember being in my bedroom after I made the decision and I heard Steve Martin from WABI and he had it on the news that I made a decision where I was going to college," Nelson said. "To me that was a huge moment."

Steve Martin had a fifty-year broadcasting career that culminated with him being the radio play-by-play announcer for the NBA's Charlotte Hornets since the franchise's inception in 1988. He retired in 2018.

Kevin Nelson was part of Skip Chappelle's "Fab Five" class at the University of Maine, which included Brian Butterfield from Orono High School. Medomak Valley's Al Baran also was recruited to Maine but transferred to Husson College before completing his collegiate basketball career at Thomas College.

Medomak Valley won its first Gold Ball in 1977 with Dean Erickson leading the way. The Panthers won another state championship game in 1980 with an undefeated season for Art Dyer. He coached Medomak Valley from 1970 to 1980, accumulating a 164–34 regular season record as the Panthers made the tournament for ten consecutive seasons. Their record was 21–9 in regional and state tournament games. Art Dyer was inducted into the Maine Basketball Hall of Fame in 2015 along with Wayne Champeon and George Hale.

Kevin Nelson and Al Baran, who played on the Black Bears' JV team, became good friends. In fact, Kevin said he wishes Al had stayed at UMO as his basketball teammate. Al retired in 2023 from his job as senior property manager at Dirigo Management Company in Portland.

"I saw a number of 6–5, 6–6 guys come through Orono. There were five freshmen my freshman year at UMO. Skip Chappelle selected five freshmen," Nelson said. "He should have selected six because we needed somebody like Al who could rebound, who was quick and could play inside and was a good teammate."

Nelson had an outstanding career at Maine. In ninety-three games and as a three-year starter, he scored more than 1,000 points and averaged 11.7 points per game plus 8.1 rebounds per game. He had a career-best 33 points in a game against the University of Buffalo and a career-best 19 rebounds in a game against Fairleigh Dickinson.

"It was fun to watch him and fun to watch his movement," Chappelle said. "When we first recruited him, he seemed to be quite physical. We were looking for that. He seemed to be able to take a knock and give a knock."

In his senior year, Nelson was team co-captain when the Black Bears hosted Marquette University in front of a sold-out Cumberland County Civic Center crowd in Portland. He scored 14 points with 11 rebounds in the 55–46 loss while holding Marquette All-American 6–9 center Bernard Toone to 13 points and 8 rebounds. Toone was selected in the second round, 37th overall, by the Philadelphia 76ers in the 1979 NBA Draft and played in the 1979–80 NBA Championship Finals against the Los Angeles Lakers. Toone fouled Magic Johnson in the final seconds of the clinching Game 6 when Magic moved to center to replace the injured Kareem Abdul Jabbar. Magic sank those two free throws to finish with a game-high 42 points along with 15 rebounds that led to him becoming the only rookie to win the NBA Finals MVP award.

Toone, who also played on Marquette's NCAA championship team in 1977, died in 2022 at the age of sixty-five.

Only two players born in Maine—Duncan Robinson of York, who plays for the Miami Heat, and Jeff Turner of Bangor, who was a first-round pick by the New Jersey Nets in 1984—have played in the NBA. They both grew up outside the state. The next native Mainer expected to play in the NBA is Cooper Flagg.

When Kevin Nelson left UMO—the only NCAA Division I basketball school in the state—he was the third-leading rebounder in Black Bears' men's basketball history (now seventh) and he ranked 20th all-time at Maine in career points through the 2023–24 season. Nelson's .545 career field goal shooting percentage still ranks among the best in Black Bears' history, though he admits that he rarely took a shot outside 15 to 18 feet and, when he was a freshman, dunking was against NCAA rules.

"The rule had been in place since 1967 and the NCAA rescinded it effective my sophomore year," Nelson said. "I remember we were playing CCNY [the City College of New York] in December 1976 at The Pit on the Orono campus when I received a pass at the top of the key, faked my defender left, drove past him to the basket and jammed it home for the first legal college dunk at UMO in almost ten years. The Pit erupted, plus I'm pretty sure we won the game. While I still have fond memories of that thrill, I wish that the NCAA had allowed the dunk four years earlier, because 6–foot-7 Bob Warner would have electrified the gym with his incredible vertical leap combined with his immense physical power. So very sad. He would have put on quite a show."

Skip Hanson attended many of Kevin's games at UMO. He coached the boys varsity basketball team at Foxcroft one more year. The 1974–75 team, Skip was reminded, was loaded with athletic players before that class graduated, perhaps the best class of athletes to come through Foxcroft Academy since the 1939–40 school year when the Ponies' football and boys basketball teams both went undefeated.

After the FA Class of 1975 moved on, there apparently were not enough good athletes left in the cupboard. The 1975 Foxcroft Academy football team went winless, 0–9. It was outscored 267–8 for the season and failed to score in its final seven games. One of the losses on the grid-iron was a 38–0 defeat to Orono.

When the 1975–76 Foxcroft Academy basketball season started, co-captain Ken Burtchell delivered a passionate and expletive-filled speech in the locker room before the season-opening game at Orono High School. It evidently had a positive impact for one night. Foxcroft came out fired up, another scuffle between players broke out in an Orono-Foxcroft game, and the Ponies prevailed 77-75 when cocaptain Peter Snow hit the game-winning shot. Snow had 30 points, and Burtchell scored 20.

"We're defending state champions, but we've never even done this before. That's a little daunting," John Champeon said. "We wind up beating Orono again in the season opener in overtime, and we're thinking in the locker room we might win the state championship again! Then, on the following Tuesday, we go to over to Milo to play Penquis Valley. I got the first two baskets of the game and they responded. They scored 20 straight points. That's when I realized this 1975–76 season has taken on a whole new meaning. We were behind by 40 at one point."

Penquis Valley—led by Dickie DeWitt, Eben DeWitt's son—won 77–47, and Patriots fans started chanting, "It's All Over, We Beat Dover." That became a common refrain throughout the season in the Penquis League.

"My brother always said Skip Hanson got the Coach of the Year Award in 1975 when they won the state championship," Joe Champeon said. "John said Skip didn't deserve it that year, but he sure as hell deserved it the next year getting six wins out of us with Tim Hanson and him as his backcourt."

Foxcroft finished the 1975–76 season with a record of 6–12, Skip Hanson's only losing season with the Ponies. Still, his six-year record of 90–47 remains the best in school history. Since the 1975 state title season, only two other Foxcroft teams have ever advanced to the Eastern Maine Boys Basketball Tournament finals. The first was the 1979 FA team coached by Rusty Clukey and led by Rick McLeish that lost to Bucksport 76–63 in the Eastern Maine title game. Bucksport went on to beat Medomak Valley 45–43 in the state championship game.

The Ponies' incredible season in 1974–75 has never been duplicated. From 1980 to 2001, Foxcroft missed the tournament seventeen times in twenty years and won only one Eastern Maine Tournament game in that span. During those two decades, there were thirteen head coaching changes at Foxcroft. No one has come close to matching Skip Hanson's enduring success with the Ponies in the Penquis League.

"Foxcroft had a thirty-eight-game league winning streak during that period of time and I played in the last victory of that streak in 1975," Ernie Clark said. "We went from a 6–9 center to about a 5–11 center. I played with Timmy Hanson—Skip's younger brother. They put up pictures of all the teams that were part of the winning streak. To this day, I say the best thing you could have done with us was to put up a picture of us all wearing paper bags over our heads. We paid for the success of the senior-ladened team before us. They, our opponents, thought they got even, but we still had that Gold Ball."

For the record, Skip Hanson coached basketball another year at Foxcroft Academy. He returned to the sidelines with the Ponies' girls basketball team in 1979–80 as a favor to FA principal Jim Steenstra who needed someone at the last minute to coach them.

"I knew they weren't very good, but I had a ton of fun. They were good kids," Skip said. "One game Rusty Clukey was walking by and joked, 'You can't win without Kevin.'"

The Ponies' girls team ended the season with a 2–16 record. The last high school basketball game Skip Hanson coached was a 72–23 loss to Stearns.

The next year, the Ponies' boys basketball team, coached by Clukey, went 14–4 and beat Van Buren and Madawaska in the Eastern Maine Tournament before losing to Orono in the semifinals. Peter Ingraham, Dave's younger brother, was a senior on that FA team.

That's the year Skip Hanson's career transitioned to school administration. He became the principal at Piscataquis County High School in Guilford. Dave Gaw, the illustrious baseball coach for the Pirates, was the athletics director at PCHS, and he had a beef with Skip when it came to Monson consolidating with Foxcroft Academy, which meant Kevin Nelson would ride past PCHS in a school bus each weekday.

"Probably twice a week Dave would say to me, 'You son of a bitch. I used to stand in the window and I would watch the SAD 68 bus go by and all I could see was a guy's shoulders and I couldn't see his head. How did you ever get him?'"

"You could have had him," Skip quipped. "I'm sorry."

Years later Skip was hired as principal at Waterville High School. He had to convince his son, Todd, to leave PCHS to play in Waterville. Todd had grown up from "Toad" into a terrific basketball player.

Al Baran also took time to visit Skip Hanson when they were both working in Waterville. Baran, who came to have so much respect for Foxcroft, Kevin Nelson, and Skip Hanson, dropped in out of the blue to say hello to Skip.

"Coach, I'm Al Baran. Do you remember me?'" Baran asked.

"Remember you?" Skip replied. "I still *fear* you."

The Maine Basketball Hall of Fame in Bangor inducted its inaugural class in 2014, which included Skip Chappelle and Jim DiFrederico. Wayne Champeon was inducted in 2015 along with Medomak Valley coach Art Dyer. George Hale was inducted among "Legends of the Game."

In 2016, Kevin Nelson was inducted into the Maine Basketball Hall of Fame along with Ed Guiski, Ron Marks, Tony Hamlin, and former boxer Dean Smith.

Finally, in 2023 in ceremonies at the Cross Insurance Center in Bangor, Skip Hanson and the 1975 Foxcroft Academy boys basketball team were inducted into the Maine Basketball Hall of Fame. It was on the same day that Skip was inducted as a "Legend of the Game" for his coaching accomplishments and his service on multiple committees for the Maine Principals' Association as an athletics director, high school principal, assistant superintendent, and school superintendent before he retired in 2011.

Skip Hanson's induction came in the same ceremony that Todd Hanson was inducted into the Maine Basketball Hall of Fame and introduced as the new executive director of the Maine Basketball Hall of Fame. Todd was inducted along with Medomak Valley's Scott Graffam. Scott's brother, Jeff, was in the group of "Legends of the Game" along with Skip.

Dennis Kiah and Dave Clement attended that ceremony as did Wayne Champeon. Skip was onstage when the 1975 Foxcroft Academy state championship boys basketball team was inducted into the Maine Basketball Hall of Fame. Skip and eight team members—Kevin Nelson, Jeff Dunn, Jeff Brown, Ken Burtchell, Peter Snow, Roger Hewitt, Scott Mountford, and Tim King—were present. Art Dyer and Al Baran were in the audience.

Kevin Nelson spoke on behalf of the newest Maine Basketball Hall of Fame team, the only boys basketball team in Maine to go undefeated in 1975 and the only one from Eastern Maine to win a state championship that year.

"Our roster was comprised of twelve kids—nine of which were seniors. We had a number of very gifted and accomplished multi-sport athletes. Football. Baseball. Track and field as well as basketball. As a group we had a very high basketball IQ. We were good friends off the court. But the characteristic that we all shared was our competitiveness. Once we stepped on the court, either in practice or games, we were all business," Nelson said.

"Now, with no disrespect to the teams we played that season, I'd have to say many of our most intense and physically draining games were our own scrimmages. Losing was not an option and this attitude carried over to the games we played against other schools during that regular season, through the Christmas tournament we held and all through the Class B tournament.

"Lastly, for those of you who may be wondering what kind of an impact an undefeated high school state championship basketball team can have on a community, particularly in rural Maine, all I can do is share with you my vivid memory of sitting on the bus as we were riding to the tournament that season. I remember looking out the bus window as we were leaving town and there it was: A huge sign on the side of the road that said: THE LAST ONE OUT OF TOWN TURN OUT THE LIGHTS."

The Ponies' state championship season has stood the test of time. Though Rick McLeish broke Kevin Nelson's single-game scoring record of 47 points with a 50-point performance against Mattanawcook Academy on February 1, 1979, and David Carey coached Foxcroft Academy to four consecutive tournament appearances leading the Ponies to the Eastern Maine Tournament championship game in 2005 when they lost to Camden Hills 76–59, the 1975 Foxcroft team is still the only boys basketball team at the school to win an Eastern Maine (now Northern) Tournament championship game and a state championship game. Given that team's remarkable success during the Kevin Nelson/ Skip Hanson era and the school's limited success on the boys basketball court in the decades before and since, the 1975 FA state title team has a unique distinction. It is unprecedented, a singular achievement in the two-hundred-year history of the school.

The pride and purpose of that team still lives within every player, coach, and manager and the unparalleled season they shared. Years later, here are their memories of the 1975 Maine State Class B Championship and the impact it has had on them.

STEVE MOUNTFORD

Steve Mountford, Scott's younger brother, was selected off the junior varsity team to suit up with the Ponies during their tournament championship run in 1975. He died in 2017 in Sanford, Florida, at the age of fifty-eight. Steve was a U.S. Air Force veteran who served in Germany. Among his life's passions was a mission in Honduras that provided clean drinking water for residents of small villages. A water well in Honduras was dedicated in his name.

"He was a lot like Scott in that he would go a thousand miles an hour even if there was a brick wall in front of him," said John Champeon, Steve's teammate.

After most games, Dennis Kiah, the Ponies' JV coach, would select a player off his team to play in the varsity game when the JV team got back to the locker room after its game. That player would usually wear varsity jersey No. 10. Steve Mountford, a sophomore guard, David Milner, a 6-foot junior forward, and Bart Sloat, a 6–1 sophomore, were the top choices. JV teammates John Champeon, Ernie Clark, Tim Hanson, and Randy Ellis also got a chance to suit up with the varsity during the 1974–75 season. Tim Hanson, Skip's younger brother, and Bart Sloat were the only ones to score points in a varsity game that season. Sloat went on to a thirty-two-year career in the U.S. Marine Corps before retiring as a Colonel in 2012.

Steve also was the last of the athletic Mountford brothers. The oldest brother, Bobby, wound up playing in the FA Band in high school, but in eighth grade on February 2, 1968, he was the unlikely hero when he made the game-tying and game-winning foul shots for Dover Grammar in a last-second win over rival Dexter.

DAVE INGRAHAM

Dave Ingraham, the 1975 team's starting point guard, attended the fortieth year anniversary reunion of the team at Foxcroft Academy in 2015. He died in 2019 in Foxborough, Massachusetts, at the age of sixty-one. He was all business on the basketball court and after high school. Dave earned his bachelor's degree at the University of Maine and worked in the banking industry for more than thirty years, mostly as a regional and branch manager at various local community banks in southeastern Massachusetts.

"It was a good career path for him. His small-town, deep community roots made him a good fit for his job. The local community was important in Dover-Foxcroft and in Massachusetts," said Dave's younger brother Peter Ingraham. "There's no question his prior experiences as a high school athlete and multiple roles as 'the quarterback' served him well as manager of a team of sometimes younger, sometimes older branch employees with limited work and life experiences. And while it's been said many times and many ways, the lessons learned from being part of a team and the team building experiences of high school athletes help prepare them for professional and personal challenges later in life. I think the concept was especially true for Dave."

Dave was never rattled, whether it was working on bank mergers and acquisitions or competing against the likes of Orono and Medomak Valley in big games.

"He also saw the value of being part of something bigger than himself, and proudly carried that approach with him for his entire life. Partly thanks to Coach Hanson, he got up and went to work every day, dressed in uniform [suit and tie], he was ready for whatever came his way," said

Peter Ingraham, who earned his master's degree in policy analysis and management at the Muskie School of Public Service and is now Director of Advancement at Foxcroft Academy.

"Dave was forever humble, never bragging or boasting about his championship team or his personal accomplishments, but fiercely proud at the same time. A true team player for the entire Foxcroft Academy community."

Dave Ingraham was inducted into the Foxcroft Academy Athletics Hall of Fame in 2016, four years after his brother Peter was enshrined.

Jim Herring

After graduating from Foxcroft Academy, Jim Herring studied business management at Husson College before working in hospital business office management. He is retired and living in Bradenton, Florida.

When he was a freshman at Foxcroft, Jim made the freshmen basketball team. He played with Scott Mountford, Jeff Dunn, Dick Hatt, Jeff Brown, Tim King, and Dave Ingraham.

Jim credits Dave Ingraham as being the unsung hero in the Ponies' undefeated season in 1974–75 and treasured the FA practice jersey that Skip Hanson gave him during his senior year.

But, at the state title game, Jim was not on the Foxcroft bench as one of the team's three managers.

"I had to play tuba in the band for the championship game in Augusta," Jim said. "I got my Gold Ball medallion while in my FA Band uniform. I was proud to serve both."

Joe Dean

Joe Dean, another team manager on FA's state championship team, is retired from a career in telecommunications and information technology, the last fifteen years running his own business providing project and program management to international companies and governments around the world. Now living in a market town called Olney, Buckinghamshire, England—birthplace of the song "Amazing Grace"—Joe drew inspiration from Foxcroft's state title season.

"One of my fondest memories, and something that stimulated me to remember that against all odds, hard work and determination will always pay off in the long run," Joe said. "I tell everyone that even though the 1975 team was special, no one on the team felt they were more special or above anyone else in all of the school."

KEITH "MAD DOG" CHADBOURNE

After leaving Foxcroft Academy, Keith Chadbourne graduated from Unity College and eventually gravitated toward California, where he has been working and volunteering.

He has kept an extensive FA Sports Folder, and his memorabilia includes game programs and participant/contestant ribbons from both the 1975 Eastern Maine Tournament and State Class B championship game, his varsity "F" letter, many team and individual photos and posters and basketball trinkets, an FA bumper sticker, a cassette tape recording of the 1975 state title game, and a "Remember the Champs" pamphlet presented by the Dover-Foxcroft Volunteer Fire Department. Keith even has the Caravelle watch by Bulova that each team member received at FA to commemorate the state championship. And, Keith said, the watch "still runs."

Keith is also dealing with right hip and right knee issues that have developed over a lifetime of living with cerebral palsy. Still memories of Foxcroft's state championship bring him joy.

"It was bigger than me. With my condition it was difficult to fit in and do those 'normal' things boys do," said Keith, who joined his brother, Mark, as a team manager as a freshman. "So this was a partial way into that world."

ROGER HEWETT

Roger Hewett described his playing in the award-winning FA Band and on Foxcroft Academy's state championship basketball team as "both exemplary experiences that had direct bearing on who I am today."

In January 2023, he retired after forty-three years in the mechanical engineering field, a career that started in 1979 as a design draftsman with a plasma welding and cutting manufacturing company called Thermal

Dynamics in West Lebanon, New Hampshire. He worked and lived in Texas, Mexico, and China before moving back to New Hampshire.

"Winning the state championship was the best I could have hoped for, for both myself and the team. The experience tied the players, coaches and managers together like nothing else could have. It's something we will always be a part of," Roger said. "I learned the value of being a team player and the result of poise and commitment. Those virtues remain with me today."

MARK JOYCE

Maybe no Pony player on the state championship team had more roles than Mark Joyce. He was a starter and the team's sixth man on the 1974 team and was a key reserve on the 1975 team. He also created the "Air Ball Chart" for the Ponies and was one of the leaders of the Foxcroft Lounge Chair Society. He was editor of the *Pony Express* school newspaper and secretly wrote Kevin Nelson's speech for his senior class presidential presentation.

"It was a great speech, but I didn't know what I was reading," Kevin quipped.

"That camaraderie from the 1975 team has stayed with me throughout my whole life. It gives you that sense of belonging, that sense of self," Mark said. "It gives you that confidence from knowing that you belonged to something that was really unique. There are state champions every year, but they don't always go undefeated. That was special, and the fact that we were all just really close made it that much more special."

Now living in Ukiah, California, Mark is an instrumentation control electronics technician for CalPine Corporation, currently working at Big Geysers, the largest geo-thermal project in the world. Mark has worked for CalPine for more than twenty-three years and, before that, worked on oil drilling rigs in the western United States and offshore.

He's traveled to some wonderful spots but, in 1975, there was no place like home in Dover-Foxcroft.

"I remember the team bus rides home. There's always that release and joking and laughing. There was a bunch of clever guys and there wasn't any clique. Everybody was part of the fun," Mark said. "There is no doubt that Kevin was the ace, but if we just had a decent center, we would have been a contender. We had a really good basketball team and clever guys. We played smart basketball. There's no doubt we lucked out and got maybe the best player in New England that year, but certainly the best in the state of Maine and probably New Hampshire and Vermont."

Scott Mountford

After years working in the oil industry in Texas, Scott Mountford founded and became chief executive officer of Yorkshore Sales and Marketing in Florida in 2002 before expanding the business to New England and York, Maine, where he now lives.

"I strongly believe that the winning attitude of my athletic career in basketball, football, Foxcroft Academy, and my outstanding parents taught me my independence and never-give-up ability," Scott said. "I truly thank all my coaches, teachers, and parents for always standing by me during those impressionable years."

Scott still maintains a family camp at Sebec Lake and remains connected to the Foxcroft Academy community and Dover-Foxcroft.

"It wasn't like we were under a lot of pressure. It was almost like, 'Wow, we're celebrities!'" Scott said. "They were rooting for us, and we didn't want to let them down. That's the love for that town. There was respect and admiration for everybody."

Tim King

After graduating from Foxcroft Academy, Tim King enlisted in the U.S. Air Force, where he served until 1995 when he retired from the military. He kept working and in 2023 left a job as a contractor with Westaff Temp Agency in Plattsburgh, New York, to join Sodexo USA, a Paris-based hospitality/catering company. An avid skier, Tim has worked events at both the Olympic Center in Lake Placid and the Cloudspin Lounge at Whiteface Mountain in Wilmington, New York.

"With regards to winning the 1975 state championship, it wasn't just that one event. For me, it was the entire season to include all the processes to get to the championship game. The practices, the school, and community rallying around the team from day one," Tim said. "In reflection, the whole support process started when Kevin started attending Dover Grammar and spearheaded our basketball team to a championship season. I'm very sure that the dream of having a great high school team was born."

Tim—along with Scott Mountford, Jeff Brown, Dick Hatt, and Peter Snow—never lost a game with Kevin Nelson as their teammate.

Some fifty years later, Tim still relishes the support he received all around him, from teammates to townspeople.

"It's more of an appreciation of all them, as fans and supporting us. If it wasn't for that I don't think if we would have succeeded if we didn't have total community involvement the whole season," he said. "The band and cheerleaders were phenomenal. The team managers. It was a total effort by everybody. If we didn't have the stellar support, I don't know if we would have been as successful. We had the tools. We had the right coach. But you've got to give credit where credit's due and that's our community. Everybody had their role. We were all role players to get to where we wanted to go."

PETER SNOW

The legacy that Peter Snow left on Foxcroft's state championship season was his unexpected scoring boost off the bench in the state championship game.

"The best 7 points I ever scored," Peter said. "I'm still pissed I missed that foul shot."

Peter was the X factor in the state title tilt. Al Baran told him so when they met face-to-face at the Maine Basketball Hall of Fame in Bangor in 2023 for the first time since the 1975 state title game.

"Seven points. He had a couple backdoor layups, and whoever passed him the ball was very smart giving it to him. I remember it well," Al Baran said. "That pretty much cost us the game. No matter what I did. No matter what Kevin did. Thirty-eight percent shooting. We couldn't make it up."

Peter played small college basketball at Eastern Maine Vocational Technical Institute in Presque Isle for a year. Starting out a career in sheet metal construction and after working with his brother Terry in the air conditioning and refrigeration business, Peter spent the final twenty-four years of his work career with Bangor & Aroostook Railroad, now Canadian Pacific, in bridge and building maintenance.

Recalling the championship year, Peter, who now lives in East Dover, said, "I remember the signs. THE LAST ONE OUT OF TOWN TURN OUT THE LIGHTS. All the signs when we were coming back from Augusta. The big one on my parents' front lawn on the Dexter Road: 22–0 THANKS STATE CHAMPS."

JEFF BROWN

Jeff Brown may have been the most confident—and motivated—player on the Ponies that they were going to win the state championship game against Medomak Valley.

"The whole season was like a dream," Jeff said. "We had our ups and downs, but not once did we have an argument among us. We might beat each other up on the floor, but there was never any discord in the locker room between anybody or anything. That's the first time I played on any team that was like that. We were all really close."

After Foxcroft Academy, Jeff became an electrician and had his own business. He worked in Maine, Wisconsin, and Washington State before finishing his career with General Electric in Bangor, where he occasionally bumped into Jeff Dunn. Retired, Brown now lives in Bowerbank.

Brown, years later, is still upset about not being called upon to play in the state championship game. Skip Hanson thought Brown would never forgive him for that decision.

When the Foxcroft Academy 1975 boys basketball team was inducted into the Maine Basketball Hall of Fame in August 2023, Brown attended. After the ceremony, he approached Skip Hanson, who saw him coming from across the room and joked about Brown ignoring him during the ceremony.

The coach and player hugged.

Did that mean that Brown has forgiven the coach?

"I'm still working on it," Jeff replied, smiling.

DICK HATT

No Foxcroft Academy player perhaps had the swing of emotions in his high school career as Dick Hatt—from considering transferring when he didn't make the varsity team to being so happy, after a spectacular senior season, that he did not.

"I think the biggest thing 1975 gave me was incredible memories and pride, how we did so much for the school and town," Dick said. "But both the school, our class, and the town helped me learn humility and love throughout my life and sharing it with my loved ones."

Dick was the only Foxcroft player on the 1975 team other than Kevin Nelson to play college basketball at a four-year program. Dick went to Thomas College on a baseball/basketball scholarship, yet the next year joined the U.S. Navy. He eventually worked his way into software implementation analyst for behavioral healthcare and supply chain hospitals in Oklahoma, Kaiser Permanente in California, and at twenty-three hospitals at Tenet Healthcare.

Now living in Dade City, Florida, Dick still reflects on the state championship season with fond memories.

"I'm so glad my mom and dad moved us back to Dover-Foxcroft back in 1968 so I could be part of the journey from seventh grade on," Dick said. "The town was so excited about the team. From day one. Smiling so much. Always filling up the gymnasium, talking to me whenever I was in town. After our last regular season game, it enhanced tenfold. It was an experience I never dreamed of experiencing and certainly have not matched it since.

"I like to share with others that we were from a small town in Maine, and had a magical season in 1975. Townspeople enjoyed it as much as we did so the winter was better for that year! Our class was tight. I share with them the sign that was built outside Dover and as we drove back to town from Augusta where the nor'easter always seems to grow."

KEN BURTCHELL

Kenny Burtchell retired in 2023 after working thirty-six years for Bangor Hydro Electric Company, the last fifteen as line supervisor. He lives in

Ellsworth and occasionally pulls out press clippings from his Foxcroft Academy playing days to show his grandchildren.

"It just seems so long ago. Everything just kind of friggin' runs together," Ken says. "They've look at scrapbooks. They're amazed."

Ken and his wife, Vicki, share a similar state championship story. Vicki, as a junior in high school, won a Gold Ball in 1976 with the fifth-seeded Freeport girls basketball team that upset Leavitt in the Western Maine Tournament title game then upset Katahdin, top-seeded team in Eastern Maine, for the state title in Class C. It was the first and last Gold Ball the Falcons' girls basketball team has won.

"Those special teams are rare, and Foxcroft certainly made history," Vicki said. "It is a special group that meshes, and those guys at Foxcroft did just that."

Ken, a humble man of few words, coached their three kids in basketball in their youth. He now works on projects around their house in Ellsworth and the Burtchell family farm in Dover-Foxcroft. In his junior year at Foxcroft Academy, he averaged 7.3 points a game during the regular season, but upped his game in the tournament with a 10.3 ppg scoring average.

In 2023, Ken attended the Maine Basketball Hall of Fame induction ceremony for the 1975 Foxcroft Academy state championship team, and his teammates were happy to see him.

"That was awesome. It was pretty amazing to hear all the stories about the Hall of Fame inductees who were there and how much time they put in and all the records and accomplishments they made," Ken said. "There were a lot of people there. A lot of people who are important to the state. Coaches. Players. The records."

JEFF DUNN

Jeff Dunn earned a bachelor's degree in business management from the University of Maine and worked in human resources. He spent sixteen years with the General Electric Company, where he was a regional manager and traveled around the country and the world supporting GE's manufacturing sites, before retiring in North Carolina.

"In looking back at our 1975 championship and the overall role basketball played in my life and career, I think the most impact came from being part of a team," Jeff said. "This established a foundation that I believe was a major contributor to successfully working in businesses and with people with very diverse backgrounds. Clearly our championship-winning team only had the success we did winning the ultimate prize because of the entire team. In fact, I would say our practices and how we pushed each other was the key ingredient. From Tim King playing relentless defense and giving 120 percent all the time, to Scott Mountford's kamikaze style of play, to Roger Hewitt's elbows and length. Every player contributed in different and similar ways."

Jeff, as a team co-captain, was the liaison between the players and the coaches.

"Jeff was one of the best players I ever coached," Skip Hanson said. "He was extraordinarily coachable, and he worked his butt off every single practice and never complained about a thing. He was smooth and graceful on the court and could dribble well and see the court well. He was one of my all-time favorites."

Hanson and his lieutenants, Dennis Kiah and Dave Clement, had a lasting impact on the players they coached and the team managers who followed their orders. Everyone was on the same page.

"Maybe most importantly, the coaching staff inspired us to work hard every minute and have the right mindset both on and off the court," Jeff said. "There were many others who contributed, including our team managers Joe and Jimmy and Keith, who I think felt just as much a part of the team as the players and coaches, and I think this is what ultimately defined us—one for all and all for one. I guess the way I would sum it up is that over the years I haven't thought nearly as much about winning a championship as I have about the fun and experience of being with this group of guys. That really was what it is all about and achieving success together."

DAVE CLEMENT
Dave Clement stayed at Foxcroft Academy as a teacher, baseball/basketball/cross-country coach, and athletics director until 2003. He then went

to work as an agent at Mallett Real Estate, which led to him purchasing a house in Bowerbank, where he and his wife Louise lived and retired.

He considered Skip Hanson to be like a brother.

"Skip was a born leader. He had a way of explaining stuff so you bought in. I instantly took a liking to him, and he was a tenacious competitor," Dave said. "Skip always stayed above the rumors and the crap. He wouldn't let it bother him. He knew he had to focus. He knew he had inherited Kevin Nelson and he took every opportunity to do his homework to make sure he didn't screw it up, and he certainly didn't. I bought into it. Skip stayed above all the ridiculousness and everything. He stayed focused and it paid off."

The state championship season stays with Dave. He can practically snap his fingers and go back to the vision of winning that game in the Augusta Civic Center.

"The 1975 state championship was absolutely thrilling," he said. "At the final buzzer, it was such an amazing and exhilarating feeling to know that the Foxcroft Academy basketball team had achieved the distinctive honor of being the best team in Class B basketball in the entire state of Maine. This team and its coaches led with their hearts and, because of that and a lot of very hard work, their dream of winning the state championship became a reality. It was such an exciting journey resulting in a bond that has lasted a lifetime."

Dennis Kiah

Like Dave Clement, Dennis Kiah considered Skip Hanson to be a mentor. Fresh out of college, Dennis was impressed with the way Skip dealt with players from day one. And Dennis says his time at Foxcroft Academy helped him become a better leader.

"The impact of being a part of the state championship team at FA has been a big part in any success I have had since in my athletic director and coaching careers," Dennis said. "I learned so much from Skip and Dave, my fellow coaches and faculty members, my administration and support people and especially from the players and managers with whom I had a great deal of contact. Learning how to mold a team from so many people with diverse backgrounds and experiences was immeasurable.

Everyone had an important role and made important contributions to the success of not just this team but to the whole program and the great FA environment."

After coaching and teaching at Foxcroft Academy for six years, Dennis returned to Brewer High School, where he taught math and coached basketball, football, and baseball for thirteen years before going to Hermon High School as the assistant principal for three years. Dennis returned to Brewer High School for nineteen more years as athletics director and assistant principal.

Though he officially retired in 2012, Dennis has been a volunteer coach at Brewer High School in football and baseball and continues to keep the scorebook for the BHS Witches in basketball and ice hockey and help maintain the playing fields. Dennis also won a courageous battle with cancer, though it took part of his jaw.

"You want to talk about a legend in Eastern Maine and throughout the state? It's Dennis," Skip Hanson said. "He worked all the tournaments as official scorekeeper and stuff like that. At one time he coached football, basketball, and baseball the same season, varsity at Brewer, and had a winning records in every sport." Dennis was inducted into the Maine Baseball Hall of Fame in 2023.

THE TOWN OF MONSON

In 1975, the year Foxcroft Academy won the state Class B championship, there were only eight schools competing in Eastern Maine Class D. In 1968, when Monson Academy won the state Class S championship, there were eighteen schools in Eastern Maine Class S.

School district consolations in the 1960s changed the landscape of small-town high-school basketball in Maine including Monson. According to the Maine Basketball Hall of Fame, of the thirty-six small-town schools during that period, only six exist today.

Though the number of schools in Maine's small school classification has dwindled, Monson still lives with the "what if" question.

"We all followed Kevin Nelson when he was at Foxcroft and at Maine. Everybody figured that Monson could have won multiple championships if he had still been at Monson Academy," said Greg Lander, a starter on the 1968 Slaters' state championship team. "I feel Monson would have won two more state championships at least, maybe three, had Kevin played in Monson."

Had Monson Academy survived on its own, Kevin Nelson could have passed the Slaters' torch down the line to other emerging star players such as Dean Smith.

"All of this happened before my time, but I was certainly aware of all the Monson players of the past and agree that Monson Academy basketball would have been formidable," Dean said. "Having now traveled all over the world, I hold dear to my heart the community, people, and history of Monson. The consolidation was, as I understand, a necessary event. But I, too, wonder what the legacy of Monson Academy would have brought the people of the community."

As it turned out the last Monson Academy state championship was in 1968. However, there are still Monson Academy class reunions, "Roller Day," and "Monson Days" that spark memories of their glory days on the basketball court. After 125 jobs were lost when Moosehead Manufacturing Co. closed in 2007, the town of Monson in recent years is having a renaissance, courtesy of the Libra Foundation. It's a private foundation based in Portland, authorized by the Internal Revenue Service to make grants and contributions to charitable organizations other than political organizations. It was the primary organization that pumped $10 million into a Monson revival project, and the town is now a destination for art and food enthusiasts. In 2022, one of Monson's restaurants, The Quarry, which opened in 2018, was named to the prestigious James Beard Foundation Award list.

That is a monumental accomplishment for a town the size of Monson and a boost to Monson's moral. So was winning a state basketball championship. That Foxcroft Academy won a state basketball championship with Monson's Kevin Nelson was of some consolation.

Constance MacPherson, esteemed English teacher at Monson Academy, joined the faculty at Foxcroft Academy. After FA won the state basketball championship and before Kevin Nelson graduated, Kevin asked Mrs. Mac, who had coached girls basketball at Monson Academy, to sign his yearbook.

"I've always been so proud of you in all the things you've done and the way you have handled all the honors that have come to you," she wrote. "It was nice to be able to say, 'He's a Monson boy!' Best luck, Mrs. Mac."

Kevin Nelson's boyhood idol also bowed to acknowledge the achievement of Foxcroft Academy winning a state basketball championship. "I was happy for them when they won," said Buddy Leavitt, who now lives outside Canton, Ohio. "It took a long time for all the bitterness to go away. I was never jealous of Kevin's or Dean Smith's accolades. My parents were chummy with Hollis and Rose. For me to not want him to win that championship would have been childish. I was very happy for them."

From an academic standpoint, the SAD 68 consolidation reaped benefits. Foxcroft Academy is a reputed private preparatory school accredited by the New England Association of Schools and Colleges and a member of the Independent School Association of Northern New England, College Board and the National Association of Independent Schools. It has been honored as an Apple Distinguished School and designated as an International Baccalaureate Program School. Foxcroft Academy was the first school in Maine to implement a 1–1 iPad classroom integration initiative.

Enrollment over the years has remained steady with an influx of about one hundred international students who board in dormitories on the hill behind the gymnasium.

From an athletics standpoint, Foxcroft Academy's facilities are among the best in the state of Maine if not all of New England. The FA gym was renovated in 2012 to install new bleachers. That project added aisles and railings for easier and safer access but eliminated about forty-five seating spaces.

In 2022, the school opened its $7 million, 80,000-square foot Jim Robinson Field House that features an indoor track and can accommodate football, field hockey, soccer, baseball, softball, and wrestling teams. It rests between Oakes Field and the Piscataquis County indoor ice rink, which FA manages for the Libra Foundation.

All this in a town of about four thousand people at a high school with a four-year enrollment of about four hundred, including dozens of student-athletes from Monson. That is not lost in the eyes of the student-athletes who competed at Monson Academy and keep track of student-athletes from Monson at Foxcroft Academy, particularly the ones who played basketball.

"We take a lot of pride in that," said Alan Bray. "Monson has a pretty impressive record of basketball going back to the '40s. We always felt we made the difference in Foxcroft. There was a long line of Monson players who made an impact at Foxcroft."

"My friends in Monson will point toward a lot of good Foxcroft teams and say there was a Monson boy on that team," said Steve Bray, who later became a sportswriter at the *Piscataquis Observer*. "The other year Foxcroft went to the Eastern Maine Tournament and there was a Sawyer. Bobby Sawyer Jr. He was a Monson boy. It was always a question to us: 'Was there a Monson boy on the team?' We have such pride in basketball. Baseball was nothing in Monson. It was like we had eleven kids just trying to fill a void in some scratchy woolen uniforms, and we didn't have a soccer team, so basketball was it. Everything was focused around basketball. There was always that sense of pride, and there still is."

Kevin Nelson started it all by greatly enhancing Foxcroft's fortunes.

"Kevin Nelson was bragging rights for Monson folks, later to be continued with Bobby Sawyer and Dean Smith. FA couldn't have done anything without the Slaters," said 1966 FA graduate Jim Harvey, another in a long line of sportswriters to follow the immortal Lou "Scoop" Stevens at the *Piscataquis Observer*.

Dean Smith still considers Monson to be his birthplace of basketball, even though his family eventually moved to Dover-Foxcroft. He knows the unique challenges still presented to students living today in Monson and the connection they will always have to Monson Academy.

"I follow Monson student-athletes particularly and eye them with pride and respect, knowing that there is an even bigger commitment required from these student-athletes in dealing with the significant travel, logistics, etc.," Dean said. "Though they may have taken the schools out of Monson, they never will take the impact of Monson out of the schools academically, athletically, or otherwise."

In 2018, the Monson 1968 state championship team observed its fiftieth anniversary with a banquet and Gary Webb, their coach, attended.

Monson Academy's success in basketball is still prominently displayed in the Monson Historical Society. The Gold Ball from 1968 sits atop a trophy case upstairs.

"If you look at that Gold Ball now, it's tarnished and old," Kevin Nelson says, "but it's still a Gold Ball."

THE TOWN OF DOVER-FOXCROFT

There's a Gold Ball in the trophy case in the lobby of the Foxcroft Academy gymnasium as well. It stands out even among all the Gold Footballs the Ponies have won on the gridiron; they had won eight prior to the 2024 season, including back-to-back titles in 2021 and 2022 coached by Danny White, Jere White's oldest son.

But, realistically, the Gold Ball for basketball was won because of one great player, Kevin Nelson, and Foxcroft fans are grateful for that.

"It's the only Gold Basketball they have ever had here in town," Ernie Clark quipped. "And they had to rob Monson of their best player in order to win the state championship."

Kevin Nelson changed the course of basketball at Foxcroft and everyone is thanking their lucky stars.

"My mom and dad used to cut the *Piscataquis Observer* clippings out for me and send them to me in Germany," said Jeff Weatherbee, who was serving in the U.S. Army in 1975. "I was always friggin' jealous. Why couldn't we have had a big guy like that when I played?"

"FA hometown fans really embraced the Nelson basketball team like no other," said Jim Harvey. "That paved the way for the Rich McLeish and Dean Smith squads."

That kept Skip Chappelle coming back to Foxcroft Academy.

"There's some great people in Dover that the people of the University of Maine had great respect for," Chappelle said.

Those who were fortunate enough to play with Kevin Nelson in high school saw his potential up close and dreamed of the possibilities of him bringing Foxcroft its first basketball state title. They feel they contributed in some small way.

"I had a real special feeling about him from the very beginning," said Jere White, who was inducted into the Foxcroft Academy Athletics Hall of Fame in 2017. "It was very gratifying. It was a proud moment. I didn't really feel like I put my stamp on it, but I kind of felt I had a little to do with his development. I felt maybe I encouraged him at the start to turn out to be the player he was. I helped out some way. We all felt like we had a piece of that championship."

Steve Lamontagne does, too, even though he was cut from the FA varsity team in Nelson's freshman year along with two of his classmates, Angus Mountain and Kenny Kelly.

"I suppose the Class of '72 was somewhat responsible for that championship," quipped Lamontagne, who was a victim of Skip Hanson's "youth movement" when he decided to keep Kevin Nelson, Kevin Saunders, and Eric Annis on varsity.

Bill Patterson was a member of that varsity team at Foxcroft Academy. Though he didn't enjoy the success he hoped for on the basketball court as a player, he appeared in Maine high school basketball state championship games as a referee. In 2023, Bill was inducted into the Maine Baseball Hall of Fame as an umpire.

When Foxcroft Academy won the state basketball championship, Bill was along for the ride.

"You actually feel like it's you and it's your team and you're part of it because you've been there and wore the uniform with them," Bill Patterson said. "You get so involved, invested, and so identified with what's going on. I might have had some bitter feelings about the way basketball ended for me at FA, but all of that was forgiven when I saw what was going on and what they were able to do. I was all in with it. You're living it."

There are many Foxcroft fans who thought the Ponies were capable of winning two state championships in basketball. Some would argue that the 1974 FA team—with Kevin Saunders—was actually better than the team that won the state championship.

"If they had won that game against Orono in the Eastern Maine Tournament finals in 1974 there wouldn't be a debate. There are always two guys who seem to be the stars on championship teams," said Duane Warren, who was inducted into the Foxcroft Academy Athletics Hall of Fame in 2023. "To me, with the '75 team, there were so many more players who contributed around Kevin Nelson. Kenny Burtchell? Man, that kid played another big man role. They all deserve recognition. They all went into the Maine Basketball Hall of Fame together in 2023. That's enormous!"

The bottom line is the 1975 state championship team touched Foxcroft basketball fans like no other team had before and has since.

"The entire community supported that team—Dover, Monson, Charleston, Sebec—it did not matter. Young and old. It was small-town community support at its best," said FA cheerleader Lindy Strout Warren, Class of 1976. "There was a large poster made into a calendar with the teams on it—and the cheerleaders. That was pretty cool."

"They were my heroes," said Peter Chase from FA's Class of 1979 who was in eighth grade when the Ponies won the state championship. "We were taught how leaders are never out of the spotlight and actions matter. As president of my senior class and recognized athlete, I was asked to live up to the standards."

For longtimers in Dover-Foxcroft, the Ponies' state championship basketball team was catching lightning in a bottle.

"I was absolutely thrilled. I think the world of Skip Hanson and I knew Kevin Nelson. Kevin went onto Maine. How could you not feel that sense of pride and community? It just goes above and beyond it," said Dave "Hawk" Anderson, who was inducted into the Maine Basketball Hall of Fame in 2024 as a "Legend of the Game." "Even though my playing days at FA had passed me by, I was so proud and so happy for the school and the community and everybody involved. That's what makes small-town Maine unbelievable. It's a first and only."

And, Anderson added THE LAST ONE OUT OF TOWN TURN OUT THE LIGHTS sign incapsulated the entire community.

"It goes back to Neil Johnston and that silly sign," Eric Annis said. "It was about everybody who was proud of the team."

TODD HANSON

Skip and Peg Hanson raised two incredible sons. Chad, who is now a judge in the State of Alabama Judicial System, and Todd, who decided to follow his dad's footsteps in basketball.

"I thought teaching was the only thing I could do because both of my parents were teachers," Todd said. "All their friends were teachers in

Dover. The Clements. The Kiahs. All the coaches. Wayne Champeon. All those guys were kind of my guides growing up, and I thought that's what you did. There was never a question in my mind that I was going into teaching and coaching, because I was around those guys at the time growing up."

When Skip became principal at PCHS, Todd played basketball in Guilford.

"He held me to a high standard and wasn't happy if my emotions got the best of me on the court," Todd said. "I got a few technicals when I was a junior in high school at PCHS, and I was always met at home with a stern reminder that that's not acceptable."

Yet Todd listened and learned from his father. He, too, had to make some difficult decisions. He grappled with the decision to leave PCHS to go play at Waterville High School when his dad became principal there. Todd's high school years shaped him for his coaching career. He won a state championship as a player at Waterville High in 1985.

"As I progressed up to be a player at the high school level and my dad was the principal at PCHS, he had to make some tough decisions administratively. And then when I was at Waterville High School and he was the principal, there were some really difficult administrative decisions. And I think I have carried that with me into my coaching career," Todd said. "In my 25 years at Brunswick High I faced similar decisions like that and I would lean on my dad for advice and I think the message was consistent from 1975 to 2015. It was the same message: You do what is right. Sometimes the easiest decision isn't the right one. The hardest thing is the right decision."

While playing for the University of Maine, Todd happened to bump into Medomak Valley star Al Baran one day in a restaurant in Portland. Todd introduced himself as Skip Hanson's son.

"And all he wanted to do was talk about that game in 1975," Al Baran joked. "I was trying to have a drink and he must have talked an hour. It was on a very good note. He wasn't rubbing it in. He just wanted to know what I thought. He was very nice, but he just wouldn't stop talking about that game."

Years later, Todd practically duplicated his father's achievement at Foxcroft. Brunswick High School won its one and only Gold Ball with an undefeated team in 2002, and he and his dad became the first father-son duo in Maine to coach teams to a state basketball championship. Todd retired from coaching in 2021 having won 314 games.

Todd thought back to the disappointment he felt when his dad stopped coaching and the joy that his dad got from the experience.

"I watched all the relationships my dad had with his players, and to me that's what it's all about. I want my players to come visit me when they are done playing for me," said Todd, who replaced Tony Hamlin as the director of the Maine Basketball Hall of Fame in 2023. "The biggest takeaway I had was the relationships he formed with his players while they were playing for him and after they were playing for him. I remember distinctly that Kevin Nelson would come to our house five or six times a year, whenever he was home from the University of Maine, and after that whenever he was home from working in Augusta."

Skip Hanson

That sense of team and building lifelong relationships with his players sticks with Skip. Winning a state championship was not the end. In a way it was a beginning.

"When he talked about it back then and today I think what he was most proud of was the players," Lionel Bishop said. "Rather than single out a player, he'd single a play out. I remember him talking about being most proud of what the players were able to do during the whole tournament."

In another way, it was a relief for Skip. Coming back to coach in his hometown and having to make gut-wrenching decisions to create a winning culture took its toll on him. It resulted in a state championship and released Skip to pursue a career as a school administrator. He earned his master's degree in education and certification of advanced study in education leadership from the University of Maine and his doctorate in educational leadership from Nova Southeastern University in Florida.

The Gold Ball set him up.

"It was a goal. It was definitely one of his long-term and short-term goals, and it boosted him onto great things. He became a great educator and had a tremendous career," Dave Clement said. "He channeled his emotions well. He knew when to celebrate and when to be serious and when to accept accolades and when to be humble. Skip is a very bright man. He handed it very well. He was a great mentor."

Skip worked as a coach, teacher, athletics director, principal, assistant superintendent, and superintendent in the Maine public school system for thirty-four years before becoming superintendent of School Administrative District Union 16 in Exeter, New Hampshire. When he retired in 2008, Exeter High School named its 1,100-seat performing arts center after him.

During that time, Skip, still impacted by his 1972 decision to dismiss co-captains Tom Largay and Steve Saunders from the team, pushed for changes in athletics policies. He recommended that if student-athletes and adults who coached them were in violation of team rules in season, they would be suspended from activities for two weeks and attend alcohol or drug counseling. After meeting requirements and successfully completing the counseling program, they would be eligible to be reinstated to the team.

Skip, who graduated from Aroostook State College in 1966 with a bachelor's degree in education, was honored by the school—now the University of Maine Presque Isle—in 2014 with the Distinguished Educator Award on its homecoming weekend.

"Everything he touched he was successful at. He was grown to be successful," Skip Chappelle said. "He was just great to be around. We always enjoyed having him at our camp at the University of Maine. He had a great demeanor."

For the team's fortieth reunion in 2015 at Foxcroft Academy, Skip Hanson wrote a personal letter to the team and created a binder for each team member, including photos, scoresheets, articles, and even pages with the play-by-play of the 1975 Eastern Maine Tournament championship and the Class B state championship games

Skip and Peg are now retired and living in Scarborough. They travel quite often to watch their grandson, Tommy—Todd's oldest son—coach football and basketball at Eldred High School in Hudson, New Hampshire.

"Thank God he's like Todd and his grandmother and stays low key," Skip said. "He doesn't get excited. He doesn't holler at anyone."

Skip also keeps tabs on the coaches and players he worked with and coached at Foxcroft. Kevin Nelson lives in Falmouth, and Al Baran and Brian Butterfield live close by, too. Inevitably all conversations and memories turn to the 1975 FA state basketball championship season. Skip, Nelson, and Baran met for lunch in 2023 and they talked for 4½ hours.

"I'm just so grateful," Skip said. "I was cleaning out some stuff years ago and I had a packet of letters that people wrote after the state championship game and one of them was from Lap Lary. He said, 'Remember when you and I met at Merrick Square Market and we were doing some shopping and I said, 'Hey, there's an opening at the Academy. Why don't you apply?'"

"I had been at Higgins for two years, and I hemmed and hawed, and he said, 'C'mon, I want you to apply.' And I said I would think about it and so I decided to apply. Lap said in the letter just think if we hadn't had met that day at Merrick Square Market."

Then Skip Hanson may have never coached Kevin Nelson.

KEVIN NELSON

Whether it was fate or destiny, Kevin Nelson came along next in Skip Hanson's life. The four years they spent together at Foxcroft Academy culminated with a state championship that has forever linked them.

"We were like this meteor in Dover-Foxcroft that came through this one season—one in the last fifty years—here it was," Nelson said. "Wow. It's a congealing factor for a small town."

After playing basketball for the Black Bears and graduating from the University of Maine in 1979 with a bachelor's degree in natural resource management and land use planning, Kevin worked for the Maine Department of Environmental Protection from 1980 to 2011. In 1988, Kevin was the department's director of Media Relations and his boss was Dean Marriott, who had been appointed commissioner by then–Maine Gov.

Jock McKernan, who was an All-State basketball player at Bangor High School. As a kid, Kevin watched Jock play at the Bangor Auditorium.

"That story is clear evidence of how small the connections and degrees of separation are in the great state of Maine," Kevin said.

Also working for Governor McKernan at the time was Dave Cheever, who had interviewed Kevin in high school and was a guest speaker at the basketball team's postseason banquet. Kevin and Dave bumped into each other.

"Kevin will tell you that as good a player as he was, it was the other team members that made the title possible," Cheever said. "They embodied the team concept in a way that small-town basketball holds dear."

Those small-town experiences sometimes morph into "it's a small world" moments. While on a trip to Florida one time, Kevin ran into Brian Butterfield and then Boston Red Sox manager John Farrell at the Fort Lauderdale airport during spring training. Brian was the team's third base coach and infield coach when the Red Sox won the World Series in 2013.

In 2011, Kevin Nelson and Skip Hanson were charter members of the Foxcroft Academy Athletics Hall of Fame. The first class of inductees also included Dave "Hawk" Anderson, Lap Lary, and Dean Smith.

"As the years have gone by, I've gained a greater appreciation of the significance of our team's achievement," Kevin said.

"First, winning a state basketball championship is not an easy thing to do and to do so without losing a game is exponentially more difficult. Everything has to go right. Thankfully we were able to avoid things like serious injuries or illnesses, suspensions due to grades or bad behavior, and probably the biggest threats of mentally losing focus and taking our opponent for granted. As the season wore on, the '0' in our loss column became a huge bull's-eye on our back. Every team we played wanted to be the one to spoil our perfect record. They would come ready to play but fortunately, so did we.

"Second, the impact of that magical 1974–75 season on the players, coaches, FA's student body, its faculty and staff, and the people in the communities of Monson, Dover-Foxcroft, Sebec, and Charleston can't be truly measured without considering the context of the world around us. At that time, there was a palpable void of optimism that existed locally and nationally due primarily to: (1) a floundering economy, (2) a political system in disarray because of the recent Watergate scandal and the unprecedented resignation of President Nixon, (3) the Vietnam War had not yet ended—I still have my draft card—and (4) waiting lines and limits at gas stations as a result of the Iranian Oil Embargo crisis of 1973–74 were still fresh in everyone's minds and 50 cents a gallon gasoline was a reality.

"I believe that our season provided a pleasant and necessary distraction from the day-to-day worries and responsibilities facing so many folks. I think we brought a little bit of fun into people's lives if only for a brief time."

Kevin now lives with his wife Marcia in Falmouth. He recently began a new job with the Catholic Diocese of Portland as a Family Service Advisor in the Office of Cemeteries.

But Kevin also has a side job with his brother Shawn, who has maintained a wood workshop on Steward Road across from the brothers' home growing up in Southeast Monson, which is now home to the Nelson Tree Farm. When their dad died, Shawn created an urn for the memorial service at Lary Funeral Home. Eric Annis, who replaced his dad as funeral director, noticed the urn and asked if Shawn had ever thought about selling the urns he made.

With Shawn's wood carving skills and Kevin's gift of gab as a salesman, the Nelson brothers created a business—Solid Wood Cremation Urns—that make and sell custom-made urns. Kevin does the marketing.

"He could schmooze the devil into selling urns to Hades," Shawn said.

Winning or losing basketball games at times may have felt like a life-or-death experience growing up. But now, as adults, the Nelsons are literally in a life-and-death business together with urns.

"I joke with Kevin, if you get one with my name on it . . ." Skip Hanson quipped.

For Skip and Kevin and the 1975 Foxcroft Academy state championship basketball team, the magnitude of that feat has mushroomed in magnificence. In 2025, there are plans to dedicate and name the gymnasium floor at Foxcroft Academy in honor of the 1975 team to commemorate the fiftieth anniversary of the school's state basketball championship.

"If we brought a little bit of happiness and pleasure into someone's life that might have been mired in a sense of despair because of the times, then maybe we did something good beyond just winning a state championship," Kevin said. "You can only look at that through a lens of age, not as a young kid."

As a kid in Monson, Kevin Nelson dreamed of a day he would win a state basketball championship. As an adult, he can appreciate and savor the fact that he did. He just had to take a detour to Dover-Foxcroft to do it.

Either way he couldn't have done it any better.

ACKNOWLEDGMENTS

To be a storyteller, one must have stories to tell.

For this book I was incredibly lucky to hear many stories, more than I could remember and realize some fifty years ago.

This book was inspired by the 1975 Foxcroft Academy state championship boys basketball team that I began covering for the *Piscataquis Observer* at age nineteen. I watched that team develop, and that team changed the course of my career.

This book would not have been possible without so many people being so willing to share stories and information with me. My thanks and gratitude go to all the people who took the time to help me and reply to dozens, if not hundreds, of phone calls, emails, and texts.

At the top of that list was Elizabeth Stevens at the Bangor Public Library, who saved me a trip from California to Maine and countless hours of research by emailing me dozens of archived newspaper clippings from the *Bangor Daily News*. Elizabeth, along with Greta Schroeder, were gracious with their time when I finally visited the Bangor library.

Another source of incredible help and assistance was Toby Nelson, director of External Affairs and Chief Communications Officer at Foxcroft Academy. The support of Toby, FA Director of Alumni Affairs Cathy Hall, FA Headmaster Arnold Shorey, and the FA library fueled my research for this book.

Thanks to Glenn Poole of the Monson Historical Society, Mary Annis and Phyllis Lyford of the Dover-Foxcroft Society, and Jon Knepp and Alex Shaffer of the Thompson Free Library. Also, athletics director Mike Archer and the library staff at Orono High School and Margaret Noel at the Augusta Civic Center.

My research also extended to Canada. Thanks to Martin Timmerman of U Sports Hoops and special thanks to Kyle Emerson in the University of Maine athletics communications office.

As this was my first venture into writing a book, I must acknowledge the *Piscataquis Observer, Lamar Tri State Daily News, Loveland Reporter-Herald, Rockford Register Star,* and *Marin Independent Journal* for taking a chance on someone without a journalism degree to provide me with a proving ground and an opportunity to pursue my passion for sports and sportswriting. Also, kudos to Dominican University of California, in particular Sarah Gardner, for believing in me and allowing me to transition to a new career in communications.

A special thanks to Jay Silverberg, my managing editor in Rockford and Marin County, and friends Lee and Marilyn Negip for their unwavering support and guidance in this project.

Being a novice as a first-time author led me to John Shea, Neil Hayes, Bob Padecky, Ernie Clark, Ron Barr, Dan Fost, Danielle Svetcov, Howard Soloman, David Hahn, Agnes Bushell, Ben Simpson, Josh Williams, Stacy Rowe, Theresa Small Sneed, Peter Ingraham, and Jeff Ryan, all of whom provided insight and helpful advice.

Thank you for the support of my two sisters (Donna and Dianne), my three children (Damianne, Drake, Brock), and my wife, Caroline, who put up with all the books, tape recorders, steno notebooks, newspaper clippings, papers, and research material I scattered across our dining room table and all the interviews I conducted from the kitchen table morning, noon, and night. My only regret is that I didn't get around to doing this book until after my brother, Dick, had passed. I would have loved to have interviewed him for this book.

A special acknowledgment to the late Susan Trevarthen Harvey, perhaps my biggest booster. She was one of the first people I told about my plans to write this book, and, though she was in a hospital bed fighting for her life, she was encouraging me at a time I should have been encouraging her.

Finally, I want to acknowledge everyone who is quoted in this book, from Tom Philbrick and Al Baran, whose honestly and insight was invaluable, to Skip Hanson and Kevin Nelson who were gracious with their time, support, and stories that shaped this book and strengthened friendships and memories of Foxcroft Academy.

In memoriam of David Ingraham and Steve Mountford of Foxcroft Academy and David Strout, Drew Butler, and Ernie Boggs of Medomak Valley

Sources

1975 Class B State Championship, DVD audio radio play-by-play
Air Force Civil Engineer Center, afcec.af.mil
Augusta Civic Center archives
Bangor Daily News sports articles and box scores 1962–76. Bangor Auditorium articles 2013, 2023
Bangor, Maine, bangorinfo.com
Bangor Public Library
Bleacher Report, bleacherreport.com
Boston College athletics, https://bceagles.com
Boston College Newspapers, newspapers.bc.edu
Central Hall Commons, centralhallcommons.org
Central Hall history. "Memories of Central Hall with Lou Stevens," DVD
Class B 1975 State Champions 22-0 binder by Arthur "Skip" Hanson, 2015
Colby College Basketball Camps, colbybasketballcamps.com
Dover-Foxcroft: A History, Louis Stevens, 1995
Dover-Foxcroft history, Bob Thorne, FA Band, Foxcroft Facts
Foxcroft Academy yearbook archives
Foxcroft Athletics history. *100 Years of Foxcroft Academy Football and Foxcroft Academy's Five Undefeated Football Teams,* Louis Stevens
Foxcroft Academy Library
Glenn Poole and Monson Historical Society (monsonmehistoricialsociety.com)
A History of Foxcroft Academy, John Glover
Husson University Athletics, https://hussoneagles.com/
Lincoln County News sports article, 2009
Loring Air Museum, loringairmuseum.com
Los Angeles Times, latimes.com
maineanecyclopedia.com
Maine Basketball Hall of Fame, www.mainebasketballhalloffame.com
Maine Memory Network, mainememory.net
Maine Policy Institute, mainepolicy.org
Maine Principals' Association, https://www.mpa.cc/
Maine Public, mainepublic.org
Mary Annis and Dover-Foxcroft Historical Society

Monson history. *Here & Every Where Else*, Andrew Witmer, University of Massachusetts Press, 1978

Monson history. *Monson Academy Revisited 1847–1997*, William R. Sawtell, 1997

The Old Town Museum of Old Town, ME, theoldtownmuseum.org

Orono High School Library

Piscataquis Observer news and sports articles 1961–1975 (doverfoxcroft.advantage -preservation.com)

Plexuss, plexuss.com

Portland Sunday Press Herald sports articles 1974–1975

Rap-Up, rap-up.com

Ryan, Jeffrey H., and Peter C. Ingraham, *We All Assemble: A Celebration of Foxcroft Academy's Bicentennial* (Indie Author books, 2022)

Saint Mary's University athletics website in Halifax, Nova Scotia, and usportshoops.ca

The Spokesman-Review, spokesman.com

Stephen King, StephenKing.com

Sun Journal sports article, 2023

Take Me Back To, takemeback.to

Thomas College athletics, https://athletics.thomas.edu

Toby Nelson and Foxcroft Academy athletics archives

Thompson Free Library

University of Maine athletics website and archives in Orono

US Army Corps of Engineers New England District, nae.usace.army.mil

WBLM 102.9, wblm.com

Wikipedia, en.wikipedia.org

About the Author

Dave Albee, a 1972 graduate of Foxcroft Academy voted "Most School Spirited" as a senior in the school yearbook, was an award-winning sportswriter and sports columnist for thirty-five years at five newspapers in four states, from Maine to California.

His first big break came while he was an attentive clerk at an A&P grocery store in his native town of Dover-Foxcroft, Maine, trying to pay off his college debt. One day in 1973 while working at the A&P, Dave was bagging groceries for the sports editor of the local weekly newspaper, the *Piscataquis Observer*, when he asked her if she was planning to cover Foxcroft Academy's big season-opening basketball game at Orono High School that coming Saturday night. When she said no and admitted she knew little about basketball, Dave on a whim and on the spot volunteered to cover the game for her. He drove to the game, wrote a game story by hand on Sunday, submitted it to the *Observer* on Monday, and on Tuesday received a phone call from its editor/publisher offering him a part-time job.

That launched Dave's long newspaper career, which included free-lance assignments with *USA Today*/Gannett News Service and *The ... News* and covering multiple Super Bowls, World Series, NBA and NFL playoff games, World Cup soccer, NCAA football bowl games and NCAA men's and women's basketball tournament games. Dave, now residing in Petaluma, California, is an honorary member of the Baseball Writers Association of America who has voted on player selection into the Baseball Hall of Fame and on selection for college football's Heisman Trophy.

Despite covering some of the world's biggest sporting events, teams, and players during the past five decades, it is Foxcroft's first and only state basketball championship season that Dave covered for his hometown *Observer* in 1974–75 that served as the inspiration for his book—*The Last One Out of Town Turn Out the Lights*. That one season is deeply personal to him compared to all the college and professional sports seasons he has experienced.

Dave was born and raised in Dover-Foxcroft and competed in football, basketball, and baseball at Foxcroft Academy. The bit of serendipity at the local grocery store provided him the opportunity to witness and now write about the 1975 state championship season.